GOVERNMENT CONTRACTING
Promises and Perils

American Society for Public Administration

Book Series on Public Administration & Public Policy

Editor-in-Chief
Evan M. Berman, Ph.D.
National Chengchi University, Taiwan
evanmberman@gmail.com

Mission: Throughout its history, ASPA has sought to be true to its founding principles of promoting scholarship and professionalism within the public service. The ASPA Book Series on Public Administration and Public Policy publishes books that increase national and international interest for public administration and which discuss practical or cutting edge topics in engaging ways of interest to practitioners, policy-makers, and those concerned with bringing scholarship to the practice of public administration.

Government Contracting: Promises and Perils, William Sims Curry

Managing Public Sector Projects: A Strategic Framework for Success in an Era of Downsized Government, David S. Kassel

Organizational Assessment and Improvement in the Public Sector, Kathleen M. Immordino

Major League Winners: Using Sports and Cultural Centers as Tools for Economic Development, Mark S. Rosentraub

The Formula for Economic Growth on Main Street America, Gerald L. Gordon

The New Face of Government: How Public Managers Are Forging a New Approach to Governance, David E. McNabb

The Facilitative Leader in City Hall: Reexamining the Scope and Contributions, James H. Svara

American Society for Public Administration
Series in Public Administration and Public Policy

GOVERNMENT CONTRACTING

Promises and Perils

WILLIAM SIMS CURRY

CRC Press
Taylor & Francis Group
Boca Raton   London   New York

CRC Press is an imprint of the
Taylor & Francis Group, an **informa** business

The subject matter included in this book should not be considered as legal advice for specific cases or for general legal guidance. Readers should seek such advice from their own legal counsel. The material in this text is provided solely for educational and informational purposes. However, all possible circumstances could not be anticipated; therefore, individual situations may require further evaluation prior to application of the solutions or recommendations presented herein.

CRC Press
Taylor & Francis Group
6000 Broken Sound Parkway NW, Suite 300
Boca Raton, FL 33487-2742

© 2010 by Taylor and Francis Group, LLC
CRC Press is an imprint of Taylor & Francis Group, an Informa business

No claim to original U.S. Government works

International Standard Book Number: 978-1-4200-8565-5 (Hardback)

Library of Congress Cataloging-in-Publication Data

Curry, William Sims.
    Government contracting : promises and perils / William Sims Curry.
        p. cm. -- (American society for public administration book series on public
        administration & public policy)
    Includes bibliographical references and index.
    ISBN 978-1-4200-8565-5 (hardcover : alk. paper)
    1. Government purchasing--Law and legislation--United States. I. Title. II. Series.

KF849.C87 2010
346.7302'3--dc22   2009053432

Visit the Taylor & Francis Web site at
http://www.taylorandfrancis.com

and the CRC Press Web site at
http://www.crcpress.com

For my wife, Kirsten
The love of my life

Contents

List of Tables

Foreword

The perils of unethical behavior and corruption in government contracting persist in the public sector, and threaten the promise of contracting with increased efficiency, improved quality and flexibility. These issues occur globally, and at all levels of American government, federal, state, and local. Corruption is viewed as such a problem worldwide that an organization, Transparency International, was established solely to track corruption. They issue a Corruption Perceptions Index annually for 180 countries. Examples of corruption in government contracting in the United States include the billion dollar sole source contracts given to Halliburton by the federal government, the selection of contractors that were influenced by elected officials in New York State, and an El Paso, Texas-school trustee who set up a shadow company that received a consulting contract. At this juncture, it is not so much that we are surprised by the existence of corruption in government contracting with the number of dollars at stake in these arrangements, but that it appears that so little attention is focused on and progress made in preventing it.

William Sims Curry's previous book on government contracting, *Contracting for Services to State and Local Government Agencies,* is a rich resource for state and local government officials. It offers rare insight into the contracting practices from a survey of all fifty states, in addition to key local governments. Curry carefully culls and presents the survey results of each step in the contracting process, and provides readers with a compilation of best practices.

This volume, *Government Contracting: Promises and Perils,* concentrates on two very important and related aspects of government contracting, ethics and corruption. These are areas that deserve attention since they undermine the goals of government contracting and sour the public's confidence in government's ability to use resources wisely and responsibly. Unethical behavior and corruption also negatively affect the reputations of the vast majority of government workers and contractors who operate within the rules and the spirit of a competitive process.

Curry uses the same thorough approach he followed in his previous book, and addresses ethics and corruption by highlighting the major elements of the contracting process, providing examples of failures, methods to overcome these failures, examples of successful models, and the benefits of success. The areas covered are the big picture, processes and issues, ethics, sole source contracts, social objectives of government contracting, solicitations and pre-proposal communications, proposal evaluation, contract administration, contracting during emergencies, and contract completion and auditing.

Curry's work also enhances the academic literature on government contracting, and can be used in courses that teach privatization and government contracting, a subject that has received increased attention in Master of Public Administration programs. This is a work that is needed in the discussion of government contracting, and it serves to move the subjects of ethics and corruption to the forefront, where they belong.

Curry has a long history of involvement with government contracting as a procurement officer in the federal government, in nonprofit and private sectors, county government, and consulting, where he both managed and advised on contracting issues, including ethics and corruption. He achieves his goal of providing detailed and practical policies and practices to government procurement officials on how to avoid situations that can provide the opportunity for corruption. He wisely understands that the steps he prescribes can greatly reduce the possibility of corruption, but not eliminate it completely. But, as he also recognizes, if many of the steps he recommends were in place, numerous incidences of corruption would probably have been avoided.

Robert A. Shick, Ph.D., Assistant Professor

Managing Director, National Center for Public Performance
Director, Executive MPA Program
School of Public Affairs and Administration (SPAA)
Rutgers, The State University of New Jersey
Newark, New Jersey

Preface

The objective of this book is to discuss the promises and perils associated with government contracting. In today's world, we cannot discuss one without the other. Promises for improvements in government operations, available through contracting reforms, include increased opportunities for successful government programs, greater value for funds expended, and enhanced integrity of government representatives. Government entities worldwide face perils such as corruption and incompetence when contracting with the private sector. An extensive list of the perils, faced by government and private-sector contractors alike, associated with government contracting is provided in Chapter 1 (Table 1.1).

The general public is rarely exposed to media reports on the overwhelming majority of honest, dedicated government representatives and government contractors involved in providing products and services required for government functioning. This book, by necessity, also highlights primarily negative examples that represent the infinitesimally small percent of the preponderance of government procurement actions that are performed in an honest, efficient manner. Despite citing primarily failed procurement actions in this book, I wish to express my appreciation to the honest, dedicated government contractors, government entities, and representatives from government and industry, especially to those who have served or who are presently serving in combat theaters, for their contributions to providing products and services needed to conduct government operations.

The perils associated with government contracting frequently result in tragic consequences for public servants and contractor personnel alike. Public agencies and private-sector companies experience significant monetary fines, penalties, and seriously damaged reputations. Private-sector companies are subject to debarment or suspension from contracting with government entities. Numerous instances of the consequences suffered by individuals and organizations are cited in this book, not to embarrass the individuals or organizations, but to caution public servants, private-sector representatives, government entities, and private-sector companies regarding these perils in the hope they heed the recommendations in this book for avoiding the nefarious, amateurish, and criminal behavior that frequently leads to harsh consequences. Promises are provided in this book by way of presenting best practices in government contracting that, upon implementation by government entities, will limit opportunities for corruption in government procurement while increasing the efficiency of contracting practices. Examples of such practices and tools include a best practices request for proposals (RFP) and a best practices contract that include provisions for limiting opportunities for corruption and for improving contracting practices. Approaches for performing advance contract planning, conducting contract negotiations, and administering contracts are provided for readers to plan for management of the contracting process throughout the contracting cycle, negotiating a contract that protects the interests of both contracting parties and best ensures successful contractor performance.

The government contracting material in this book is presented primarily from the government perspective. However, a considerable amount of information presented in this book is considered essential for government contractors that seek performance excellence. Recommendations provided for contractors include proactive efforts to increase government sales and the calculation of profit on government contracts. This book includes recommendations for actions for contractors to avoid government sanctions, corporate fines, seizure of employee assets, and suspension or debarment of contractors. Additional recommendations are provided to prevent behavior that results in actions taken against corporate executives, officials, and employees. The actions that can be taken against contractor personnel include fines, forfeiture of assets, and imprisonment. The recommendations are made in the chapters dealing with the applicable topics.

Presenting improved contracting techniques and tools to the readers necessitates an element of technical contracting discussions. Readers whose interests do not include technical details have been spared some of the particulars by the inclusion of a CD with the book that contains some of the most detailed discussions. Providing contracting documents and tools on the CD also facilitates their downloading and modification for implementation by individual government entities and government contractors. The CD also includes a glossary of terms and several other tools to assist those involved in government contracting.

William Sims Curry
Chico, California

Acknowledgments

I wish to acknowledge the support and encouragement I received from Dr. Evan Berman, distinguished professor at National Chengchi University in Taipei, Taiwan, and editor-in-chief, American Society for Public Administration (ASPA) Book Series in Public Administration & Public Policy, Taylor & Francis Group, who, just as he did for my first book, tirelessly read and critiqued several versions of the text prior to sanctioning it for publication by Taylor & Francis/CRC Press. I would like to thank Maura May, publisher, Business Improvement, Productivity Press, CRC Press, Taylor & Francis Group; the late Raymond O'Connell, acquiring editor, Auerbach Publications, Taylor & Francis Group; and Stephanie Morkert, project coordinator, Taylor & Francis Group, LLC, who performed the multitude of tasks required to bring the rough manuscript to a state where it was ready for production and marketing. Finally, I'd like to acknowledge the efforts of Andrea Demby, project editor, and other members of the production staff who took the manuscript through the final stages of editing and composition to present the book for publication.

The states and local government agencies named below participated in a project to develop a best practices services contract and a best practices request for proposals (RFP) for my earlier book, *Contracting for Services in State and Local Government Agencies*. The best practices developed through that research project were instrumental in developing the promises in this book that are presented here to address the perils of government contracting that confront government officials and employees as well as government contractor officials and employees.

Considerable research was conducted to identify the perils faced worldwide by contracting professionals and by other government officials and employees who participate in the contracting process. However, reliance was placed on the research project conducted in preparation for writing the earlier book on contracting for services, and for preparing methodologies for confronting those perils. Therefore, I wish to again express my sincere gratitude to the states and local government agencies that responded to the questionnaire and provided templates for their RFPs and contracts in support of the research project that was conducted in preparation for my earlier book. The letters requesting participation by the states were addressed to the Office of the Governor. The governors' offices referred the requests for participation in the research project to the state offices with overall responsibility for the state contracting process. Following is a list of participating states and local government agencies:

State of California
State of Connecticut
State of Hawaii
State of Iowa
Commonwealth of Kentucky
State of Maryland
Commonwealth of Massachusetts
New York State
State of North Carolina
State of Ohio
Commonwealth of Pennsylvania
State of Rhode Island and Providence Plantations
State of South Dakota
State of Texas
State of Utah
Washington State
State of West Virginia
City of Des Moines, Iowa
City/Borough of Juneau, Alaska
City of Montgomery, Alabama
City of Richmond, Virginia
Maricopa County, Arizona
Oklahoma County, Oklahoma

About the Author

William Sims Curry authored the 2008 book, *Contracting for Services in State and Local Government Agencies*. Prior to that book he wrote numerous articles for periodicals published by professional contracting and public administration associations. He also conducted seminars and workshops on the topics discussed in his articles. Curry developed the curriculum for and taught college courses in materials management.

Curry was first introduced to the contracting field as an Air Force systems procurement officer while participating in the procurement of or staff support for command, control, and communications programs as well as space systems and ballistic missile programs. Following his retirement from the Air Force, he worked in contracting and purchasing for the Stanford Linear Accelerator Center on the Positron Electron Project and for several private-sector corporations in the aerospace and defense fields on the Hubble Space Telescope and various Department of Defense programs. Curry's first exposure to state and local government contracting began when he became a county purchasing services manager and continued through his subsequent positions as a county deputy administrative officer and then as a county general services director. Following his retirement as general services director, he has continued his involvement in federal, state, and local government contracting through independent research projects and consulting assignments.

Curry has been a long-term member of the National Contract Management Association (NCMA). He was designated by the NCMA as a certified professional contracts manager (CPCM) and received the award of NCMA Fellow. Mr. Curry served on the board of directors for the Industry Council for Small Business Development (a not-for-profit corporation established to assist small businesses, small disadvantaged businesses, and woman-owned small businesses) and held various elected offices including president. Curry also held or holds membership in the American Society for Public Administration (ASPA), Counties General Services Association (CGSA), National Institute for Governmental Purchasing (NIGP), and the California Association of Public Purchasing Officers (CAPPO), where he also wrote and presented professional development papers.

Curry received a bachelor of science degree in business management from Florida State University, Beta Gamma Sigma, and a master's in business administration from The Ohio State University.

Chapter 1

Big Picture — Big Issues

On the other hand however, the contractor in order to get a contract will give a bribe, while at the same time the contract will be inflated to line the pockets of both the giver and the receiver of the contract. In such an arrangement there is a lot of public money.

Dr. Abubakar H. Kargbo[1]
Deputy Coordinator
National Long-Term Perspectives Studies
Sierra Leone

1.1 The Big Picture: International Implications of Procurement Corruption

The value of individual high-value contracts for government entities ranges from millions to billions of dollars,[2] depending on the magnitude of the budget for any particular government entity. Government enlists the participation of private-sector companies and individuals to provide products, services, and capital projects that cannot, or cannot economically, be provided solely by government entities or government personnel. Best practices of the government entities participating in the research project introduced in the preface, referenced throughout this book, and thoroughly described on the CD accompanying this book are presented for implementation to improve the efficiency and integrity of their contracting programs. Government contractors, prudent government officials, and government employees are *not* inherently corrupt or incompetent. The colossal sums involved in government contracts, however, attract a measure of unscrupulous participants and magnify the consequences from that minority of contractors or government representatives who are corrupt or incompetent. Considering the seemingly infinite barrage of media accounts of corruption associated with government contracts, the temptation to be personally enriched by culling a share of those millions to billions is apparently too great for some officials and employees to resist. A World Bank report[3] indicates that progress has been made in reducing corruption in Europe and Central Asia; however, there has been no significant decline in bribery to obtain government contracts. Media accounts of the consequences of accepting improper contractor gratuities range from fines, ruined careers, forfeiture of assets, imprisonment, and broken families through the extreme consequence of suicide. Government representatives with contracting responsibilities, in virtually all cases, are sufficiently compensated to support themselves and their families comfortably without accepting illegal gifts or gratuities. Yet, seemingly intelligent and rational women and men continue to risk the consequences included in Table 1.1 in return for rewards that normally represent a pittance in comparison to the risked assets.

Procurement fraud is prevalent worldwide, from developing countries to countries with the most advanced economies. Even the United Nations (UN) is not exempt from procurement corruption. A former UN procurement officer, Alexander Yakovlev, pleaded guilty to soliciting a bribe under the $64 billion oil-for-food program.[4] The oil-for-food program was initiated after the 1990 invasion of Kuwait and was intended to help ordinary Iraqis who were adversely affected by UN sanctions. Yakovlev's activities included the award of UN contracts funded by the oil-for-food program as well as other UN contracts. The investigators found that Yakovlev received approximately $1.3 million in kickbacks from UN contracts that were not funded by the oil-for-food program.

Yakovlev cooperated with authorities by testifying against Vladimir Kuznetsov, a Russian UN diplomat, who was subsequently convicted of laundering a portion of $300,000 provided by Yakovlev as bribe proceeds from companies seeking UN contracts. Kuznetsov was sentenced to 51 months in prison and assessed a fine of $73,000 for money laundering. However, he was later turned over to Russian justice officials and returned to Russia, where he is expected to serve 16 months in jail.[5]

The UN Procurement Task Force, an ad hoc group that was established within the UN Office of Internal Oversight Services (OIOS), has been investigating procurement irregularities and exposed over $630 million in tainted UN contracts during a recent three-year period.[6] The UN Procurement Task Force's results are commendable; however, it is troubling that Russia and Singapore led an effort to block an extension to the term of the task force.[7] Funding for the task force ended and investigations appear now to be the responsibility of OIOS. Former members of the task force, however, are experiencing UN bureaucratic delays in their attempts to be hired by OIOS, which lacks expertise in contract fraud. Impediment of the UN Procurement Task Force by UN members has, tragically, restricted transparency of the UN's procurement function.

Table 1.1 Government Procurement Corruption Wall of Shame

Abuse of power	Favoritism	Nefarious behavior
Aggrieved contractor	Gratuities	Partiality
Amateurish behavior	Greed	Patronage
Bias	Fraud	Payoffs
Bribery	Illicit payments	Political influence
Cash payments	Incarceration	Poor planning
Conflict of interest	Incompetence	*Quid pro quo*
Conspiracy	Ineptitude	Protest
Contract fraud	Intimidation	Restitution
Corruption	Irresponsibility	Sham contracts
Criminal Acts	Kickbacks	Lack of transparency
Deceit	Larceny	Sole source contractors
Duplicity	Malfeasance	Suicide
Escort services	Misinformation	Neglect
Extortion	Misrepresentation	Slovenly conduct
Extravagance	Mismanagement	Waste

Inappropriate expenditures of tax receipts, however, are not limited to illegal acts. Taxpayer resources are oftentimes wasted through ineffective and misguided actions by government officials and employees who are not motivated by greed, but who merely lack the requisite knowledge or skills for acquiring needed products or services from the private sector. Certain knowledgeable and skilled government officials, additionally, squander taxpayer resources through abuses with apparently no motive other than the ruthless exercise of power. The quotation at the beginning of this chapter was made at a workshop addressing corruption in English-speaking West Africa. Procurement corruption, however, as discussed earlier, is a worldwide problem afflicting countries with emerging economies through nations with the most advanced economies. Although it would be presumptuous to assume that reading this book will resolve all procurement corruption issues, following the recommendations and using the tools provided here and on the accompanying CD will assist government officials and employees in managing the contracting function and limit opportunities for corruption. The contract management tools presented in this book are intended to improve the likelihood that government officials manage successful programs and decrease the likelihood that they or their reports cross the threshold from ethical, competent, and lawful behavior to nefarious, amateurish, and criminal behavior. A list of ethical and professional lapses, too common in government contracting, is provided in Table 1.1.

Big issues contributing to the reprehensible situation, wherein vast monetary sums are squandered, include mismanagement of the government contracting workforce, inappropriate actions of both contracting professionals and government representatives in disciplines other than contracting but who influence contracting decisions, sole source contracting, corruption, misguided contracting activities conducted during emergencies, and the mismanagement of contracts and contractor performance. These issues are introduced in this initial chapter; however, each issue is addressed in considerably more detail in subsequent chapters.

1.2 The Case against Abandoning Government Contracts

Private-sector companies represent a valuable resource for government. These companies design, manufacture, and market products that either fully meet the needs of government or can meet government requirements through value-added effort. With respect to the majority of products sold to government, the private-sector market is vastly larger than the government market, thus permitting government the advantage of large-scale manufacturing. Private-sector companies also design and build capital projects requiring similar skills and resources needed for government construction projects. Experts available through the private sector provide needed expert services to government. The problems, or perils, associated with government contracting, as reflected in Table 1.1, however, give one pause to consider abandoning government contracts altogether. The alternative to contracting from the private sector is to provide government resources to produce, or otherwise provide, all systems, services, and commodities required by the government. However, mere consideration of the magnitude of the tasks involved in designing, developing, and manufacturing aircraft should convince most readers that government cannot reasonably obtain the resources necessary to provide all systems and services required for mission accomplishment. In addition to the near impossibility of recruiting government employees qualified to design and manufacture such aircraft, there is also the lack of government-owned specialized facilities that are required for manufacturing aircraft. The advantage of large-production-scale orders for commercial aircraft permits private-sector contractors to significantly reduce the cost and the time that would otherwise be necessary for the government to design and manufacture aircraft solely for government use. The existence of large production orders for commercial aircraft makes private-sector manufacturing especially economical for law enforcement or military aircraft that are variations of commercial aircraft. Private-sector manufacturers and professionals are positioned to provide high-quality legal and financial counseling, mental health services, automobiles, computers, furniture, medical supplies and equipment, farm implements, educational equipment, and virtually every service and product procured by government at competitive pricing.

The government can often obtain the skills of experts on a part-time basis from individuals employed full time by private-sector companies. When government does not have need for full-time experts, it is likely more economical to benefit from the experts' skills through service contracts with private-sector employers, or directly from the expert, as an independent contractor. Addressing the problems associated with contract corruption, despite the enormity of the challenges, is more practical than developing government resources to provide all needed systems, services, and commodities.

Numerous contracting terms are defined as they are introduced in this book; however, to facilitate review of the terms when they recur following the introductory definitions, they are repeated in alphabetical order in the glossary at the end of the book. A compact disk accompanying this book includes the glossary, a description of the essential elements of a contract, details of the research project that was conducted to establish the best practices in government contracting referenced in this book, templates for a request for proposals (RFP) with a contract, and other useful information and contract management tools. Reference is made in subsequent chapters to more detailed material on the CD relating to the topics discussed. Readers who are not thoroughly familiar with government contracting are invited to review the material on the CD regarding the glossary of terms, essential elements of contracts, and best practices research prior to proceeding with the following discussion of individual contracting issues.

1.3 The Scourge of Procurement Corruption

Participation in government procurement corruption schemes is not limited to government contracting professionals and their private-sector counterparts. Others with potential for participating in such corruption include those officials and employees, such as engineers or other technical personnel, who influence contracting decisions by writing procurement specifications, serving on proposal evaluation teams, reviewing or approving contracts, or evaluating the acceptability of contractors' work but who are not considered part of the contracting workforce. Still other government representatives with potential involvement in government procurement corruption include those officials who approve high-value contracts, finance or accounting professionals who review contracts for financial and budgetary matters, and attorneys who review contracts for conformance to legal form. Private-sector representatives, other than contracting professionals, with potential for involvement in procurement corruption include finance professionals, engineers and other technical professionals, and executive personnel. The training and expertise of the individuals in these professions is not generally in question. However, government officials or employees with authority to write specifications, who serve on proposal evaluation teams as well as approve and execute high-value contracts, may have little or no training in ethics. This problem requires definitive attention. Training for individuals in these positions, with the exception of attorneys, is nearly devoid of contracting courses. Ethics training is too often concentrated on the maximum value of gifts and gratuities that may be accepted and the penalties for exceeding statutory limitations. Concentrating ethics training on the value of acceptable graft is akin to teaching what bribes one can accept without consequence. Perhaps concentrating on the development of personal responsibility and the establishment of a personal ethical code that includes refusal of all gratuities, despite statutes that permit acceptance of gifts below the established thresholds, would reduce the incidence of corruption and malfeasance that oftentimes results in termination of government service, arrest, conviction, imprisonment, fines, forfeiture of assets, the devastation of families, or even suicide in rare instances.

A number of cases and problems associated with problematic government contracting are included in the following discussion because they are representative of the *big picture — big issues* theme of this chapter. The first set of cases illustrates the range of gratuities offered by government contractors and accepted by government representatives.

The level of corruption spans a large range of monetary values. Selecting the lower end of the range appeared to be a simple task when a *Chicago Sun Times* story from January 23, 2004, described a *Sun-Times* investigation finding that the City of Chicago had a list of dump trucks used for questionable city jobs. The article indicated that some truck owners have political clout and some are mob (organized crime) figures or relatives of mob figures. The story quoted one of the drivers who indicated that he just sat on the job all day and that there was no cost for fuel and no truck wear and tear. The disclosure in the article, however, that there were 165 such trucks on contract with the city, valued at approximately $40 million per year, eliminated the dump truck case from representing the bottom of the monetary range for procurement corruption.

The case selected to represent the bottom of the range (although arguably), as reported in a U.S. Department of Justice press release,[8] involved a $5,000 payment to obtain a Cherry Hill, New Jersey, township employee's assistance in obtaining a contract. The now-former president of the company vying to secure the inspection services contract pleaded guilty to making a cash payment of $5,000 in exchange for the township employee's alleged agreement to throw out bids that had been received for the inspection services contract. The township employee allegedly was then to assist the contractor with winning the contract based on a new set of bids. In addition to the $5,000 cash payment, there was allegedly also payment by the contractor to cover the township employee's personal expenses for attendance at conferences in Reno, Nevada, and Atlantic City, New Jersey. Both defendants were released on $50,000 unsecured bonds. The charge of bribery carries a maximum statutory penalty of ten years in federal prison and a fine of $250,000.

The case selected to represent the top of the range involves Randy "Duke" Cunningham. This case was selected based on the lofty position from which Mr. Cunningham tumbled and the exceptionally high value of his illegitimate compensation. Mr. Cunningham was an authentic war hero who had been nominated for the Medal of Honor and awarded the Navy Cross, two Silver Stars, and a Purple Heart. Duke Cunningham shot down five MiGs over North Vietnam and became the first "Ace" of that conflict. He eventually retired from the Navy as a commander. He was subsequently elected for eight terms to the U.S. House of Representatives from San Diego County. Upon reading or viewing the media reports of Congressman Cunningham's confession to accepting bribes valued at $2.4 million from Defense Department contractors, one might ask how a person who sacrificed so much for his country could have capitulated to such greed at this stage of his life. However, upon reading the psychiatric evaluation[9] prepared for consideration in his sentencing, one cannot help but comprehend the calamitous nature of his case, which may hopefully provide a lesson to others who might otherwise succumb to similar temptations.

Duke Cunningham was one of four F-4 fighter pilots who were engaged in battle by twenty-two MiG-17s, MiG-19s, and MiG-21s. After shooting down three of the MiGs, his aircraft was heavily damaged by a SAM2 missile, thus causing him to crash into the Gulf of Tonkin. He suffered significant injuries resulting in the long-term use of numerous medications with considerable side effects. Following his retirement from the Navy, Duke Cunningham volunteered for various humanitarian causes and refused initial requests to run for a congressional seat. He eventually agreed to run for congress after being asked personally by President Reagan. While subsequently serving as a congressman, he supported programs for medical research, education, military, and intelligence. It was only when he was working with U.S. Department of Defense (DoD) contractors in an effort to increase military funding that he developed personal friendships with representatives from DoD contractors that led to his descent to criminal behavior. Had Mr. Cunningham attended ethics training that concentrated on personal responsibility and establishment of a personal zero tolerance ethical standard, as introduced earlier in this chapter and explored in-depth in a subsequent chapter, he may have escaped his calamitous fate.

In a public health related case involving alleged false claims and inducements paid to doctors and other healthcare professionals, the U.S. Department of Justice announced early in 2008 a $399 million settlement with Merck & Company, Incorporated.[10] In the settlement, Merck allegedly underpaid the federal government, forty-nine states, and the District of Columbia for Zocor and Vioxx. Merck allegedly offered discounts amounting to less than 10% of the average manufacturers' price for certain drugs on the condition that the hospitals achieved and maintained an established volume of the drugs. Merck did not report the discounted prices to the Medicaid program. The case also involved allegations that Merck paid fees, remuneration, and other valuable consideration to doctors and other healthcare professionals to influence the doctors to prescribe Merck drugs. The former Merck employee (a whistleblower) who instigated the suit based on the False Claims Act[11] received over $44 million as his share of the settlement.

1.3.1 Mismanagement of the Government Contracting Workforce

Government contracting workforce members require extensive government contracting and ethics training. In the United States, military and civilian government members of the federal contracting workforce are provided with and required to take meaningful government contract management classes beginning at the commencement of their federal government employment and continuing throughout their careers. The National Contract Management Association (NCMA) is a professional association that provides seminars, workshops, conferences, and publications that complement primarily the federal government contracting classes to further enhance the knowledge of contracting matters for federal contracting professionals. However, federal employees who influence contracting decisions, but who are not a part of the contracting workforce, often receive considerably less, if any, formal training on contracting matters or ethics.

Virtually every government contracting professional is assigned to an organization headed, at some level, by a government official who is not a contracting professional. One easily visualized example of such an organization is the combat arena with ongoing significant contracting activity, such as present-day Afghanistan and Iraq. An overwhelming percentage of military personnel engaged in combat arms, contract management, and other career fields, as well as private-sector contractor personnel, who serve in a combat theater perform their duties as patriotic acts while risking their lives. They are commended for their patriotism and their courage. In a combat theater, however, top contracting officials are accountable to field commanders who are engaging the enemy and oftentimes attempting to make alliances with local leaders. In the absence of authority for field commanders to make direct monetary payments to local leaders to help win their support, providing monetary aid through sham contracting is a tempting alternative for field commanders. Pressure from field commanders on their subordinate contracting officials to approve payment for uncompleted work under the sham contracts would create a difficult choice between refusing a superior's request to approve payment for uncompleted work and incurring damage to one's career.

The *Federal Acquisition Regulation* (FAR) is a comprehensive set of procurement rules, applicable to virtually all federal agencies, that has evolved over many decades to provide rules and exceptional guidance for federal procurement professionals. The FAR is regularly updated and is available in print or online.

Exceptional training, professional development opportunities, and a comprehensive reference (i.e., the FAR) are available to members of the federal government contracting workforce. However, there is a serious staffing deficiency in relationship to the workload. This situation affecting the federal civilian procurement workforce was aptly described by David Drabkin, a deputy chief acquisition officer and senior procurement executive at the General Services Administration, in a FederalTimes.com commentary on September 7, 2008 ("Commentary: More Contract Specialists, Better Tools Needed") wherein he compared the staffing and workload between 1991 and the present day. His description was summarized by the following statement:

> These numbers tell their own story: Fewer people are doing almost 300 percent more work.

Mr. Drabkin continues his commentary by describing how the cited 300% increase in workload does not consider the added factor of increased complexity of the work necessitated by the transition from traditional, and relatively simple, selection of contractors based on lowest price to the more complex selection of contractors based on best value. Increased emphasis on best value is based on the reality that lower ownership costs may justify paying a slightly higher initial price to achieve lower total costs over the expected life of the product or service. As might be expected, calculating best value is considerably more complex than merely determining the lowest price. The added complexity of calculating best value may also result in differing interpretations regarding the assumptions and calculations employed in this more subjective determination. Accompanying this greater level of subjectivity is the correspondingly greater potential for protests from aggrieved contractors. Protests are normally filed by contractors that unsuccessfully competed for award of a contract and claimed that a competing contractor was improperly selected. Occasionally, protests are filed by prospective contractors that review a solicitation and determine that the provisions of the solicitation provide an advantage to one or more of their competitors. The need to react to protests, naturally, further increases the workload of contracting professionals, thus further compounding the impact of the shrinking federal contracting workforce.[12]

More recently, however, it appears that the DoD is addressing this problem by making a significant increase in its acquisition workforce.[13] Secretary of Defense Robert Gates announced that 20,000 acquisition personnel would be added to the DoD workforce beginning in 2010. The increase (15% over the present workforce) is planned to be completed by 2015.

State and local government contracting professionals have far fewer training opportunities than their federal counterparts. Although the FAR provides federal contracting professionals, and other federal officials who influence government contracting decisions, with a concise set of rules in a single volume or online, there is no all-encompassing counterpart available for state and local government contracting. Although the body of knowledge for state and local government contracting is ever expanding, the oftentimes conflicting rules and statutes among the various states and agencies within states make it virtually impossible to develop an all-encompassing counterpart to the FAR for states and local governments.

Although numerous professional associations that provide training and professional development opportunities for the state and local government workforce have been formed, professional association attempts to develop professionalism among state and local contracting practitioners is also complicated by the aforementioned conflicting provisions in state and local government statutes and regulations. Further complicating the competency of the state and local contracting workforce are budgetary pressures that have resulted in reductions, in many agencies, to their centralized contracting function and the resultant need to decentralize certain contracting responsibilities to the department level. The requirements for training and qualifications for contracting personnel in departments where contracting authority has been delegated may reflect lower standards than the standards provided in centralized contracting functions. The position description, discovered on a county website, for a contracts specialist in a county department with delegated contracting responsibilities reflects specifications for education, experience, certifications, and licenses, as noted below:

> High School Diploma or GED equivalent and two (2) years experience
> in clerical, accounting or administrative duties.
> State of … driver's license may be required.

Passing a General Educational Development (GED) test combined with two years of clerical duties and a driver's license is adequate for the entry level in certain government clerical positions, but it is entirely inadequate for a contracts specialist with responsibilities that include development of contracts, terms and conditions, contract amendments, and additional contracting functions, as outlined in the position description.

1.3.2 Sole Source Contracting

The need to award government contracts through competition is a long-standing axiom. However, further substantiation of the need for competing government contracts is contained in the June 2007 Majority Staff report, "More Dollars, Less Sense," prepared for the Committee on Oversight and Government Reform of the U.S. House of Representatives, which includes the statement:

> Competition in federal contracting protects the interests of taxpayers by ensuring that the government gets the best value for the goods and services it buys. Competition also discourages favoritism by leveling the playing field for contractors while preventing waste, fraud, and abuse.

Despite this obvious need to maximize competition in government contracting, the same report provides the following finding with respect to trends in noncompetitive contracting:

> In 2000, the federal government spent $67.5 billion on contracts awarded without full and open competition. By 2006, federal spending on these no-bid and limited-competition contracts had grown to $206.9 billion, an increase of 206%. In total, the dollar value of contracts awarded without full and open competition more than tripled between 2000 and 2006.

Reasons frequently provided for awarding contracts without competition are provided in Table 1.2, along with recommended responses to each justification by agency officials who approve or deny sole source procurements.

The lack of full competition is not unique to U.S. federal contracts. Seemingly perpetual media reports describe questionable sole source or limited competition in contracts awarded by national and local governments in virtually every country.

1.3.3 Misguided Contracting Activities Conducted during Emergencies

Protection of constituent lives and property during natural or contrived disasters is a fundamental government responsibility. Once the emergency is progressing there is no time for government entities to follow their standard procurement practices involving formally written solicitations and responses. Provisions for procurement of supplies and services needed during emergencies, in the interests of efficiency and economy, need to be included in advance planning for all foreseen government operational requirements in future emergencies. Failure to plan in advance for purchasing during emergencies ensures delayed receipt of needed supplies and services as well as excessive pricing and possibly substandard quality.

Table 1.2   Recommended Reaction to Justifications for Sole Source Procurement

Justification Provided for Sole Source Procurement	Response of Agency Approving Official
Insufficient time to obtain competitive proposals or bids for first-time procurement.	Deny: Competitive proposals or bids can be obtained concurrently from multiple contractors in the same timeframe as a sole source proposal or bid. Competitors may be able to provide products or services earlier than presumptive sole source contractor.
Insufficient time to obtain competitive proposals or bids for follow-on procurement.	Deny: If department waited too long to solicit proposals or bids for contract nearing the end of its term, the present contract can be extended for a month or two to provide time for competitive proposals or bids.
Only known source able to provide this product or service.	Deny: Need to conduct a search to discover potential competitors. The agency contracting department may be able to assist in the search.
Contractor consistently offers the lowest pricing.	Deny: Lowest pricing can normally be established only in a current competitive procurement. Contractors that were unsuccessful in the past due to high pricing may now be willing to offer more competitive pricing.
Current supplier has been performing well and had the most competitive pricing when last competed.	Deny: Current supplier may elect to increase pricing due to inflation and previously unsuccessful contractors are likely to lower pricing to become more competitive.
Only the software developer is able to support the computer software.	Possibly approve: While this is often a valid reason for approving a sole source contract, the sole source approving official may wish to verify this with competitors. Also, it is possible that a competitor may be able to propose alternative software that is superior or more economical or both.
Only the manufacturer can maintain the equipment.	Deny: Most equipment can be maintained by competitors of the manufacturer. However, if a search fails to identify a qualified maintenance contractor, it may be necessary to approve the contract on a sole source basis.

Table 1.2   Recommended Reaction to Justifications for Sole Source Procurement (Continued)

Justification Provided for Sole Source Procurement	Response of Agency Approving Official
The equipment will be leased; therefore, it is not subject to competitive requirements for purchased equipment.	Deny: A lease is merely for the purchase of equipment that is financed by the contractor or a third party. Therefore, competitive purchasing rules do apply.
The building is available for leasing now and is suitable for the department's needs.	Deny: Placing an advertisement in a local newspaper or hiring a real estate agent may identify a building that is better suited, more economical, or both.
The building was severely damaged during a declared disaster and must be completely refurbished through emergency contracting procedures.	Deny: Competitive bids may be obtained concurrently from multiple contractors in the same timeframe as a sole source bid. A competitor may be able to refurbish the building sooner than the presumptive sole source contractor.
The supplies or services are needed to respond to a declared disaster.	Deny: Competitive bids or proposals (even if informal or verbal) may be obtained in the same timeframe as a sole source bid or proposal and competitors may be able to provide supplies or services sooner than the presumptive sole source contractor. Competitors may also be able to provide superior quality supplies or services.
A thorough search revealed that there is just one contractor that is able to provide the needed supplies or services.	Possibly approve: If the statement is true, then it is a valid reason for approving a sole source contract. However, the agency's contracting staff may be aware of a competitor or may be able to locate a competing contractor through a search for qualified contractors.

1.4 Corruption Avoidance

Subsequent chapters include numerous recommendations for avoiding perils inherent in government contracting. Several of the recommendations are introduced here because they are representative of the big picture — big issues theme of this chapter. A summary of the recommendations and perils that will be avoided through implementation of the recommendations is provided in Table 1.3. A brief introduction to each of these recommendations is provided here.

Table 1.3 Peril Avoidance and Resultant Promises

Recommendations	Resultant Promises
Advance contract planning	Incorporates consideration of actions affecting all phases of the contracting cycle, thereby preparing the government to implement all the subsequent recommendations, thus resulting in the promises stated below
Enhanced ethical standards and practices	Helps avoid the costs arising from the need to compensate corrupt government representatives Helps avoid significantly greater costs associated with increased contract costs needed to compensate corrupt contractors
Full and open competition	Provides government with the best opportunity to obtain the optimal combination of price, quality, and timeliness Minimizes opportunities for corruption
Equal opportunity techniques to implement socioeconomic contracting	Complements full and open competition, resulting in low pricing, high quality, and timely delivery Minimizes opportunities for procurement corruption
Best practices request for proposals (RFP) template	Ensures equal treatment of prospective contractors Minimizes opportunities for procurement corruption Facilitates selection of the best contractor for the needed materials or services Results in award of a contract with provisions well balanced between responsibilities and risks for the government and the contractor Results in homogeneous proposals, thus simplifying proposal evaluation Avoids protests from aggrieved contractors
Proposal evaluation process	Avoids undue influence by individual proposal evaluation team members Facilitates fair and impartial contractor selection process Leads to selection of contractor offering the best value to the government

Table 1.3   Peril Avoidance and Resultant Promises (Continued)

Recommendations	Resultant Promises
Proposal evaluation process (continued)	Avoids unnecessary protests
	Provides a clear, unambiguous score to identify the contractor best meeting the government's requirements
Contract administration techniques	Effective contractor performance monitoring contributes to program success
	Protection against contractor overpayments
	Detection of potential cost overruns in sufficient time for implementing corrective action
	Discourages corruption
Emergency contracting practices	Expedites delivery of needed materials and services
	Facilitates availability of high-quality materials and services
	Minimizes costs associated with responding to emergencies
	Helps avoid procurement corruption
Contract closeout and audit approach	Frees excess funds for other purposes
	Provides information on contractor performance for use in future contractor selections
	Identifies contracting process weaknesses to foster continuous improvement

Advance contract planning represents planning conducted in advance of efforts to draft the solicitation sent to prospective contractors to determine their interest in competing for a contract to provide the needed products, services, or capital project. This planning is not considered *advanced* contract planning. Advance contract planning denotes planning for future events whereas advanced contract planning implies a newly conceived innovative approach to contract planning. Certain government entities, however, have a long history of carefully planning their procurement efforts before they begin drafting the solicitation, similar to the contract planning approach presented in this book. Therefore, advance contract planning is not considered an innovative concept. The recommended advance contract planning encompasses planning for features included in the solicitation and contract, a format for the contractors' proposals or bids, weighted criteria and the proposal scoring technique applicable when an RFP is used as the solicitation document, and reports to be submitted by the contractor during the term of the contract to facilitate contract administration.

Enhanced ethical standards and practices are recommended as two of several approaches designed to address the significant procurement corruption problem that exists. Ethical transgressions decimate not only the lives, families, and careers of affected government and contractor representatives, but also damage the reputations and diminish the resources of government entities and private-sector contractors.

Full and open competition has an undeserved reputation for obtaining inferior products at bargain basement prices. However, when intelligently planned and implemented, full and open competition results in the acquisition of needed products, services, and capital projects at the optimal combination of price, quality, and timeliness.

Socioeconomic contracting also has an undeserved reputation for excluding mainstream contractors from the government procurement process while purchasing inferior products or services from targeted companies at inflated prices. Readers, however, will be introduced to a socioeconomic contracting approach that resulted in significant increases in participation in government contracting by historically underrepresented companies while reducing the cost of materials, increasing the rate of on-time deliveries, and improving the quality of purchased materials.

The best practices RFP recommended for adoption by government entities includes features to discourage procurement corruption, facilitates equal treatment of contractors, includes a model contract with provisions balanced to not favor contractors over government, has a requirement for prospective contractors to prepare homogeneous proposals to simplify proposal evaluation according to the criteria in the RFP, and has numerous other features for improving contract management effectiveness.

The recommended proposal evaluation process includes features to prevent individual proposal evaluation team members from exerting undue influence during the proposal evaluation process, assigns weighting to the criteria to place more emphasis on the criteria that are more critical to program success, discourages unnecessary protests from aggrieved contractors, converts the price (or alternatively, life cycle cost) to a weighted value that can be incorporated in the scores for subjective criteria to provide a single score for each competing contractor representing their relative rating according to the government's criteria. The single score provides the source selection authority or other government official a clear differentiation between the competing contractors to simplify the contractor selection process. The term *source selection authority* (SSA) is used by some government organizations to identify the official with authority to award the contract.

Contract administration techniques and tools are recommended to ensure that contractors are not overpaid, milestones and deliverables are tracked to avoid schedule slippages, measures are in place to discourage corruption, and overruns on cost reimbursement contracts are prevented by detection of probable overruns prior to contract completion.

Implementation of the recommendations for contracting during emergencies eliminates the authority to award sole source contracts except when fully justified, may result in more timely delivery, may result in better quality products and services, and controls costs. This is a fact that appears to be counterintuitive because most government entities waive competitive purchasing during emergencies. Prior to awarding a contract, however, the government requires information from the prospective sole source contractor on the nature of the services or supplies the contractor is able to provide, when the services and supplies can be delivered, and the prices charged by the contractor. Because this information must be obtained from the presumptive sole source contractor, it is logical that the same information necessary to award a contract or purchase order on a sole source basis can be obtained concurrently from multiple contractors, thus permitting a competitively awarded contract. It is genuinely possible for one of the alternative contractors to commence delivery of the needed supplies or services sooner than the presumptive sole source contractor. A process for awarding contracts in the absence of a declared emergency for activation during emergencies is described to minimize the need to locate contractors and award contracts after future emergencies are declared.

Although the Federal Emergency Management Agency (FEMA) reaction to Hurricane Katrina may be considered by many to be the archetype for government dereliction, FEMA has since taken effective corrective actions, as evidenced by its reaction to the wildfires in Southern California. On November 2, 2007, Robert Brodsky reported the following on GovernmentExecutive.com:

> The Federal Emergency Management Agency said it learned a lesson from Hurricane Katrina, where the dearth of precompeted contracts slowed the delivery of goods and led to a number of hastily arranged sole-source deals.
>
> Over the past two years, the agency inked a number of indefinite delivery, indefinite quantity contracts that were then available after President Bush declared much of Southern California a federal disaster area in late October.

This is a lesson learned that has likely been carried over into President Obama's administration.

A process for closeout of completed contracts and conducting audits is recommended to make excess funds available, provide data on contractor performance that is available for future source selection activities, and identify contract management weaknesses that can be addressed on future contracts to achieve continuous improvement to the contracting process.

1.5 Conclusion

The topics discussed previously are explored in greater depth in subsequent chapters by citing additional examples of problems actually encountered in government contracting, recommendations for avoiding or mitigating problems, and the consequences of participating in government contracting without first developing either requisite contracting skills or respect for laws protecting the public from corrupt officials.

Nefarious, amateurish, and criminal behaviors contaminate government contracting globally, from the smallest villages to national governments and multinational organizations. An excellent description of the nature and extent of the problem is provided in the following material from the Transparency International website:[14]

> An avoidable misuse and abuse of public funds results from corruption. Corruption in public contracting leads to a distortion of fair competition, the waste of scarce resources and the neglect of basic needs, perpetuating poverty. Massive market inefficiencies can also arise from corruption and, in the extreme, lead to the destruction of development opportunities. If corruption in public contracting is not contained, it will grow. It is estimated that systemic corruption can add 20–25% to the costs of government procurement, and frequently results in inferior quality goods and services and unnecessary purchases.
>
> It is argued that, on average, approximately 70% of central government expenditure turns in one way or another into contracts. Contracts are sources of power to those who give them out, and targets of ambition for those who may receive them, making public contracts particularly prone to abuse at the expense of public need. The risk of corruption in public contracting exists even before the contracting process has started, perhaps even at the moment when public budgets are allocated, and it perpetuates beyond the awarding of a contract to its implementation.
>
> For all these reasons TI [Transparency International] has been working on alerting governments, the business community and civil society worldwide about the importance of curbing corruption in public contracting and on developing a number of anti-corruption tools. Most importantly, TI has demonstrated that corruption in public contracting can be reduced.

This opening chapter has explored the extent of the problem and introduced recommendations for improving ethics and efficiency in government contracting. Further discussion of the problem and expanded descriptions of the proposed solutions are contained in subsequent chapters.

Notes

1. Taken from a presentation by Dr. Abubakar H. Kargbo entitled, "Corruption: Definition and Concept Manifestations and Typology in the African Context" at the 2006 Sierra Leone Workshop for members of Civil Society for English-speaking West Africa.
2. Dollar figures are shown in U.S. dollars throughout this book.

3. "Strengthening Bank Group Engagement on Governance and Anticorruption," September 8, 2006.

4. *The Seattle Times*, "Former U.N. Procurement Officer Pleads Guilty to Taking Bribes from U.N. Contractors," by Nick Wadhams and Edith M. Lederer (Associated Press), August 8, 2005.

5. *Moscow New*, "From NY — With a Prison Sentence," November 11, 2008.

6. *The Washington Post*, "U.N. Cites $20 Million in Fraud," by Colum Lynch, October 21, 2008.

7. WebMemo published by the Heritage Foundation, "The Demise of the U.N. Procurement Task Force Threatens Oversight at the U.N.," by Brett D. Schaefer, February 5, 2009.

8. "President of Private Inspection Service Company Admits Paying a Bribe to the Former Cherry Hill Director of Code Enforcement and Inspections," April 22, 2009.

9. The psychiatric evaluation is contained in a letter from Dr. Saul J. Faerstein, M.D., Re: Randall Harold "Duke" Cunningham, to The Honorable Larry Alan Burns, United States District Judge, February 13, 2006, and was prepared for Judge Burns' consideration in the sentencing of Mr. Cunningham.

10. The Merck case was announced in a Department of Justice media release, "Merck Agrees to Pay $399 Million to Resolve Allegations of Improper Medicaid Billing and Improper Inducements to Healthcare Professionals," February 7, 2008.

11. The False Claims Act provides for nongovernment personnel with insider information on procurement fraud, normally employees or former employees of government contractors, to file a suit against a government contractor. The federal government then joins the suit and the insider (or whistleblower) receives a share of the proceeds received by the government.

12. The problem of the shrinking federal government workforce has been recognized and is being addressed, as evidenced by the GovernmentExecutive.com article, "Army Increases Ranks of Contracting Personnel, but Gaps Remain," Elizabeth Newell, March 26, 2009.

13. FederalTimes.com, "DoD to Add 20,000 Acquisition Personnel," Elise Castelli, April 13, 2009.

14. Adapted from "Global Priorities: Public Contracting," Copyright June 5, 2009, Transparency International: The Global Coalition against Corruption. Used with permission. For more information, visit http://www.transparency.org.

Chapter 2

Processes and Issues in Contracting

2.1 The Contracting Cycle: Overview of the Contracting Process

> Each thing is of like form from ever lasting and comes round again in its cycle.
>
> **Marcus Aurelius**

Prior to discussing the promises and perils of advance contract planning, the cycle of activities in the contracting cycle is described to provide readers with an overview of the contracting process and how advance contract planning influences the balance of activities included in the contracting cycle. Although Marcus Aurelius was likely not thinking of government contracts when he uttered the remark about cycles, as quoted above, his observation is most fitting for this subject. Describing the various phases of the contracting cycle provides an overview of the subject matter and helps provide a meaningful framework for consideration of the big picture and government contracting issues. The material in this book is presented in the sequence of the contracting cycle. The contracting cycle begins with the pre-solicitation phase and proceeds through development of the solicitation, proposal evaluation, contract award, contract administration, and contract closeout.

2.1.1 Pre-Solicitation Phase

The pre-solicitation phase of the contracting cycle begins immediately following the government's decision to send a solicitation to qualified, or apparently qualified, prospective contractors. Extensive planning for all phases of the contracting cycle is required prior to release of the solicitation. Failure to plan for each phase increases the likelihood of problems leading to unsatisfactory performance or absolute program failure. The specific problems that are likely to occur in a poorly planned or poorly executed contract will be addressed in the following discussion of each phase of the contracting cycle. The generic promise resulting from a well-planned contract is the increased likelihood for program success. Specific promises emanating from well-planned and well-executed contracts will also be addressed in the discussion of the contracting cycle.

For high-value or high-risk projects, an advance contract planning team is normally formed to establish the methodology and parameters for soliciting and selecting the contractor. For lower value or lower risk contracts, the contract planning team may be limited to one or two individuals. The term "advance contract planning team" is used in this book to represent either a traditional team or just one or two individuals performing the contract planning functions. A list of problems that are most likely to occur during the pre-solicitation phase is provided below:

- If available competitors are not identified, and a sole source contract is approved inappropriately, the agency is not able to obtain the numerous benefits available through full and open competition.
- Problems can also occur in a competitive environment:
  - The RFP may not contain features that guard against conflicts of interest.
  - The lack of a model contract in the RFP invites prospective contractors to submit their contract format with provisions favoring the contractor at the government's expense.
  - Proposal evaluation criteria may not accurately reflect the agency's needs, thus leading to selection of a less than optimal contractor.
  - Selection of a flawed proposal evaluation process may result in selection of a contractor that does not best meet the agency's requirements.
- Failure to establish an effective pre-proposal communications management plan may result in uneven treatment of prospective contractors or protests from aggrieved contractors, or provide opportunities for conflicts of interests including perils, such as those included in Table 1.1.

Advance contract planning is essential to program success. Failure to effectively plan for a solicitation document with the requisite provisions discussed above can not only contaminate the solicitation phase, but also is likely to result in selection of a less than optimal contractor. The problems associated with selecting other than the optimal contractor will be compounded if an effective contract document was not planned. A contract with inadequate provisions for assigning contractor responsibility, ill-defined contractor reporting requirements, inadequate deliverables and milestone schedules, and a lack of provisions for improving the performance of an underachieving contractor foretell a less than optimal contract outcome. Effective advance contract planning provides promise for selecting the contractor proposing the optimal combination of price, quality, and on-time delivery, thus greatly improving the probability for program success.

2.1.2 Solicitation Phase

The solicitation phase commences when the RFP is released to prospective contractors and terminates when the proposals are received by the contracting agency. Although one might believe intuitively that activities conducted during this phase of the contracting cycle are restricted to prospective contractors, agency personnel do have specific responsibilities during the solicitation phase. This can truly be one of the most problematic contracting phases for government representatives. Prospective contractors may elect to engage in intelligence-gathering activities during the solicitation phase. The probability for intensive intelligence gathering is heightened when the market is highly competitive. Although most contractors do not possess criminal intent during intelligence gathering, the potentially sensitive nature of activities at this time requires government management of communications between agency personnel and contractors to ensure equal treatment for all prospective contractors. Information relayed to one contractor that is not provided to all other prospective contractors is considered favored treatment. Failure to treat contractors equally constitutes a serious variation from agency protocol and can result in a protest from an unsuccessful contractor. Protests that have been filed on a sound basis have potential for reflecting poorly on the professionalism and ethics of agency officials. Subsequent chapters include recommendations for managing pre-proposal communications and agency reaction to the receipt of protests.

There is a far greater potential for perils than promises during the solicitation phase. This phase begins following completion of government's intense efforts to complete advance contract planning and develop the RFP. The principal documentation prepared during this phase of the contracting cycle consists of proposals prepared by prospective contractors. Government's primary responsibility during this phase is management of pre-proposal communications. Government's failure to adequately manage communications during the solicitation phase can result in less than equal treatment of prospective contractors, which can lead to otherwise unnecessary protests from aggrieved contractors. Protests, as in the U.S. Air Force aircraft refueling tanker program that is discussed in detail in a subsequent chapter, can create huge expenses for the government, significantly delay program commencement, and result in the need to use obsolete equipment for an extended period of time. Delays in contract award can result in the loss of funding leading to cancellation of the program. The promise for managing pre-proposal communications well is limited to the avoidance of unnecessary protests. Although there is no guarantee that there will be no protests during this phase of the contracting cycle, the potential for protests is lessened for government entities that effectively manage pre-proposal communications.

2.1.3 Proposal Evaluation Phase

The proposal evaluation phase begins upon receipt of proposals from prospective contractors and ends when the proposal evaluation team selects a contractor or recommends a contractor for contract award. Although the previous contracting cycle phase is sensitive and may involve unethical behavior or criminal acts, the proposal evaluation phase is where most procurement corruption occurs. The unethical behavior or criminal acts referred to in the pre-proposal phase involve less than equal treatment of prospective contractors. Unequal treatment can range from the relatively innocent response to a question that is not provided to all prospective contractors to the more serious transgression involving advice limited to one contractor on how it might structure its proposal to ensure contract capture. The proposal evaluation phase of the contracting cycle involves considerably more significant risks for contract corruption. It was in this phase of the contracting cycle that Duke Cunningham, who was improperly involved with Defense Department contractors, and the Cherry Hill township employee, who was allegedly involved in tampering with the award of inspection services contracts, allegedly committed the illicit activities that led to their plea bargaining or guilty pleas. One serious peril faced during the proposal evaluation phase of the contracting cycle is the possibility of a government representative steering the contract award to a particular contractor in exchange for a gratuity or kickback. Although such illicit steering of a contract award is the most egregious peril, government is also subject to the relatively more innocent peril of selecting a less than optimal contractor through use of a deficient proposal evaluation process. Perils faced when employing a deficient proposal evaluation process include not only the chance of selecting the wrong contractor, but the increased probability of receiving a protest from an aggrieved contractor. Perils faced during the proposal evaluation phase can lead to program commencement delays; less than optimal program results; program failure; prosecution of government and contractor personnel if their actions constitute criminal activity; as well as fines, restitution, suspension, or debarring of contractors. Although no proposal evaluation process can promise selection of the optimal contractor, the avoidance of unethical behavior or conflicts of interests, or even the commission of criminal acts, implementation of the proposal evaluation process recommended in a subsequent chapter will significantly reduce the potential for selecting the wrong contractor or receiving a protest due to a faulty proposal evaluation process, conflict of interest, unethical behavior, or a criminal act. The promise from implementing the recommended proposal evaluation process is a greater potential for selecting the best-qualified contractor and for success of the government program.

A subsequent chapter provides details on the advantages and disadvantages of various methods for evaluating proposals. A well-disciplined approach to evaluating proposals helps government avoid improper contract awards. One of the more salient considerations when evaluating proposals is the importance of basing contractor selection solely on the evaluation criteria contained in the RFP. Deviations from the criteria in the RFP for evaluation of proposals can result in a protest from an aggrieved contractor or be an indicator of an attempt to improperly steer a contract to a favored contractor.

2.1.4 Contract Award Phase

The contract award phase begins when the proposal evaluation team completes the evaluation of proposals and selects a contractor or recommends a contractor for award of a contract and ends when there is an uncontested contract award. High-value contracts are normally awarded by a high-ranking agency official who did not participate in the proposal evaluation process. The goal of the proposal evaluation team is to select the contractor that submitted the proposal reflecting the best value to the government and present their recommendation to the SSA. The goal of the SSA is to award the contract to the contractor that submitted the proposal reflecting the best value to the government. The proposal evaluation team may dedicate hundreds or thousands of hours evaluating proposals to present the SSA with their recommendation. The best practices research project, referenced earlier, revealed that a significant number of government entities that assign weighted evaluation criteria fail to assign a weight to price or life cycle cost. Presenting the SSA with one or more numbers representing the weighted scores plus a separate number representing the price or life cycle costs confounds the recommendation. The SSA receiving such vague or even contradictory indicators of the proposal evaluation team's results may feel that contract award to any of the competing contractors is justified. An example of contradictory information that might be presented to the SSA is reflected in Table 2.1. Other government agencies that weigh price or life cycle cost oftentimes fail to calculate a single score to identify the recommended

Table 2.1 Conflicting Information Provided to Source Selection Authority

Criteria	Weight	Contractors		
		A	B	C
Technical	25	85	83	79
Management	20	86	80	88
Past performance	20	81	80	82
Life cycle cost (billions)	35	$9.2	$9.4	$9.0

contractor, and present the SSA with multiple scores, such as reflected in Table 2.1, to consider when selecting the winning contractor.

The SSA presented with the information provided in Table 2.1 faces a difficult choice. Contractor A received the highest technical score and the second highest score for all the other criteria. Contractor C proposed the lowest life cycle cost (which is assigned the highest weight) and also has the highest scores for management and past performance. In this case the SSA may feel some flexibility to award the contract to either Contractor A or C. The perils resulting from conflicting information presented to the SSA are that the SSA may inadvertently award the contract to the wrong contractor, the proposal evaluation team members may believe that the SSA merely awarded the contract to a favorite contractor, the SSA may actually award the contract to a favorite contractor, or one of the unsuccessful contractors may file a protest based on the belief that the information presented in Table 2.1 indicates that the contract should have been awarded to their company.

The promise results from implementation of the proposal evaluation process described in Chapter 7, which provides a formula for converting the price or life cycle cost to a score that reflects the appropriate criterion weighting and that can be combined with scores for the other criteria. Providing a single combined score reflecting the weighting for all the criteria clearly reflects the proposal evaluation team's recommendation for contract award and provides the SSA with unambiguous results that clearly reflect the contractor recommended for contract award. Removing ambiguity from the proposal evaluation team's recommendation for contract award is likely to discourage protests from aggrieved contractors, provide the SSA with a clear indication of the recommended contractor, and discourage that rare SSA who might be tempted to award a contract to his or her favorite contractor.

Opportunities abound globally for fraud during the contract award phase of the contracting cycle, as evidenced by the guilty plea by the German industrial company Siemens AG for violating the Foreign Corrupt Practices Act (FCPA).[1] According to an article in *The Washington Times*, Siemens AG officials carried suitcases filled with cash to pay over $1 billion in bribes to receive public works contracts in Argentina, Bangladesh, and Venezuela. As a result of Siemens AG's guilty plea, they were required to pay fines of $1.6 billion, to be divided between U.S. and German authorities. Additionally, Siemens AG is required to be under the supervision of an independent monitor for four years.

2.1.5 Contract Administration Phase

The contract administration phase begins upon the uncontested award of the contract and continues until the contractor has fulfilled all its contractual responsibilities. The contractor provides services, delivers products, or constructs a capital project. This phase of the contracting cycle oftentimes extends over a period of time that exceeds the combined time for all previous phases. Virtually all of the contractor's responsibilities are fulfilled during the contract administration phase.

Agency personnel are generally involved in numerous activities during this phase of the contracting cycle. These activities include attending project meetings with the contractor if applicable, monitoring the contractor's performance, evaluating contractor billings for approval of periodic payments, evaluating proposed changes to the contract provisions, negotiating contract changes, and preparing modifications to the contract. Significant involvement on the part of agency personnel is required to deal with problem solving when a contractor's performance is substandard. In the case of the $40-million-per-year dump truck contracts discussed in Chapter 1, basic monitoring of the contractors' performance would likely have revealed that numerous trucks were idle during virtually the entire contract administration phase. Had the fact been reported that the trucks were not needed, this wasteful practice might have been stopped sooner. Recommendations for reacting to underperforming contractors are provided in a subsequent chapter.

Failure to establish an effective contract administration program exposes government entities to numerous problems. Many problems are made possible by ineffective agency contract administrators. A more dangerous situation, however, occurs when dishonest agency and contractor personnel collude to:

- Approve payment for incomplete work
- Approve payment for inferior work
- Fail to identify a probable cost overrun
- Fail to identify an underperforming contractor
- Make unauthorized changes to the contract
- Negotiate inflated pricing for contract modifications

Contract administration phase promises result from implementation of the recommendations provided in Chapter 8, which provide government with an approach and tools for administering contracts to best assure contractor performance according to the provisions of the contract. The recommendations include contractor prepared reports that are verified by the government and then used to analyze the contractor's progress. Implementation of recommendations to analyze contractor invoices helps ensure that contractor payments do not exceed the amount earned for work actually performed.

2.1.6 Contract Closeout Phase

The contract closeout phase normally involves routine matters beginning upon completion of the contract work or termination of the contract and is completed when the records are destroyed because the records retention period has elapsed. Activities performed during this phase include preparation of the contractor's performance report, if applicable, relief of financial encumbrances, if any, maintenance of the contract records, contract audit, and eventual destruction of the contract records.

Contractor performance reports are recommended to record government's observations regarding the quality of the contractor's performance. Contractor

·ts are valuable when evaluating contractors for award of future
g financial encumbrances makes those funds available for other
Auditing completed contracts may provide government with
_____ation on deficient contracting practices that can be modified to enhance
efficiencies and ethical practices in the award of future contracts.

Table 2.2 provides a summary of the events that occur during the contracting cycle.

Table 2.2   Phases of the Contracting Cycle

Phase	Events during Each Phase
Pre-solicitation	Advance contract planning Initiate list of prospective contractors Develop guidelines for RFP and proposal evaluation Establish strategy for management of pre-proposal communications
Solicitation	Contractors prepare their proposals Respond to inquiries from contractors Manage pre-proposal communications
Proposal evaluation	Receive proposals and treat them confidentially Evaluate proposals according to criteria in the RFP Conduct negotiations as appropriate
Contract award	Guard against unlikely event of collusion Respond in a timely and complete manner to contractor protests Award contract
Contract administration	Monitor contractor's performance Evaluate contractor's invoices prior to payment approval Ensure that deliverables meet contract specifications Guard against collusion
Contract closeout	Relieve financial encumbrances Prepare contractor performance report Audit contract if applicable Maintain records for specified time period Destroy records at completion of retention period

2.2 Consequences of Failed Contract Planning

> An individual who is observed to be inconstant in his plans, or perhaps to carry on his affairs without any plans at all, is marked at once, by all prudent people, as a speedy victim in his own unsteadiness and folly.

Alexander Hamilton

Criticizing the results of failed procurements after the fact is immeasurably simple when compared to planning for the future. When assuming the role of second guesser, one might feel the need to apologize for taking advantage of the benefit of hindsight. However, the recounting of an actual contract planning failure is a convenient means for illustrating such failures and the consequences thereof. The benefits derived from learning from the mistakes of others, therefore, appear to justify the second guessing involved in illustrating past contract planning errors. Rather than use numerous examples to illustrate the multitude of perils inherent in the failure to include predictable events in the contracting process, just one example from an odious case is employed to illustrate the consequences of failed contract planning. The now infamous, yet ongoing, program selected for this purpose is the U.S. Air Force air refueling tanker procurement. The Air Force and The Boeing Company have made significant admirable contributions to the defense of the free world. The nefarious behavior of two individuals, one a former USAF representative and one a former representative of Boeing, represents an infinitesimally small percentage of the USAF and Boeing workforce and is not considered as representative behavior for officials from these organizations.

There was considerable reluctance to select a USAF program as an example of contract planning that repeatedly went awry. This reluctance is based on the fact that it was the late General Bernard Schriever (USAF retired) who as commander of the Air Force Systems Command and guiding force behind the revolution in systems procurement contributed immeasurably to the effort that enabled the United States to achieve a lead in the development of intercontinental ballistic missiles during the arms race in the 1950s and 1960s.

2.2.1 Basic Advance Contract Planning and the Need to Obtain Full and Open Competition

A 2003 Boeing media release, "U.S. Air Force — Boeing 767 Tanker Lease Explained," provided background information on the air refueling tanker program, beginning with the Air Force's concern regarding the condition of the aging aircraft and the cost effectiveness of operating, maintaining, and upgrading the air refueling fleet. Congress authorized the Air Force to explore the viability of leasing 100 Boeing 767 tankers in 2001. Of course, Congress would not have authorized this exploration unless the Air Force had performed some preliminary analysis and then pitched the concept to Congress for authorization. Presenting a multi-billion dollar aircraft leasing scheme to Congress appears to have been in direct conflict with basic contract planning practices that demand full and open competition. Leasing aircraft that require extensive modification of passenger aircraft to meet air refueling tanker capabilities consistent with the Air Force's needs actually constitutes a purchase that is distinguished from other procurements merely by manufacturer or a third-party financing. The reality of a purchase rather than some temporary lease is based partially on the fact that the aircraft would never be converted back to passenger service. The colossal expenditure of funds required for the lease, regardless of whether the Air Force keeps the aircraft permanently or eventually returns them to Boeing, demands the introduction of competition to ensure that taxpayer funds are spent intelligently. The Department of Defense Inspector General (DoD IG) report (Report no. OIG-2004-171, May 13, 2005) included the finding that although senior Air Force officials argued that an operational lease was justified because the aircraft was a commercial item, this action did not meet the commercial item standards specified in Section 403 of title 41, U.S. Code. Therefore, basic logic and the DoD IG report clearly show that the lease was actually a multi-billion dollar procurement. With a high-value procurement, one of the very first actions of the advance contract planning team is to establish a list of prospective contractors. The DoD IG report indicated that the tanker lease deal was being guided for the Air Force by Ms. Darlene Druyun (then principal deputy assistant secretary of the Air Force [Acquisition and Management]) and for Boeing by Mr. Michael Sears, Boeing chief financial officer. Despite the basic requirement to investigate the availability of Boeing competitors, the Air Force presented its proposal for a multi-billion dollar sole source procurement. The fact that the proposed procurement was based on a lease from Boeing and financed through a third party did not justify negotiation of the agreement on a sole source basis. The same DoD IG report also includes acknowledgment by DoD officials of the need for competition and the fact that the aircraft were actually being purchased. The text of an e-mail regarding the tanker lease from a Pentagon comptroller's office official to a deputy undersecretary of defense included the following statement: "The key of course is to include some *competition* into the *purchase* process." [emphasis added]

2.2.2 Personal Consequences Stemming from Corrupt Practices

In November 2002, Ms. Druyun recused herself from further negotiations with Boeing, tendered her retirement, and accepted an executive position with Boeing. The National Defense University and the Defense Science Board reviewed the tanker lease deal and found five statutory provisions that were not met while conducting this procurement. Those provisions relate to commercial items, two testing provisions, cost-plus-a-percentage-of-cost contracting, and leases. The deputy secretary of defense placed the Boeing KC-767A tanker program on hold. In a tentative agreement between Boeing and the Department of Justice, Boeing agreed to pay $565 million for civil claims and a penalty of $50 million. In November 2003 Boeing dismissed Ms. Druyun and Mr. Sears. Mr. Sears pleaded guilty to illegally helping Ms. Druyun land the executive position at Boeing (while she was employed by the Air Force). Mr. Sears was sentenced to four months in prison, was fined $250,000, and received two years probation. Ms. Druyun pleaded guilty to favoring Boeing in numerous contract negotiations, including the tanker lease, because she felt indebted to Boeing for giving jobs to her daughter, her son-in-law, and herself. Ms. Druyun was sentenced to nine months in prison and seven months in a halfway house, and she was fined $5,000. One week following the firing of Sears and Druyun, the Boeing chief executive officer resigned from his position.

In January 2007 the Air Force continued to rely on the aging fleet of tankers and released an RFP for a competitive purchase to finally replace the air refueling tankers.

Although not directly related to advance contract planning or the consequences of failed contract planning, brief mention of the fate of Charles Riechers is worthy in this chronology of the problems plaguing Air Force procurement. Mr. Riechers was a retired Air Force officer who was appointed as the principal deputy assistant secretary for acquisition after Ms. Druyun's departure. Mr. Riechers died at his home of an apparent suicide. There was an ongoing inquiry into payments being made to Mr. Riechers by another defense contractor; however, it was unclear if there was a relationship between his apparent suicide and that inquiry.

2.2.3 Organizational Consequences Stemming from Failure to Guard against Protests

In February of 2008, the Air Force announced the award of a contract to the Northrop Grumman/European Aeronautics Defence and Space Company (Northrop/EADS). Boeing protested the award, and the investigation of the protest by the Government Accountability Office (GAO) upheld Boeing's protest. Although it is impossible to determine the details of the advance contract planning that transpired for the air refueling tanker program, it is possible to gain insight into the planning process through review of the reasons the GAO stated (GAO press release of June 18, 2008, and in their published decision of the same date) for sustaining Boeing's protest. The GAO cited seven reasons for sustaining Boeing's protest. The first two are the result of advance contract planning failures. Two of the remaining five are tied to planning failures, but no attempt is made to illustrate that relationship here. The first two reasons from GAO's press release for sustaining Boeing's protest are presented below, followed by the rationale for tying these reasons to advance contract planning failures:

> Finding 1: The Air Force, in making the award decision, did not assess the relative merits of the proposals in accordance with the evaluation criteria identified in the solicitation, which provided for a relative order of importance for the various technical requirements. The agency also

did not take into account the fact that Boeing offered to satisfy more non-mandatory technical "requirements" than Northrop Grumman, even though the solicitation expressly requested offerors to satisfy as many of these technical "requirements" as possible.

Finding 2: The Air Force's use as a key discriminator that Northrop Grumman proposed to exceed a key performance parameter objective relating to aerial refueling to a greater degree than Boeing violated the solicitation's evaluation provision that "no consideration will be provided for exceeding [key performance parameter] objectives."

2.2.3.1 Rationale for Tying Finding 1 to Poor Contract Planning

The first sentence of Finding 1 indicates that the proposal evaluation team varied from the weighting of evaluation criteria stated in the solicitation. This variance from the stated weighting for the evaluation criteria suggests that the proposal evaluation team did not agree with the weighting of the criteria that is normally established by the advance contract planning team. The failure to conform to evaluation criteria or weighting of evaluation criteria is a serious infraction of the evaluation rules established by the contracting agency. It is essential that determinations made during the contract planning process do not require modification to match the agency's actual requirements after the proposals are received. The second sentence in Finding 1 indicates that the solicitation referred to "non-mandatory technical requirements." Such a term, including both "non-mandatory" and "requirements," is a blatant oxymoron. Based on the finding, it is apparent that the proposal evaluators gave more importance to "non-mandatory" whereas the GAO gave more importance to "requirements." It is essential that evaluation criteria be expressed clearly to avoid any possibility of misinterpretation.

2.2.3.2 Rationale for Tying Finding 2 to Poor Contract Planning

Finding 2 relates to the fact that the Air Force provided a higher score to Northrop/EADS because the fuel-carrying capacity of the aircraft proposed by Northrop/EADS significantly exceeded the fuel-carrying capacity of the aircraft proposed by Boeing, but the solicitation indicated that no consideration is provided for exceeding objectives. The concept of not providing consideration for exceeding objectives is a basic maxim in the evaluation of systems proposals. However, it is the responsibility of the contract planning team to establish objectives that reflect available technology and sought-after mission performance. When aircraft manufacturers can deliver aircraft capable of significantly exceeding historical fuel-carrying capacity, and when greater fuel-carrying capacity is favorable, then the evaluation criteria must be structured to consider the advantage of greater fuel-carrying capacity. In this case, the fuel-carrying capacity objective stated in the RFP apparently approximated the capability of existing tankers, and the

RFP stated that consideration would not be given for exceeding that objective. However, when the proposal evaluation team realized the advantages of the greater fuel-carrying capacity, they elected, although contrary to solicitation provisions, to give extra consideration to the Northrop/EADS proposal. The advance contract planning team ideally would have taken into consideration the fact that aircraft manufacturers are capable of providing air refueling tanker aircraft with fuel-carrying capacity significantly greater than the 1950s-era aircraft and determine whether that would benefit the government. Had Boeing been made aware of the desirability of a greater fuel-carrying capacity, it might have proposed a larger aircraft.

2.2.4 Additional Topics for Consideration

Once it is determined that significant changes to the specifications for an existing system are advantageous, there is the need to evaluate all advantages and disadvantages of other changes necessitated by that change. When increasing the fuel-carrying capacity specification for aircraft that will replace an existing fleet, for example, it is necessary to consider the probability of the need to acquire significantly larger aircraft than those in the existing fleet. When replacement aircraft are larger than aircraft in an existing fleet, it is necessary to evaluate the cost and practicality of increasing the size of hangars, aircraft parking aprons, and runways to accommodate the larger aircraft. It is possible that some or all of the existing bases where refueling tankers are based cannot accommodate the larger aircraft or that the cost associated with accommodating the larger aircraft is prohibitive. Of course, it is also possible that the larger aircraft may have greater range, in addition to their greater fuel-carrying capacity, which would contribute to reduced operating costs and a reduction in the number of bases where the aircraft are based. When these factors are included in the advance contract planning process, however, it is necessary to include them in the solicitation and in the evaluation criteria. Only then can prospective contractors determine the appropriate aircraft to propose to best meet the contracting agency's requirements.

Although these observations are made through the benefit of hindsight, and there were problems not associated with inadequate advance planning, it is evident that improved advance planning for the air refueling tanker program would likely have provided a considerably lower priced replacement aircraft and earlier replacement of the aging air refueling tanker fleet. Although Congress authorized the Air Force to explore replacement of the air refueling tanker fleet in 2001, repeated missteps through 2008 made it virtually impossible to award a contract prior to 2009. The contract award may even be delayed until 2010 or later. In the intervening years, taxpayer dollars have been fettered away, careers have been ruined, families have been devastated, significant monetary fines have been imposed, and people have been sentenced to prison. It is hoped that government learns from these past shortcomings and applies the lessons learned to future contracting actions.

2.3 Program Success through Effective Contract Planning

Strategic planning will help you fully uncover your available options, set priorities for them, and define methods to achieve them.

Robert J. McKain[2]

The advance contract planning effort normally begins immediately following the government's decision to release solicitations to prospective private-sector contractors. For high-value or high-risk projects, an advance contract planning team is normally formed to establish the methodology and parameters for soliciting and selecting the contractor, preparing the initial list of firms to be solicited, establishing a strategy for managing pre-proposal communications, defining the content and format for proposals, establishing criteria and criteria weighting for evaluating proposals, awarding the contract, and determining reports required to manage contractor performance. A summary of these activities is provided here. Readers who wish to have more detailed information on these activities are referred to the file entitled "Detailed Advance Contract Planning Team Considerations" on the CD that accompanies this book. The CD also contains templates for RFPs and contracts that incorporate the features described in this section.

2.3.1 Appoint the Advance Contract Planning Team

As discussed earlier in this chapter, advance contract planning may be a team project for high-value critical programs or it may be performed by one or two individuals for less significant programs. The advance contract planning team is responsible for all the activities outlined here and detailed on the CD that accompanies this book, to include planning the actions required to solicit proposals, defining criteria for evaluating proposals received from contractors, establishing the process for evaluating proposals received from prospective contractors, and defining contractor reports that will be required to administer the contract after it is awarded. Selection of a well-rounded team allows for diverse expertise, which contributes to successful project management including technical aspects, contract management, finance, and oversight of the contractor's performance. Failure to select a multidisciplinary team increases the probability of overlooking consideration of certain disciplines that are essential for project success. Selecting team members who can commit to team participation beginning with advance contract planning and continuing through contract award helps ensure continuity throughout the contracting cycle. Continued participation of advance planning team members through the contract administration phase permits firsthand knowledge of the reasoning behind the decisions made during the advance planning phase throughout all key phases of the contracting cycle. The preferred timing for assigning the project manager to the team is during the advance contract planning phase. The project manager is the central figure involved in all decision making during the term of the contract, and his or her participation in the advance planning, contractor selection, and contract award activities provides valuable background for decision making during the contract administration phase.

2.3.2 *Prepare the Project Background Statement*

The advance contract planning team normally evaluates conditions leading to the decision to solicit private-sector companies, or individuals, to perform a particular service or provide a specific product for the agency. Those conditions form the basis for the background statement included in the solicitation informing the prospective contractors of the project's background. This need not be a lengthy document, but is best reduced to writing to permit future reference by team members. The best practices RFP includes a section where the background statement, or a variation thereof, is inserted. The next step is to develop the project objectives. The objectives, understandably, are closely correlated with the project background and agency policy. Development of the project objectives may be accelerated through a brainstorming session and a review of the objectives established for similar projects. Once the project objectives are completed, the actions needed to meet those objectives can be established.

2.3.3 *Establish a Website*

Agency websites are often provided for contracting matters to keep contractors and prospective contractors informed of ongoing contracting efforts, to provide general information about the agency and its contracting function, to permit companies and individuals to register with the agency as prospective contractors, and to announce the award or recommended award of contracts. However, managing pre-proposal communications through an agency website is one of the greatest benefits with respect to the contracting process. Requiring all prospective contractors to submit questions regarding the solicitation and proposal process via e-mail to one designated agency official is the first step in managing pre-proposal communications. The agency official receiving the questions and posting both the questions and the agency responses on the website completes the pre-proposal communications management process. This process helps ensure that all prospective contractors are treated equally during the pre-proposal phase of the contracting cycle and prevents communications that favor one contractor over its competitors.

2.3.4 *Prepare List of Contractors to Be Solicited*

Development of a list of prospective contractors early in the planning process is recommended because preparation of the list is normally time consuming and a delay in the availability of this list delays both the release of the solicitation and project commencement. A comprehensive list of prospective contractors is essential for obtaining full and open competition, thus ensuring competitive pricing and minimizing opportunities for contract corruption. A search of the government entity's database containing contact information on companies that have been awarded government contracts or expressed an interest in performing government contracts is normally the initial step to identify prospective contractors. Members of the advance contract planning team and the government's central contract management office may be able to suggest additional companies for inclusion on the list of contractors to be solicited. Internet searches, trade directories, and even telephone yellow pages are other good sources. Qualified companies for highly complex or technical products or services may not have a presence in developing countries. However, international companies providing such products and services are likely to be discovered during Internet searches.

2.3.5 *Develop Solicitation Ground Rules*

Proper use of terminology in the RFP and contract, such as referring to the contractors' response to an RFP solely as a "proposal" and not as a bid, and referring to contractors as "contractor" or "prospective contractor" and not as vendor, helps avoid incongruities within the contract documents. Establishing effective proposal scoring techniques, avoiding ineffective scoring techniques that might enable ineffective or fraudulent contractor selection, establishing weighted proposal evaluation criteria, including price or life cycle cost as one of the criteria, and ensuring that proposals are evaluated solely by the criteria in the RFP helps avoid the filing of protests by aggrieved contractors. Establishing a format for proposals submitted by contractors, and describing the proposal format in the RFP, results in more homogeneous proposals that are relatively simple to evaluate. Establishing page limits for each specified proposal topic adds to the homogeneity of the proposals and further simplifies the proposal evaluation process. Defining the terms "responsive" and "responsible" in the RFP minimizes delays caused by confusion when the agency elects to determine any proposals to be nonresponsive or determine any contractors to be not responsible. Describing a debriefing procedure as well as a process for filing a protest in the RFP likely avoids the filing of a protest and also avoids an improper protest filing.

2.3.6 *Decide Model Contract Provisions*

A one-page contract format consists of a single-page contract document with all essential contract information such as pricing, contracting parties, contract price, nature of the contract, and incorporation of contract attachments such as the scope of work and the agency's terms and conditions provided on the same page as the contract signatures. This one-page contract format is recommended because it avoids errors on contract documents and ensures the official signing the contract that she or he is not signing the equivalent of a blank check. The agency terms and conditions that are commonly attached to the contract do not normally require modification because that is a recurring document periodically reviewed by legal counsel. The scope of work, however, is typically prepared specifically and independently for a single contract. Therefore, more care is often given, while preparing the model contract, to the proper structuring of the scope of work than to the agency terms and conditions. Common errors that occur in drafting a scope of work are the failure to use the word that best compels a contractor to perform, such as "shall" for the federal government and most states, and the failure to define the contractor as the party required to perform mandatory tasks described in the scope of work. The inclusion of a statement in the RFP to the effect that the agency intends to award a contract essentially in the form of the enclosed model contract helps avoid the problems associated with contractors proposing their own contract format. Government entities are urged to avoid use of contractor formats for contracts because contractor-prepared provisions likely favor contractor rights over the rights of the government. The terms and conditions in the model contract on the CD are not intended as substitutes for FAR clauses or any other provisions that may be mandatory for certain government entities.

2.3.7 *Proposal Evaluation Guidelines*

Contracting agencies generally benefit from providing information in their solicitations that describes how the contractor selection process is conducted. In most agencies, late proposals in response to an RFP are acceptable and all proposals are treated confidentially; therefore, there is no public opening of proposals. Bids in response to an invitation for bids (IFB), however, are normally opened publicly, read aloud, and rejected if received late. Because some prospective contractors may be confused by the differences in the treatment of bids and proposals and by treatment differences between various government entities, it is recommended that prospective contractors be advised in the solicitation on the acceptability of late bids or proposals, the confidential treatment of proposals, and if there is a public opening of the bids or proposals. When agencies advise prospective contractors that late proposals may be accepted, it is recommended that contractors also be advised that delivery of proposals on time is recommended because the agency may reject late proposals. The second part of the recommendation discourages the late submittal of proposals by permitting summary rejection of late proposals.

Proposals are normally treated confidentially until the contract is awarded or recommended for award because proposals are subject to negotiation. Releasing proposals to the public prior to selection of the successful contractor permits competing contractors access to one another's proposals, thus compromising negotiations. The advance contract planning team may wish to develop contingency planning in the event that the contractors submit bids or propose prices that exceed the budgeted amount for the contract. If added funding cannot be made available or if a scaled back scope of work cannot be developed before the bids or proposals expire, it may be necessary to repeat the solicitation process, thus delaying contract award and project commencement. If no significant difference exists between the pricing in a negotiable proposal and the budget, it may be possible to negotiate a price within the budget. Because agencies are more susceptible to protests when proposals are not evaluated strictly according to the criteria in the RFP, the advance contract planning team might consider establishing processes to ensure evaluation of proposals based solely on the proposal evaluation criteria. The team may wish to include flexibility within an RFP that permits, but does not require, the agency to request presentations from prospective contractors to gain more insight into the contractors' qualifications.

2.3.8 *Establish Contract Administration Strategy*

Advance contract planning prepares the project team not only to prepare the solicitation and the contract, but for all phases of the contracting cycle that follow the contract planning phase. Tools that enable the agency to perform effective contract administration and contractor monitoring include periodic progress meetings, establishment of critical milestones, reports of contract deliveries, and contract status meetings. These tools are available to the agency merely by including contractor reporting responsibilities in the scope of work, which are, in turn, incorporated in the model contract included in the RFP.

Contract administration, including the monitoring of the contractor's performance, does not begin until the contract is awarded; however, prudent advance contract planning includes specifying tools for managing the performance of contractors after the contract has been awarded. The advance contract planning team may specify what contractor-prepared reports are to be submitted during the term of the contract. Chapter 8 includes a recommendation for contractor reports and a methodology for evaluating those reports to estimate contractor expenditures through contract completion. The need to perform this level of analysis is based on the extent of government-assumed risks, the criticality of the project, and the value of the contracts. While performing analyses of contractor-prepared reports, prudent government officials consider the possibility that the contractor may not be totally forthright when reporting the percentage of completion for contractor tasks. Readers are advised to follow President Reagan's adage regarding the former Soviet Union's dismantling of nuclear weapons when considering contractor-prepared status reports:

> *"Trust, but verify,"* or the old Russian proverb, "Doveryai, no proveryai"
> ("Доверяй, но проверяй")

The reported information most subject to exaggeration by the contractor is the completion percentage for tasks. However, in their defense, contractors may

Table 2.3 Activities Conducted during Advance Contract Planning

Appoint the advance contract planning team
Prepare the project background statement
Establish a website
Prepare list of contractors to be solicited
Develop solicitation ground rules
Decide on model contract provisions
Develop proposal evaluation guidelines
Establish contract administration strategy
Additional activities included on the CD that accompanies this book

report the percentage of task completion estimated by the date that the government receives and takes action on the contractor reports. Therefore, erroneous reporting may be attributed to excessive optimism rather than a lack of veracity.

Table 2.3 provides a summary of the activities conducted during advance contract planning.

2.4 Robust Contract Planning's Contribution to Efficiency and Ethics

A man who does not plan long ahead will find trouble at his door.

Confucius

The benefits from a robust contracting plan are common globally and result from maximizing the benefits of full and open competition, a well-constructed solicitation that results in homogeneous proposals to facilitate selection of the optimal contractor, and management of pre-proposal communications to ensure equal treatment of prospective contractors and the avoidance of protests and fraudulent activities. Added benefits of a robust contracting plan include selection of the contractor that most likely best meets the government's requirements, award of a contract instrument that clearly expresses the rights and responsibilities of all parties to the contract while minimizing the government's risks, and establishment of the framework and availability of information required for effective contract administration.

2.4.1 Comprehensive List of Prospective Contractors

The advance contract planning team has the initial opportunity to create a comprehensive list of prospective contractors to ensure the government, thus the constituency, has the comprehensive benefits of full and open competition. As explained elsewhere in this book, the benefits of competition are not limited to obtaining the lowest pricing. Contractors that enjoy the position as sole source provider for certain commodities or services are prone to not only charge whatever pricing the market will bear, but also provide less-than-optimal quality and timeliness. The overall objective of developing a comprehensive list of prospective contractors is to achieve the maximum benefit from obtaining, through full and open competition, the optimal combination of price, timeliness, and quality that maximizes the probability of program success.

2.4.2 Well-Constructed Solicitation

The benefits afforded through a well-constructed solicitation, a purview of the advance contract planning team, include the establishment of proposal evaluation criteria that ensure contractor selection based on attributes best representing the qualifications required to meet the government's needs. The advance planning team can, furthermore, establish weighting of proposal evaluation criteria to provide greater emphasis on those criteria that are more significant in the selection of the best-qualified contractor.

The agency further benefits from a solicitation that requires homogeneous proposals, resulting in all the contractors' proposals discussing the same topics, in the same sequence, and with the same maximum number of pages for each topic. Homogeneous proposals greatly increase the efficiency and decrease the level of effort involved in proposal evaluation while maximizing the equal treatment of contractors.

Intelligent construction of the solicitation, in addition to ensuring selection of the contractor that best meets the government's requirements and simplifying the proposal evaluation process, also helps avoid protests from aggrieved contractors. Protests are discouraged when the solicitation is designed to facilitate the contracting agency's maximization of objective proposal evaluation techniques and equal treatment of competing contractors. Avoidance of protests from aggrieved contractors is a universal goal because receipt of a protest is a challenge to the legitimacy of the agency's source selection process or efficacy of the government's practices during the evaluation of proposals. Government benefits from protest avoidance because, in addition to questioning the government's proposal evaluation practices, protests can result in program delays, contribute to added program costs, and possibly result in termination of the program.

2.4.3 Management of Pre-Proposal Communications

Effective management of pre-proposal communications also contributes to protest avoidance. A subsequent chapter contains an extensive discussion of the advantages and disadvantages of various methods for managing pre-proposal communications, cautions readers to shun questions posed in person or by telephone, and recommends that prospective contractors be limited to communicating with the contracting agency solely through the agency's project manager via e-mail. The recommendations also include posting all contractor questions and agency responses on the agency's website. Although adoption of this recommendation does not guarantee the complete avoidance of protests or unethical behavior, it greatly benefits the contracting agency by avoiding some protests and the workload increases, added costs, and time delays associated with protests.

2.4.4 Selection of the Contractor That Best Serves the Government's Requirements

The advance contract planning team has the opportunity to establish proposal evaluation guidelines to help ensure selection of the contractor that best meets the agency's needs. The most obvious benefit from selecting the contractor that best serves the government's requirements is the associated increased probability for program success. The recommended proposal evaluation guidelines include acceptance of late proposals, confidential treatment of proposals, negotiation of ground rules, no public opening of the proposals, establishment of criteria for evaluating proposals, consideration of weighted criteria to ensure that the more significant criteria have a greater influence on contractor selection, and use of a scoring technique that avoids problems associated with selecting a suboptimal contractor.

2.4.5 Award of an Effective Contract Instrument

The advance contract planning team has an opportunity to decide whether it includes a model contract, including the government's terms and conditions, in the RFP and states that the agency intends to award a contract substantially in the form of the model contract. Doing so greatly benefits the agency through award of a contract that clearly specifies the contractor's responsibilities and protects the agency from unnecessary risks. Failure to employ the model contract in this manner greatly increases the probability that a contractor or contractors will propose their own contract with terms and conditions likely to favor the contractor at the agency's expense. In a competitive procurement, competing contractors are likely to propose dissimilar contract provisions, thus introducing the impossibility of evaluating contractors on an equal basis.

Awarding a well-crafted contract incorporating the features discussed in this book, including the one-page contract format, carefully considered and fully staffed agency standard terms and conditions, standard insurance provisions, and a scope of work that unequivocally describes the contractor's responsibilities, provides the government with a contractual instrument that minimizes its program risks immeasurably when compared to acceptance of a contractor-prepared contract.

2.4.6 Availability of Information Needed to Ensure Adequate Contractor Performance Monitoring

Planning for contract management activities and monitoring the contractor's performance during the term of the contract provides the advance contract planning team an opportunity to ensure optimal contractor performance. Directing the agency's personnel responsible for drafting the scope of work to proscribe periodic contractor reporting of performance progress and expenditure status is the first step to ensure that the contractor meets its contractual responsibilities. Categorical acceptance of the contractor's information is folly. The contractor-reported information, however, provides the contractor's view of its progress and serves as a starting point in determining the actual progress to date. Determination of the actual progress achieved requires agency monitoring to ensure accuracy of the contractor's achievement of objectives, entitlement to claimed compensation, and detection of unethical activities. Contractor reporting combined with government verification and analyses best ensures effective contractor performance, leading to program success.

The benefits of a well-conceived contracting plan are worthy of the efforts expended to properly plan for soliciting contractors, selecting the contractor that submitted the proposal that best meets the government's needs, and administering the contractor's performance to ensure that the work is performed according to the contract provisions.

Failure to properly plan for anticipated events during the contracting cycle, or failing to conform to the government's ethical standards, is likely to result in predictable, undesirable outcomes.

2.5 Conclusion

Advance contract planning, also referred to as "advance procurement planning" and "acquisition planning," which involves planning prior to implementing the contracting process, appears to be a common-sense approach to government contracting requiring little discussion. There are, however, instances when government representatives are overly eager to proceed with program initiation and rush into preparation of the solicitation document without adequate planning. Astute government representatives who recognize the need for planning do not begin a procurement effort without planning. Planning in advance for contract administration is the phase of the contract cycle most likely to be overlooked, and experienced personnel occasionally fail to plan for administering the contract. A report by the GAO[3] recognized the need to plan in advance for contract administration by noting that the DoD recently established guidance on contract surveillance, recommending the appointment of surveillance personnel during the *early contracting planning phase* to help improve oversight of cost-reimbursable and time and materials service contracts. Advance planning of all activities during the entire contracting cycle is essential. Failure to plan in advance often leads to unforeseen complications if not program failure. Planning for the contract administration phase is overlooked most frequently, yet this crucial phase in the contracting cycle requires thoughtful planning to ensure adequate monitoring of the contractor's performance.

Notes

1. *The Washington Times,* "Siemens Guilty of Global Fraud," Ben Conery, December 16, 2008.
2. Robert J. McKain is the author of *How to Get to the Top and Stay There*, New York, AMACOM, 1981, and *Realize Your Potential*, New York, AMACOM, 1975.
3. "Opportunities to Improve Surveillance on Department of Defense Service Contracts," Report number GAO-05-274, March 2005.

Chapter 3

Ethics in Contracting

> Corruption in public procurement is a particularly important issue in Asia and the Pacific, where it is estimated that governments pay from 20% to 100% more for goods and services because of corrupt procurement practices. That shift of income from the public purse to private firms means government will have far less money to fund the infrastructure, education, health, and other public investments needed to reduce poverty and deliver much needed public services.
>
> **Lawrence Greenwood, Jr.**[1]
> *Vice President*
> *Asian Development Bank*

3.1 Global Need for Ethical Government Contracting

Individuals reading this book are predominantly honest public servants and aspiring public servants throughout the world who do not accept gratuities offered merely because of their government position, or government contractors that do not offer gratuities to public servants to win government contracts. Despite the readers' honesty, the material covered in this chapter on ethics in contracting is valuable to public servants worldwide with any degree of influence or potential influence regarding any aspect of government contracts. The material is crucial for government contractors as well. The potential to influence government contracts occurs when public servants are responsible for:

- Serving on an advance contract planning team
- Serving on a contract management staff

- Serving as a project manager for contracted work
- Writing or contributing to writing specifications or a scope of work
- Writing or contributing to writing a request for proposals (RFP) or invitation for bids (IFB)
- Serving on a proposal evaluation team to select a contractor
- Performing financial or legal review of a pending contract or contract amendment
- Voting for approval or disapproval of a contract award or amendment
- Signing a contract or contract amendment for the government
- Managing or assisting in the management of a contract or contractor
- Verifying that a contractor provided adequate products or services
- Approving contractor invoices for payment
- Writing a contractor performance report
- Auditing a completed contract

The process for corruption of public servants likely begins in small steps, such as the acceptance of low-value gratuities from government contractors. A report from the Office of the Inspector General from the Government of the District of Columbia[2] enumerated gratuities accepted by an associate director of a DC agency. The gratuities she accepted included food, beverages, golf tournaments, theater tickets, and promotional items. The gratuities were offered by one company that was competing for a contract wherein the associate director was involved in the evaluation and selection phase. She also attempted to make payments, without benefit of a contract, to another contractor that had provided her with gratuities. Two of the associate director's staff members were also found to have accepted gratuities from government contractors. Gratuities, however, need not be limited to low-value items such as food, beverages, and golf tournaments. An employee of the U.S. Federal Bureau of Investigation (FBI) pleaded guilty to acceptance of a gratuity of a Caribbean cruise, including lodging and airfare, valued at approximately $7,500. The gratuity was accepted by the FBI employee shortly after he reviewed and approved the bid for a contract valued at approximately $2 million. Later in this chapter readers are introduced to an approach for dealing with offers of gratuities in a manner that prevents government employees from being lured into the acceptance of gratuities of ever increasing values that might eventually cause them to feel obligated to give the contractor preferential treatment. Readers are introduced to recommended features for an ethics policy and an ethics training program, an approach to establishing personal ethical standards, and a recommendation for reacting to the acceptance of an inappropriate gift by a colleague.

That minority of public servants who mistakenly believe that acceptance of gratuities is an appropriate benefit of public service will also be provided valuable information. For the benefit of any individuals who are not dissuaded from engaging in corrupt practices despite the tragic outcomes described in Chapter 1, additional cases involving public servants who were discovered violating ethics laws are discussed in this and subsequent chapters.

Federal, state, and local government officials and employees in the United States are all subject to federal law with respect to contract fraud and related crimes involving ethics and conflicts of interest. Director Robert J. Mueller stated in his speech of April 17, 2008, at the American Bar Association Litigation Section Annual Conference in Washington, DC:

> Public corruption is our top criminal priority, for the simple reason that it is different from other crimes. Corruption does not merely strike at the heart of good government. It may strike at the security of our communities.
>
> The vast majority of public officials are honest in their work. They are committed to serving their fellow citizens. Unfortunately, some have abused the public trust.
>
> We have more than 2,500 pending public corruption investigations—an increase of more than 50 percent since 2003. In the past five years, the number of agents working public corruption cases also has increased by more than 50 percent. We have convicted more than 1,800 federal, state, and local officials in the past two years alone.
>
> For a nation built on the rule of law—and on faith in a government of the people, by the people, and for the people—we can and should do better. Ultimately, democracy and corruption cannot co-exist.
>
> The FBI is uniquely situated to address public corruption. We have the skills to conduct sophisticated investigations. But more than that, we are insulated from political pressure. We are able to go where the evidence leads us, without fear of reprisal or recrimination.

The last quotation above regarding the insulation from political pressure is a primary reason that the FBI handles virtually all cases involving procurement corruption at the state and local level. The FBI's expertise, combined with the lack of resources at the state and local level, also contributes to this rationale.

Ethical lapses by public officials are not recent aberrations. The propensity for conflicts of interest and other ethical lapses on the part of public officials was recognized by the framers of the U.S. Constitution. Article I, Sections 6 and 9, of the U.S. Constitution includes prohibitions against profiting from such lapses. Subsequent provisions in federal statutes, state constitutions, laws and codes, as well as local ordinances further prohibit profiting personally by elected and appointed government officials and other government employees. In addition to these statutory prohibitions against conflicts of interest, moral values instilled through families, religious institutions, friends, and educators also caution against enriching oneself at the expense of others. Despite these constitutional, statutory, and moral prohibitions against profiting through ethical lapses, continuing media coverage of arrests, trials, convictions, incarcerations, and even occasional suicides by government officials and employees attests to the persistence of unethical practices to influence the award of contracts in return for personal gain.

Governor Rod Blagojevich of Illinois was impeached by the Illinois House of Representatives and convicted (removed from office) by the Illinois Senate. The proposed report prepared for the Illinois House of Representatives[3] in preparation for the impeachment proceedings included wiretap evidence regarding attempts to sell the U.S. Senate seat vacated by Barack Obama when he was elected to the office of President of the United States. However, the wiretap evidence also revealed attempts to obtain contributions to Governor Blagojevich's campaign in exchange for action on government contracts. In the case of a $1.8 billion project for new express lanes for the Illinois Tollway, the wiretapped telephone recording indicated that the governor intended to seek a $500,000 campaign contribution from the contractor. The report included numerous instances of redacted expletives that were characteristic of the ex-governor's speech pattern in the wiretapped conversations.

Michel Roussin, a former French minister who admitted knowledge of payments to politicians for 1½–2% of any greater Paris region school building and maintenance contracts, was fined €50,000 despite his denial of running the scheme. Michel Roussin served as President Jacques Chirac's chief of staff during the president's term as Paris mayor and as prime minister.[4]

The large number of individual statutes worldwide makes it impractical to describe global restrictions regarding ethics and conflicts of interest. Additionally, such detailed information on individual statutes is beyond the scope of this book. Lacking details on individual statutes is not problematic, however, because there are global similarities in laws applicable to ethics and conflicts of interest. Because state and local officials in the United States are generally tried based on violation of federal laws, and because of the similarities of statutory limitations in the various jurisdictions throughout the United States and in other countries, it is not necessary to delve into individual statutes. Commonly shared characteristics in ethics and conflict of interest legislation include prohibition against illicit enrichment not only of the government representatives but their close family members as well, a maximum value of gifts that may be accepted, penalties for violating statutory limitations, and the need to file periodic financial disclosure statements. In certain cases, lying on a financial disclosure form can result in a conviction. David H. Safavian, the former chief of staff for the U.S. General Services Administration (GSA), was convicted[5] of lying on a financial disclosure form, along with several other counts.

Although notable contract corruption scenarios generally involve remuneration paid to government employees in exchange for award of a contract, for a higher than market price for a contract, or for overlooking substandard contract performance, a more unique approach involves contractors that invite government employees to visit their facilities for three to five days to evaluate their manufacturing processes. The trips are fully paid by the contractor and the employees typically write a sole source justification shortly following their return from the trip. When challenged regarding the appropriateness of their trips, the employees invariably attempt to justify the trip as a necessity to ensure their purchase of well-manufactured equipment.

An alternative approach to ensuring that equipment is well manufactured, without compromising the integrity of government representatives, is for the agency to fund visits to the facilities of all competing contractors. This approach also rewards the government with the benefits of full and open competition. One-day visits to evaluate manufacturing processes will suffice for most equipment purchases. The cost savings achieved through competitive procurements will likely more than offset the cost of visits to the contractors' facilities.

More information is provided in this section on agency training in ethics and conflicts of interest. Incorporation of mandatory ethics training is recommended to discourage ethical lapses by all government officials and employees involved either directly or indirectly in agency contracts. It is possible to mandate ethics training through legislation.

3.1.1 Ethics for Government Negotiators

Rather than merely dickering over prices, as practiced by some individuals when negotiating prices for commodities purchased for personal use, a more comprehensive approach to negotiations is recommended for government contract negotiators. Government negotiators are normally expected to maintain higher professional and ethical standards than private-sector negotiators. Government negotiators are generally required to treat all prospective contractors equally, not reveal features of one contractor's proposal to potential competitors, refrain from engaging in auctioneering techniques,[6] and conduct ethical negotiations. Although ethical negotiation policies are likely included in the continuing training for contracting professionals and other government officials who regularly participate in contract negotiations, this does not justify excusing contracting professionals from receiving negotiation ethics training along with other negotiation team members. Ethics training is appropriate for all team members whenever an ad hoc negotiation team is formed. The receipt of ethical negotiation training in a group setting increases the consciousness with respect to ethical issues that arise during team activities. When ethical negotiation training is not provided by the agency, the negotiation team leader may develop instructions, based on the agency's policies, for negotiation team members to conduct ethical negotiations. The instructions should be consistent with agency policy with respect to maintaining the confidentiality of proposals, equal treatment of all prospective contractors, and disclosure of any actual or apparent conflicts of interest, yet reinforce the objective of striving to meet the agency's negotiation objectives.

3.1.2 Professional Negotiations

Government negotiators are expected to present their rationale for their differences from the contractor's offer when making counteroffers. Failure to provide such an explanation is counterproductive to completing successful negotiations and can result in an impasse. It provides a basis for acceptance of the agency's counteroffer or for pursuing negotiations further. Blind exceptions to a contractor's offer jeopardize further negotiations, whereas providing the rationale for exceptions facilitates reaching a meeting of the minds. When making a complex offer or counteroffer, government negotiators might consider making the counteroffer verbally, but providing the contractor with a written summary of the differences between the contractor's position and the government's position.

3.1.3 Equal Treatment of Contractors

A basic tenant of government contracting is that contractors are treated equally. The government negotiator who deals differently with one contractor than with another or other contractors risks a presumption of favoritism that is counter to reaching the best arrangement for the agency and for the constituency. Negotiations conducted inconsistently between two or more competing contractors will likely lead to a protest.

It appears to be in the nature of humans to identify a favorite team or participant when observing a competitive event. Developing a favorite contractor during a competitive procurement is, however, a dangerous practice that can result in an embarrassing, time-consuming, and expensive protest. The danger is that the favored contractor status may cause a government representative to give preferred treatment to the favored contractor. During certain competitive procurements the representatives from one contractor may appear to be so obnoxious that the government official or employee may abhor the thought of rewarding their negotiation team with a contract. Whenever the government official or employee suspects that she or he has developed a favorite contractor, in such a competitive situation, recusing oneself from participation in that contracting action is recommended. Failure to recuse oneself in this situation constitutes a conflict of interest. If such recusal is considered too severe a reaction, the government official or employee might consider advising the government negotiation team leader of the potential conflict of interest. However, in this situation, recusal is the preferred alternative.

3.1.4 Confidential Treatment of Proposals

Revealing the features of a competitor's proposal is not condoned for government negotiators. Permitting one contractor to know the content of a competitor's proposal goes beyond favoritism and may actually constitute outright fraud. Condoning this behavior constitutes entirely unacceptable conduct that threatens to damage the negotiators' career and possibly initiate a protest, thereby delaying the commencement of project work. The agency's team responsible for negotiating a new contract is oftentimes a holdover from the proposal evaluation team. However, adjustments to team membership might be made prior to commencement of negotiations. Efforts to ensure that information in one prospective contractor's proposal is not revealed to a competitor during the proposal evaluation phase are expected to continue throughout the negotiation phase of the contractor selection process. Government officials or employees who are experienced in contract negotiations are generally conditioned against violating the precept of proposal confidentiality. However, lesser experienced government officials and employees, when called on to participate in or even lead the government's negotiation team, benefit from training with respect to treating proposals confidentially.

3.1.5 Avoidance of Auctioneering Techniques

Although the relatively recent technique of holding reverse auctions has proven acceptable for purchasing commodities, the more traditional auctioneering technique will likely prove counterproductive in the long term. The more acceptable reverse auctions are customarily held online wherein the prospective contractors can freely access their company's resources while determining the price to offer. However, traditional negotiation auctioneering techniques are conducted face-to-face at the agency's facility, where the prospective contractors experience considerable pressure to reach agreement with limited, if any, access to their company's information resources. In some cases, the government negotiator may have several prospective contractors in different rooms while the government representative goes from room to room advising the prospective contractors that their offer is not the lowest. This auctioneering technique places great pressure on prospective contractors to offer prices lower than any of their competitors. The danger in this approach is that contractors may decide to offer pricing that covers their variable cost plus a small contribution to their fixed cost, but actually represents a financial loss when total revenue is compared to total costs. Although a contractor may be able to use such pricing occasionally, repeated pricing in this manner will likely result in company failure and the loss of one of the agency's contractors.

3.1.6 Government Employees or Officials Who Initiate Consideration of Gratuities

Although the discussion of gratuities thus far has involved a contractor offering the gift, favor, or "courtesy," cases of government representatives soliciting gift giving also exist. Contractors that do not condone such possibly illegal behavior find that their company is placed in an awkward situation by such a solicitation. Although outright refusal to provide a gratuity may result in a loss of business, granting such a request potentially subjects the contractor to significant disciplinary action that might include suspension, debarment, termination of existing contracts, or punishment as serious as criminal prosecution.

There are not nearly as many cases involving the conviction of a public official for solicitation of kickbacks as there are convictions for actually accepting kickbacks. This lower rate of convictions for soliciting kickbacks is likely due to the reluctance of prospective contractors to refuse to pay the kickback, or to report the kickback solicitation to a law enforcement agency. One such case, outlined below, was reported in the *Los Angeles Times.*[7] Added details were found in the Department of Justice press release[8] announcing additional corruption charges and in the Department of Justice press release[9] announcing the guilty plea.

Mr. Joseph Impastato, a councilman from St. Tammany Parish in Louisiana, arranged to receive payment of 50% of the proceeds from a government subcontract to haul away debris from Hurricane Katrina. The government's prime contract was with Omni Pinnacle, and Councilman Impastato was charged with convincing the prime contractor to enter into the subcontract with Pontchartrain Chipping Yard to haul away the waste. Council Impastato allegedly pressured Pontchartrain Chipping Yard to pay him 50% of the payments they received from Omni Pinnacle. Either the prime or subcontractor apparently notified the authorities because, according to the *Los Angeles Times* article, the FBI taped Councilman Impastato accepting two $85,000 cashier's checks. The article indicated that Impastato did not deny accepting the cashier's checks. However, he unsuccessfully argued that the funds were not a kickback that subjected him to a maximum penalty of twenty years imprisonment and a fine up to $500,000, because he was acting as a private businessman, not as a public official. The press release announcing Impastato's guilty plea indicated that he pleaded guilty to federal bribery through the illegal solicitation and receipt of payments in connection with a Hurricane Katrina debris removal contract and making false statements on his 2001 federal income tax return.

3.2 Pummeled by Corruption: Consequences for Government and Contractors

> If you can't drink a lobbyist's whiskey, take his money, sleep with his women and still vote against him in the morning, you don't belong in politics.[10]

Jesse Unruh
Former Speaker of the California State Assembly

Jesse Unruh's ethics philosophy and deportment, as reflected in the above quotation, are fortunately not commonplace in public service. However, all government entities are cautioned to be alert to the possibility that their organization has been targeted for the ethical lapses reflected in Table 1.1.

Just as the benefits of an effective ethical contracting program are applied differently to the government itself than to government officials and employees, the consequences of failing to maintain ethical standards apply differentially to the government itself and to the government officials and employees at the agency.

Therefore, the discussion regarding the consequences of failing to maintain ethical standards is presented separately for agencies and individuals. The discussion of the consequences for individuals is followed by the perils faced by government contractors that fail to conform to government ethical standards.

3.2.1 Consequences Applicable to Government Entities

The consequences applicable to government entities include consideration of the fact that although illicit compensation may be significant, it is normally a small percentage of the increased cost of the program due to other corruption-related factors. The other factors detracting from program budgets include inflated pricing, damaged agency reputation, costs associated with lowered morale of employees who become aware of ongoing corruption, canceled or scaled-back government programs necessitated by excess costs resulting from corruption, corrupt practices by other officials or employees who feel empowered to engage in similar corrupt practices, and the likelihood that disenfranchised prospective contractors will protest the improper selection of a competing contractor.

Therefore, although the illicit compensation paid to corrupt government representatives may be calculable, when discovered, it is considerably more difficult to determine the government's monetary cost resulting from the corrupt contract transaction. However, one can be certain that the overall government cost from involvement in a corrupt transaction is significantly greater than the value of the illicit compensation paid to an individual. The certainty of this assertion is based on the logical argument that a corrupt company, or corrupt individual, is unlikely to become involved in a high-risk transaction that has the potential for damaging the company's future existence or result in the incarceration of contractor representatives unless the expected revenue gain greatly exceeds the costs. The greater majority of companies, which refrain from involvement in unethical or illegal contracting transactions, have avoided such transactions despite the ratio between rewards and risks.

News regarding a government's corrupt contracting activities certainly damages the government's reputation. A government entity with such a reputation is likely to experience difficulty recruiting qualified, honest employees, who fear that their employers' reputation will affect their personal reputations. This potential impact on the reputation of officials and employees is likely to endanger retention of honest and respectable representatives. The damaged reputation of a government entity is likely to harm an elected official's reelection chances.

Lower employee morale also likely results from a belief that corrupt practices are tolerated by the government entity. Decreased morale may lead to lessened productivity, employees seeking alternative employment, whistleblowers reporting suspected transgressions to law enforcement, or possibly even the belief by some employees that they are likewise entitled to a share of the largess. Regardless of the employee reaction, with the possible exception of whistleblowing, the impact on the agency is negative.

The value of canceled or scaled-back government programs is expected to approximate the expense of the excess costs associated with the corrupt practices. The excess costs from corrupt practices are the sum of the added contractor remuneration, gratuities received by the corrupt official or employee, lessened productivity and employee turnover costs associated with lessened morale, and the expense associated with reacting to an increase in the number of protests resulting from corrupt practices. The added contract costs are likely to exceed all other added costs; however, in the event of a particularly infamous case, the costs of dealing with the aftermath are likely to exceed the excess contract costs.

Recognizing the existence of corrupt practices within a government organization is likely to cause certain officials or employees to feel empowered to also unjustly enrich themselves by engaging in similar corrupt practices. If government officials or employees feel empowered to engage in corrupt practices, it is likely that the costs of corruption will spiral upward until the level of government services provided the constituency is seriously compromised.

Prospective contractors that feel disenfranchised by their perception that contractors are being selected contrary to agency standard practices are likely to file protests. The receipt of protests always involves added staff effort to respond to them. An unusually large volume of protests, especially when the aggrieved contractors have a sound basis for filing the protests, can result in significant agency costs if it becomes necessary to engage outside counsel, reimburse contractors for their costs of filing and pursuing protests, and incur costs associated with the termination of improperly awarded contracts.

3.2.2 Consequences Applicable to Government Representatives

The consequences applicable to government officials and employees include fines, restitution, forfeiture of assets, imprisonment, ruined careers, damaged reputations, devastated family relationships, and occasionally suicide.

According to an *Army Times* staff report posted April 19, 2008, and a U.S. Department of Justice press release of May 8, 2008, five individuals were convicted in one case, referred to here as the Sphinx case, that was investigated by at least four civilian and military criminal investigative agencies. In addition to the initial five convictions, the son of one of the convicted public officials was sentenced at a later date. The son admitted to accepting a $90,000 payment from a contractor on behalf of his father. Additionally, child pornography images were found on the son's home computer while officials were investigating the corruption case. The sentences resulting from the Sphinx case are summarized in Table 3.1.

One of the public officials directed contracts to the contractor, Sphinx, beginning in 2002. In 2003 the defendants made arrangements with a Native American tribally owned business that was eligible for noncompetitive contracts regardless of the value. Contracts were then awarded to the tribally owned company, which kept

Table 3.1   Summary of Sphinx Case Sentences

Position	Prison	Supervised Release	Restitution	Community Service	Forfeiture of Assets
Public official #1	7 years	3 years	$2.7 million	500 hours	Yes
Contractor consultant	7 years	3 years	$2.7 million	1,000 hours	Yes
Public official #2	7 years	3 years	$2.7 million	500 hours	No
Company owner	5 years 2 months	3 years	$2.7 million	No	No
Contract public employee	5 years	3 years	$265,560	500 hours	No
Son of public official	5 years 6 months	3 years	$2.7 million	No	No

a portion of the proceeds but transmitted most of the funds to Sphinx. In 2004 three of the defendants were given a 75% interest in Sphinx, and millions of dollars in government contracts were then directed to Sphinx.

In similar cases, family members are usually impacted primarily by the penalties imposed on their public service relatives. In this case, however, one family member became involved by accepting a contractor payment on behalf of his father. One can hardly imagine how devastating it is to involve one's child in a scheme on their behalf that results in that child being incarcerated in federal prison for over five years. In this particular case, however, the public official's son is unlikely to receive any compassion because child pornography images were found on the son's home computer during the contract corruption investigation.

Fines, restitution, and forfeiture of assets are the direct financial consequences of being convicted of or pleading to corruption charges. The amount determined for restitution and forfeiture of assets, when applicable, is normally directly related to the value of the ill-gotten proceeds, whereas fines are penalties for committing crimes. Indirect financial consequences from involvement in corrupt contracting activities are discussed below.

Many individuals beginning a career in government service likely have not the slightest concern that through their actions they might be subject to imprisonment. However, imprisonment is not an unusual punishment for public servants, and contractor representatives, who become involved in contract corruption. In the Sphinx case, the six defendants received a total of more than thirty-six years in prison. Of those sentenced to imprisonment, two were traditional public officials, one was a contract public employee, two worked in the private sector, and one was the relative of a public official. Ex-congressman Randy "Duke" Cunningham was sentenced to eight years in federal prison for accepting over $2.4 million in bribes. This seemed an exceptionally long sentence when compared to the typical contract corruption case; however, the value of the bribes he accepted was also greater than typical bribe values and his sentence exceeded the longest sentences in the Sphinx case by merely one year.

Ruination of one's career is an obvious consequence of being convicted of, or pleading guilty to, procurement fraud. However, likely not so obvious is the possibility of restrictions against future government employment for a specified number of years. In the absence of such a restriction against future government jobs, there is the additional problem of finding employment in either government or the private sector when it is necessary to list previous convictions on job applications. Hiring officials are likely to be hesitant to make a job offer for any position involving significant responsibilities to otherwise promising candidates who have a record of enriching themselves at the expense of their employer.

Perceived contracting irregularities short of procurement fraud can also result in career damage. Procurement scandals such as those that tormented ex-Governor Gray Davis of California were instrumental in his recall and replacement by Governor Arnold Schwarzenegger in 2003. There was considerable voter discontent from the energy contracts negotiated in secret during the electricity crisis. However, the catalyst for the recall was most likely the fundraising scandal regarding a $95 million sole source Oracle Corporation contract. A state audit report indicated that rather than save money for the state, as intended, the contract might actually cost the state an added $41 million. Testimony from the governor's top aides indicated that an Oracle lobbyist gave a $25,000 campaign contribution to the governor's former e-government director shortly after the contract was signed.[11]

Damage to one's reputation is also an expected result from involvement in contract fraud. Although a damaged reputation will likely contribute to career problems, it also impacts family, friendships, and community relationships. If public officials considered the impact of a damaged reputation prior to engaging in criminal activities, such consequences might be sufficient to dissuade them from becoming involved in procurement fraud.

Devastation of familial relationships, to most individuals, is an extreme consequence. The concept of subjecting family members to such consequences is impossible to fully visualize prior to becoming involved in contract corruption. However, it is not that difficult to imagine the personal and financial impact on one's spouse, and possibly their children, when a previously respected and financially secure public servant proceeds through the ordeals associated with an investigation, arrest, arraignment, trial, conviction, fines, restitution, forfeiture of assets, imprisonment, and eventually probation or parole. Experiencing these ordeals is especially devastating to a spouse who had either abandoned or suspended his or her own career opportunities to help support the spouse who, following the corruption entanglement, can no longer provide for the family.

Although relatively rare, suicides naturally have the gravest of impacts. The apparent suicide of U.S. Army Major Gloria Davis instigated investigations into massive contract fraud committed by numerous Army personnel who were awarding contracts in support of operations in Iraq and Afghanistan from Camp Arifjan in Kuwait. As of this date there have been three apparent suicides by Army officers resulting from the ongoing procurement fraud investigations stemming from the suicide of Major Davis.

Incessant media accounts of contract fraud would logically alert any reasonable person tempted to enrich him or herself through an illicit arrangement with a government contractor to realize the potential devastating consequences. However, rather than learning from the mistakes of others, some government officials persist in risking grave consequences by accepting or soliciting kickbacks. The following material is quoted from a speech by Robert S. Mueller, III, director of the FBI, April 17, 2008, at the American Bar Association Litigation Section Annual Conference in Washington, DC. It provides some surprising statistics that illustrate the magnitude of the problem:

> We have more than 2,500 pending public corruption investigations—an increase of more than 50 percent since 2003. In the past five years, the number of agents working public corruption cases also has increased by more than 50 percent. We have convicted more than 1,800 federal, state, and local officials in the past two years alone.

Contract corruption cases often appear to reflect a relationship that developed between the government and contractor representatives over an extended time period. Initial contractor gifts are likely to be of limited financial value; however, a pattern of gift giving may evolve from initial gifts of modest value to gifts of ever increasing value. Naturally, such a pattern does not normally evolve unless the corrupt contractor determines that there is some benefit to providing gratuities. Eventually, the value of the gifts is likely to exceed the acceptable threshold. Of course, the $2.4 million cumulative value of gifts accepted by Randy Cunningham is on the upper range of gratuities. Had Randy Cunningham, perhaps, established a zero tolerance policy before he became involved with the contractors, he would not have become caught up in this notorious case that resulted in the downfall of this once extremely high-level government official. The personal zero tolerance standard, if followed, would have resulted in his refusal to accept initial gifts with a relatively modest value and likely would have prevented the offering of the more expensive gifts that led to his conviction and imprisonment.

George Ryan, the former governor of Illinois, was sentenced to six and one-half years in federal prison for fraud and racketeering. Earlier in his career, Ryan was nominated for the Nobel Peace Prize for commuting the death sentences of prisoners in Illinois. He represents yet another example of a public official who was held in exemplary esteem prior to being tempted to seek what he perceived as even higher rewards than he earned through his legitimate accomplishments. As a result of the same investigation, former governor Ryan and his lobbyist friend Larry

Warner, as well as seventy-three other state officials and employees and lobbyists, were convicted of crimes associated with fraud and racketeering. Two other defendants involved in this investigation became fugitives.

The prosecution claimed that, in addition to having his staff work on his campaign while on the state payroll, George Ryan received cash, gifts, and vacations from lobbyists in return for requiring state contractors to pay fees to lobbyists.

Another ex-governor, John Rowland, the former governor of Connecticut, also lost his office and freedom. Rowland resigned from his position as governor in 2004, admitted to accepting vacations valued at over $100,000, and pleaded guilty to one count of conspiracy to steal honest services. He also faced a concurrent impeachment inquiry. Rowland served ten months in prison. The contractors that were involved in his case consisted of one state contractor and a charter jet company that obtained a tax break.

The most outrageous consequence from an apparent case of procurement fraud concerned R. Budd Dwyer, who was the state treasurer of Pennsylvania. According to a *New York Times* article ("Official Calls in Press and Kills Himself," January 23, 1987), Mr. Dwyer was convicted of bribery in connection with the offering of a payoff to obtain a $4.6 million computer contract. Shortly before he was to be sentenced for up to fifty-five years in federal prison, he called for a news conference. While the reporters were gathered, and while still and motion pictures were being taken, he revealed a .357 Magnum revolver that had been hidden in an envelope, and he fatally shot himself.

Although the outcomes of most procurement corruption cases are not nearly as notorious as the R. Budd Dwyer case, one would think that the rate of more than three convictions of public officials per business day (1,800 in two years according to FBI Director Mueller) would discourage agency officials from becoming involved in corruption. Media reports, however, continue their seemingly inexhaustible accounts of public officials suffering criminal convictions, imprisonment, fines, destroyed careers, decimated families, and personal impacts so troubling that the disgraced officials have taken their lives rather than suffer the pain of facing family, friends, and society following or anticipating criminal corruption convictions.

3.2.3 Perils for Government Contractors That Do Not Establish Strict Ethical Standards

Examples have been presented regarding corporate personnel who were fired or resigned under pressure, fined, and imprisoned as a result of procurement fraud. There are, however, also serious consequences that apply directly to corporations involved in procurement fraud. Corporations can be suspended or debarred from contracting with the government as a result of their participation in procurement fraud. Significant fines can also be imposed on corporations. As described below in the NetApp case, corporations can receive significant financial penalties for failing to conform to government rules. In this case, an ex-NetApp employee took advantage of the *qui tam* legislation and received a monetary reward for initiating a lawsuit against his ex-employer.

The Department of Justice reported[12] that NetApp, Inc., and NetApp U.S. Public Sector, Inc. (NetApp), agreed to pay the United States $128 million plus interest following the investigation of alleged false claims and contract fraud. The NetApp contracts in question involved the sale of hardware, software, and computer network storage management services to government entities through GSA's multiple award schedule (MAS) program. The settlement revolved around NetApp's failure to disclose discounts offered to other customers during negotiations with the GSA, and that NetApp knowingly made false statements about their sales practices and discounts. The former NetApp employee who initiated the lawsuit on behalf of the U.S. government is entitled to receive $19,200,000.

3.3 Optimal Government Service and Increased Contractor Profit

Wise men learn by other men's mistakes, fools by their own.

H. G. Wells

There are innumerable examples of men and women who have made serious ethical mistakes while serving in positions of trust within the government. Opportunities abound for learning from poor examples. The benefits derived from an effective agency contracting ethics program apply differentially to the government itself and to the government officials and employees. Therefore, the discussion regarding the benefits to be derived from an effective ethical contracting program is presented separately for agencies and for individuals. A discussion of the promises available to government contractors follows the discussion of promises for government representatives who conform to ethical standards.

3.3.1 Agency Benefits

The benefits for government entities that maintain an effective ethical contracting program include improved budgetary opportunities, enhanced agency reputation, elevated employee morale, strengthened government services, as well as opportunities for just compensation of agency officials and employees.

Improved budgetary opportunities can be expected for agencies with an effective ethical contracting program. Although the amount of budgeted funds that are diverted to corrupt employees and officials may not appear sufficient to impact the agency's budget, corporations do not normally make such payouts unless their return is many times the value of the gratuities. No reliable information is available on the ratio between the value of the payout to the corrupt government representative and the added cost of the program as a result of the corrupt practices. However, based on what can be gathered from actual cases, it is reasonable to use a ratio of 20:1. This ratio would result in $2,000 in added program costs for every $100 received by corrupt agency officials or representatives. If this is the correct ratio in the Randy Cunningham case, then the added program cost was $48 million (20 times $2.4 million).

Agencies that establish a credible program for ethical contracting standards are likely to earn an enhanced reputation. The public may become aware of such ethical practices through the agency's transparent contracting program. Transparency is an essential element for an effective ethical contracting program. One approach to establishing transparency is to post future contracting opportunities on a website to advertise opportunities to compete for agency contracts. Posting the results of competitive contracts awarded on a website, along with the rationale for selecting the successful contractor, also contributes to transparency. Providing a website or an agenda that reflects the identification of the program, contractor name, and contract value for contracts that were awarded provides useful information, but does not constitute sufficient transparency. Transparency requires an indication of the level of competition, justification for sole source, justification for pricing if the price was not established through competition, and the basis for contractor selection if the contract was not awarded to the company offering the lowest price.

Elevated employee morale is evident in employees who are confident that contracts are being awarded on the basis of best value to the agency rather than through practices that are, or appear to be, corrupt. Employees with high morale are more likely to be productive and innovative, thus providing greater benefits to the agency and the constituency. Retention and recruitment also likely benefit from elevated employee morale. Improved retention is self evident; however, recruitment benefits from high employee morale more indirectly through recommendations from employees to acquaintances and family members.

Strengthened government services are achieved primarily through increased funding that is available because funds are no longer being diverted to corrupt contractors and government representatives. Contractors selected through corrupt practices without full and open competition are less likely to provide the timeliness and high quality that is more characteristic of honest contractors selected on the basis of the best value to the government. However, corrupt practices are not limited to the selection of contractors. Corrupt contractors are also willing to provide illicit compensation to government representatives who are willing to overlook substandard contract performance. Government representatives, if they also are corrupt, are willing to accept illicit compensation. Therefore, the government may be paying full price, or more likely inflated prices, for inferior products or services.

Establishing just employee compensation packages depends heavily on available funding. When funding is diverted by inflated payments to corrupt contractors and illicit payments to corrupt government officials, there is less funding available for legitimate employee compensation packages. Curtailing payments to corrupt agency and company representatives frees funding for justly compensating agency officials and employees on the basis of their legitimate contribution to agency goals.

An example of the benefits to agencies having effective ethical contracting practices is the avoidance of cases such as the one described here, involving a former state fire college president.[13] William Luther Langston was found guilty on thirty-eight counts including mail fraud, wire fraud, conspiracy, money laundering conspiracy, and theft from an organization receiving federal funds. The former state fire college president was ordered to pay approximately $1.4 million in restitution. A partial list of the specific acts that he was found guilty of includes:

■ Diverting approximately $100,000 to partially pay for his house
■ Having paid contractors' work on his house through state funds
■ Hiring "ghost employees" who did little or no meaningful work, and receiving kickbacks from each ghost employee
■ Diverting funds to a former member of the Alabama House of Representatives: a co-conspirator (The funds were then diverted to a foundation and finally back to the co-conspirator through phony scholarships to the co-conspirator's daughter.)

Numerous examples have been provided wherein the corrupt official received exceptionally high-value illicit rewards. However, the value of most contractor gifts and gratuities is not sufficient to significantly impact the official's or employee's standard of living. The constituency providing financial support and being served by the agency expects their government representatives to pay for their livelihood through their agency compensation without reliance on additional contractor contributions. In the absence of an agency zero tolerance gift and gratuity policy, public servants are encouraged to establish their own personal zero tolerance policy and not accept anything of value from any contractor or prospective contractor. If such a personal zero tolerance policy appears incompatible with traditional business lunches, contracting professionals might question whether business lunches are more productive than office meetings. If agency officials or employees firmly believe that business lunches are truly more productive than office meetings, then business lunches are justified. When agencies determine that business lunches are productive, they might consider evenly sharing that cost with the contractor. Such cost sharing avoids the possibility that agency employees might feel indebted to contractors that provide free lunches. Continuing the practice of contractor-provided lunches might result in the expectation that government representatives feel obligated to make decisions favoring the contractor. The earliest known reference to free lunches, with respect to ethical practices of government representatives, was the statement by Mayor Fiorello La Guardia during his 1934 inauguration, *"E finita la cuccagna!"* That exclamation translates from Italian to English as "No more free lunch!" It was generally believed that this was Mayor La Guardia's proclamation that there would be no graft during his administration. A variation of that statement appeared in an editorial in the *Reno Evening Gazette* on January 22, 1942: "Mr. Wallace neglects the fact that such a thing as a 'free' lunch never existed. Until man acquires the power of creation, someone will always have to pay for a free lunch." The phrase "There's no such thing as a free lunch" was later popularized by Milton Friedman.

3.3.2 Officials' and Employees' Benefits

The benefits applicable to government officials and employees who embrace their agency's ethical contracting practices include continued government career opportunities, improved personal and professional reputation, enhanced family relationships, retained compensation, preserved personal freedom, and increased self-confidence.

Continued government career opportunities are obviously available to employees who avoid disciplinary actions, terminations, or incarceration resulting from investigations, arrests, and conviction for violating statutes intended to curtail procurement corruption. Depending on the strength of the evidence when government representatives are investigated for corruption, the employee is likely to be placed on either paid or unpaid administrative leave during the investigation. Upon conviction, the employee normally resigns or is involuntarily terminated on the basis of the conviction. Whether the employee is placed on probation or incarcerated, there is also the distinct possibility that the employee is prohibited from working for any government organization for an extended time period. However, in the absence of such a government employment prohibition, it is unlikely that any government organization would hire an individual who has been convicted of an egregious crime.

Improved personal and professional reputation is achieved by individuals who are employed by an organization that is known to maintain stringent ethical standards. This fact was demonstrated to this author by observing the opposite reaction to representatives from a contractor that had recently been suspended from receiving further government contracts due to contract fraud. Two representatives of the suspended contractor appeared at a joint government/contractor gathering that included representatives from a relatively large number of government entities and contractors. Although a cold reaction for the contractor representatives may seem a normal reaction to representatives from a contractor suspended for fraud, the specifics of this case are likely to lead most readers to consider their cold reception to be an overreaction. The offending division of the suspended contractor was located on the opposite coast from the division represented by the attendees at the joint gathering, and the sales of the offending division represented less than one-half of 1% of the corporation's total sales. Although the representatives of the suspended contractor may have felt some trepidation knowing that likely all their associates, many of whom were also friends, had heard of the suspension, their surprise and disappointment were quite evident when, upon their arrival, the gathering fell silent and they received hard stares in lieu of their normal friendly greetings.

Enhanced family relationships are enriched through employment with a respected organization. Ethical public servants who are employees or officials of a government organization that benefits from a reputation of fair and transparent contractual activities share in their agency's reputation, and that reputation sharing contributes not only to their personal reputation but to their relationship with family members, who are also judged by their loved one's reputation.

The avoidance of fines levied against corrupt public servants is certainly one indicator that individuals maximize retained compensation by ensuring that their dealings with contractors strictly conform to agency policies. Although compensation may be maximized in the short run by participating in corrupt activities, it hardly seems worth the risk when one considers the FBI's conviction rate for public corruption, as mentioned earlier, at more than 900 federal, state, and local officials convicted each year.

Preservation of personal freedom and avoidance of imprisonment often imposed on corrupt public servants seem to be obvious incentives for individuals to conform to agency ethical contracting practices. Duke Cunningham, who as of this writing remains incarcerated for his ethical transgressions discussed in Chapter 1, certainly would have benefited from personal freedom and avoidance of imprisonment had he established personal ethical standards that either conformed to or exceeded his agency's statutory requirements.

Increased self-confidence is gained through knowledge of how to react if offered a gratuity. Government representatives with responsibility for drafting specifications or solicitations; writing sole source justifications; evaluating proposals; selecting contractors or recommending contractors for agency contracts; negotiating, reviewing, or executing contracts and amendments; monitoring contractor performance; or approving contractor payments are likely to be offered a gratuity at some time during their career. Employees or officials that have a zero tolerance personal ethics standard are able to develop a predetermined response in the event that a gratuity is offered. Having a predetermined response when a contractor gift is offered is personally reassuring because the official or employee knows the proper response to the offer of a gratuity. The lack of a personal ethical standard and lack of a predetermined response may place the government representative in the awkward position of weighing the pros and cons of accepting a surprise gift offer from a contractor representative and making the decision to accept or decline the offer in that moment.

The establishment of a personal zero tolerance policy with respect to acceptance of gifts and gratuities is consistent with ethical codes established by professional procurement or contract associations. Contracting professionals and other agency officials and employees who establish such a personal zero tolerance policy certainly are worthy of the respect of their contemporaries for making such a commitment.

3.3.3 Benefits of Ethical Standards for Government Contractors

Although there are disadvantages to being a private-sector company that provides products or services to the government,[14] and instances of noncompliance with government contracting regulations are frequently reported by the media, there are numerous little-known advantages available to government contractors that conform to government regulations. Strict compliance with socioeconomic subcontracting requirements and maintenance of a subcontracting program that conforms to *Federal Acquisition Regulation* (FAR) requirements are considered, even by some corporate executives, as excess costs incurred by government contractors, but they actually have benefits that can far outweigh the added costs. The benefits of conforming to FAR requirements include the negotiation of higher profit percentages, improved opportunities for award of government contracts, and the ability to award most subcontracts and purchase orders without undertaking the added effort and time required for obtaining prior government approval. Details on the nature of these benefits and recommendations on measures for increasing profits on federal contracts are addressed in subsequent chapters.

Government contractors that develop zero tolerance ethical standards earn the respect of the overwhelming majority of government officials who do not expect to be rewarded with gifts and gratuities for performing their public service. However, contractors that do not widely publicize their rigid ethical standards prominently in their facility, in advertising materials, on their websites, and in their responses to government solicitations may not receive the complete benefits earned through the establishment of a strict ethics program.

3.4 Essential Features for Ethical Contracting Programs

> Character, in the long run, is the decisive factor in the life of an individual, and of nations alike.
>
> **President Theodore Roosevelt**

Most individuals who decide to embark on public service do not begin that career to receive contractor gifts that are proffered merely because of their position of responsibility in government. However, because certain employees will accept contractor gifts, it is necessary to develop organizational standards for ethical behavior and establish limits on the value of acceptable contractor gifts. Placing limits on contractor gifts is intended to discourage elaborate gifts and establish a threshold that, if exceeded, may result in disciplinary action.

The policies and regulations applicable to the agency also normally specify the dollar threshold at which the reporting of gifts and gratuities is required. Another view of ethics policies and procedures is that they describe the maximum value of gifts and gratuities that can be accepted from contractors attempting to influence decisions regarding the contractor's business dealings with the agency. Or, more directly, the agency's ethics policies and regulations describe the level of remuneration that public servants can accept from contractors with impunity.

Government restrictions typically establish a dollar threshold that represents acceptable values for gratuities that can be accepted and for gratuities that must be reported. The problem with such restrictions is that they concurrently establish a limit under which gratuities *are* acceptable and reporting requirements are avoided. The frequency at which gratuities may be accepted is not consistently established and the thresholds may be too high. However, establishing very low thresholds or zero tolerance policies is also challenging.

Development of organizational standards for ethical contracting practices and the avoidance of conflicts of interests are needed to ensure that agency officials and personnel are informed of the agency's ethical standards, and that lapses in ethical behavior by government representatives are not tolerated. Definitions for various types of conflicts of interest [actual, potential (or possible), and apparent (or perceived) conflicts] are provided in the glossary at the end of this book.

In addition to standards regarding the various types of conflicts of interest, organizational ethical contracting standards typically include applicable statutes, thresholds for acceptable gratuities, financial reporting, and training requirements. Although whistleblower protection, solicitation and contract provisions to discourage conflicts of interest, establishment of personal ethical standards that are more restrictive than the statutory thresholds for acceptable gratuities, procedures for dealing with violations and suspected violations, and periodic reviews and updates of the standards are not routinely included in organizational ethical contracting standards, agencies are encouraged to include them. Government entities require reasonable guidelines for officials and employees. Suggested ethical guidelines for government entities are reflected in Table 3.2. Acceptance of the recommendation for government officials and employees to establish personal zero tolerance ethical standards would necessitate standards that differ from the government entity standards. Suggested ethical guidelines for government officials and employees are reflected in Table 3.3. A third set of ethical guidelines is necessary for government contractors because contractors confer the gratuities provided to government officials and employees. Recommendations for government contractor ethical guidelines are reflected in Table 3.4.

3.4.1 Applicable Statutes

Officials who draft organizational ethical standards benefit from conducting research on gift-giving restrictions and including statutory and other conflict-of-interest restrictions that flow down from higher government levels to local ethical standards established for agency officials and employees. In recognition of the FBI's role in the investigation and prosecution of corruption at the federal, state, and

Table 3.2 Agency Guidelines: Ethical Guidelines for Government Entities

Offer of Gratuity	Recommended Policy
Inexpensive office supplies suitable for government office use (such as pens, pencils, letter openers, note pads, calendars, etc.) with contractor name and contact information	Recommended if truly inexpensive (no platinum, gold, silver, or gemstones), contains contractor name and contact information, and does not exceed established cumulative monetary limits
Coffee, pastries, and working lunches	Recommended if infrequent and provided at contractor's facility or public place (not in government offices), at work-related meeting or seminar, and does not exceed established cumulative monetary limits
Dinners with or without adult beverages	Not recommended unless approved in advance in writing and does not exceed established cumulative monetary limits
Participation at contractor hospitality suite	Not recommended unless approved in advance in writing and does not exceed established cumulative monetary limits
Sporting and cultural events	Not recommended unless approved in advance in writing and does not exceed established cumulative monetary limits
Use of contractor-owned or -provided aircraft, boats, or motor vehicles	Not recommended unless approved in advance in writing and does not exceed established cumulative monetary limits
Contractor-provided honorarium for speech or writing	Not recommended
Contractor-provided meals, housing, or entertainment	Not recommended
Contractor reimbursement of expenses	Not recommended
Nightclub entertainment	Not recommended
Charitable contributions in name of agency or agency representatives	Not recommended
Furniture	Not recommended
Contractor-sponsored golf tournaments	Not recommended
Visits to contractor hunting/fishing lodges	Not recommended
Escort services	Not recommended
Cash or negotiable instruments	Not recommended

Table 3.3 Agency Representatives Guidelines: Ethical Guidelines for Government Officials and Employees

Offer of Gratuity	Minimal Policy	Recommended Policy
Inexpensive office supplies suitable for government office use (such as pens, pencils, letter openers, note pads, calendars, etc.) with contractor name and contact information	Recommended if truly inexpensive (no platinum, gold, silver, or gemstones), contains contractor name and contact information, and does not exceed established cumulative monetary limits	Assumptions: Government officials and employees are sufficiently compensated such that it is not necessary to receive anything of monetary value from government contractors.
Coffee, pastries, and working lunches	Recommended if infrequent and provided at contractor's facility or public place (not in government offices), at a work-related meeting or seminar, and does not exceed established cumulative monetary limits	The constituency expects government representatives to refuse anything of monetary value from government contractors that provide such gratuities merely because of the government representative's position with the government.
Dinners with or without adult beverages	Not recommended unless approved in advance in writing and does not exceed established cumulative monetary limits	The contractor's motivation for providing gratuities to government representatives is to receive favorable treatment in return.
Participation at contractor hospitality suite	Not recommended unless approved in advance in writing and does not exceed established cumulative monetary limits	Minimal acceptable values for gratuities have been established, not as approval of gratuity acceptance, but as a basis for disciplining those who exceed the established monetary limits.

(continued)

Table 3.3   Agency Representatives Guidelines: Ethical Guidelines for Government Officials and Employees (Continued)

Offer of Gratuity	Minimal Policy	Recommended Policy
Sporting and cultural events	Not recommended unless approved in advance in writing and does not exceed established cumulative monetary limits	Recommendation: Based on these assumptions, and despite the existence of agency policy permitting acceptance of gifts within established limits, government representatives are cautioned against accepting anything of value from government contractors.
Use of contractor-owned or -provided aircraft, boats, or motor vehicles	Not recommended unless approved in advance in writing and does not exceed established cumulative monetary limits	
Contractor-provided honorarium for speech or writing	Not recommended	
Contractor-provided meals, housing, or entertainment	Not recommended	
Contractor reimbursement of expenses	Not recommended	
Nightclub entertainment	Not recommended	
Charitable contributions in name of agency or agency representatives	Not recommended	
Furniture	Not recommended	
Contractor-sponsored golf tournaments	Not recommended	
Visits to contractor hunting/fishing lodges	Not recommended	
Escort services	Not recommended	
Cash or negotiable instruments	Not recommended	

Table 3.4   Contractor Guidelines: Ethical Guidelines for Government Contractors

Offer of Gratuity	Minimal Policy	Recommended Policy
Inexpensive office supplies suitable for government office use (such as pens, pencils, letter openers, note pads, calendars, etc.) with contractor name and contact information.	Recommended if truly inexpensive (no platinum, gold, silver, or gemstones), contains contractor name and contact information, and does not exceed established cumulative monetary limits	Assumptions: The majority of government representatives are honest people who strive to obtain the best bargain for their agency and constituency without any expectation of personal enrichment from contractors.
Coffee, pastries, and working lunches	Recommended if infrequent and provided at contractor's facility or public place (not in government offices), at a work-related meeting or seminar, and does not exceed established cumulative monetary limits	Government representatives who expect personal enrichment from contractors based on their position with the government are likely in conflict with their agency's policy.
Dinners with or without adult beverages		
Participation at contractor hospitality suite		
Sporting and cultural events		
Use of contractor-owned or -provided aircraft, boats, or motor vehicles	Not recommended unless use is provided in connection with legitimate business and is consistent with customer's policy	
Dinners with or without adult beverages	Not recommended	Providing gratuities to government employees that exceed monetary limits established by government customers is likely illegal and can result in loss of contracts, fines, payment of restitution, debarment, and imprisonment of contractor employees.
Contractor-provided honorarium for speech or writing	Not recommended	
Contractor-provided meals, housing, or entertainment	Not recommended with exception of coffee, pastries, or working lunches	
Contractor reimbursement of expenses	Not recommended	
Nightclub entertainment	Not recommended	

(continued)

Table 3.4 Contractor Guidelines: Ethical Guidelines for Government Contractors (Continued)

Offer of Gratuity	Minimal Policy	Recommended Policy
		Recommendation:
Charitable contributions in name of agency or agency representatives	Not recommended	Based on these assumptions, contractors are cautioned against offering anything of value to government representatives. Contractors should also publicize a "no gratuity" policy in promotional materials and on bids and proposals sent to government customers.
Furniture	Not recommended unless furniture is a contractor product that is provided for demonstration purposes for less than a full month	
Contractor-sponsored golf tournaments	Not recommended	
Visits to contractor hunting/fishing lodges	Not recommended	
Escort services	Not recommended	
Cash or negotiable instruments	Not recommended	

local level in the United States, it is appropriate to cite applicable federal laws in ethical standards for all levels of government.

3.4.2 Thresholds for Acceptance of Gifts

Organizations faced with the task of developing thresholds for differentiating between acceptable and unacceptable ethical behavior, or updating existing ethical thresholds, face difficult decisions regarding the value that differentiates acceptable and unacceptable behavior. Another consideration is the subjectivity for the value of personal gifts. The subjectivity involved in establishing the difference between acceptable and unacceptable gifts tends to inject unfairness into ethical standards. In light of this subjectivity, some employees or officials may be tempted to err in favor of accepting a particular favor. However, more conscientious employees may decline the same or similar contractor-offered favors. The acceptance of low-value favors may lead to less reluctance to subsequent acceptance of more valuable favors and rationalization over the apparent value of gifts offered by contractors or prospective contractors.

When the agency's policy permits receipt of a certain value for gifts or gratuities, it is recommended that the policy also address the frequency that such gifts may be accepted. Certain agencies may elect to establish differing gift and gratuity thresholds based on an official's or employee's status or position title.

The zero tolerance approach to gratuity standards refers to a zero tolerance for accepting any gift. Although a zero tolerance approach appears to eliminate the problem of establishing the distinction between the value of personal enrichment that would constitute acceptable or unacceptable behavior, it is difficult to enforce such severe restrictions. If an agency official or employee accepts a cup of coffee from a contractor or prospective contractor, despite a zero tolerance policy, the agency officials responsible for enforcement of the policy may feel that they are viewed as petty for disciplining the offender. However, when agencies ignore enforcement for the unacceptable receipt of a cup of coffee, they subject themselves to criticism for uneven enforcement when they discipline another offender for a more serious infraction.

Another problem associated with enforcing ethics policies involves an agency official or employee who maintains a friendship with a contractor or prospective contractor representative that predated her or his agency employment, or who has a relative who works for a contractor or prospective contractor. Such relationships likely involve frequent social interaction and a historical exchange of gifts. One solution for dealing with such relationships is to require such agency officials or employees to recuse themselves whenever the prospective contractor in question is being considered for award of a contract or when decisions are made that affect current contractors that employ friends or relatives of agency officials or employees. If the official or employee is recused in these cases, however, there remains the appearance of a conflict of interest if the recused official's subordinate assumes the decision-making role. If the recused official is the chief elected or chief appointed official, then there is little choice but to have a subordinate assume the decision-making role. If the contractor in question competes for a large number of agency contracts, the effectiveness of the official or employee who is frequently recused might also be questioned.

3.4.3 Financial Reporting Requirements

Organizational ethical standards that establish the threshold at which gifts may or may not be acceptable may include differing thresholds for gratuities that may periodically be accepted and the frequency for reporting gifts and gratuities. A listing of the nature of gifts and gratuities that may or may not be accepted and those that may or may not require public disclosure is recommended for inclusion in the organization's ethical standards. Unambiguous standards help guard against claims that officials or employees failed to understand that a particular gift was reportable.

Monitoring compliance with and consistent enforcement of violations of the organization's ethical standards are essential for a successful program that guards against activities that inappropriately enrich public officials and employees for selfish actions they take in their official capacity. The report element pertains to the reporting of income or other revenue received from sources other than the employee's or official's agency compensation. The reporting forms used by most agencies indicate that the person completing the form is subject to disciplinary action if there is knowing and willful falsification of the reported information. Conviction of corrupt officials is often based on falsification of gift reporting. The need to report gifts is intended to be a deterrent to accepting gifts over the established thresholds. However, deterrence was apparently not effective in the case of David Safavian, the former GSA chief of staff. Notwithstanding the occasional failure of the deterrence factor, the ability to prosecute officials for failing to fully disclose gifts on financial disclosure forms was, in Mr. Safavian's case, effective.

3.4.4 Ethics Training

Implementing the recommendations presented in this chapter will inform government officials and employees unequivocally of their agency's commitment to professional contracting standards, demonstrate proactive measures to guard against contract corruption, and contribute to professionalism in management of the government's contracting function. Individuals who intend to design an ethics training program, or update an existing ethics training program, are encouraged to review additional sources prior to reflecting on the material to cover, the approach to presenting the material, and the desired impact on those receiving the training. Jonathan P. West and Evan M. Berman authored an excellent article[15] that is recommended for this purpose. For those who are interested in researching in even greater depth, the materials in the notes to the West and Berman article identify additional resources.

Ideally, agencies provide training on their policies and regulations regarding ethics for newly hired employees, periodically for those employees who are apt to be exposed to ethical challenges, and refresher training for employees assigned to advance contract planning or proposal evaluation and negotiation teams. In contrast to agencies with formal ethics training, some agencies merely rely on their employees and officials to read the policies and regulations on their own. It is preferable for agencies to conduct initial, periodic, and refresher ethics training in a classroom setting.

The incorporation of training in ethics and conflicts of interest is recommended for agencies' new-hire training programs. Reliance on annual or other periodic training may result in the placement of new employees in situations where they are confronted with an ethical decision-making situation, such as the offer of a gratuity, before they have attended their initial ethics training. It is inexcusable for agencies to place their employees in such situations, and it is unfair to new employees who are faced with reacting to the offer of a gratuity prior to learning about the agency's ethical standards.

Refresher training is recommended upon assignment of employees or officials to an advance contract planning, proposal evaluation, or negotiation team. If considerable time has elapsed since the previous ethics training was completed, officials or employees who are likely to be exposed to ethics decisions, on the basis of their ad hoc advance contract planning or proposal evaluation assignments, may require refresher training on the agency's ethical standards. Such refresher training need not be conducted separately from other briefings regarding the project or program that is the subject of the advance contract planning or proposal evaluation effort. Combining the ethics refresher training with project or program briefings, in fact, may be preferable to a separate ethics training program, because combining the two tends to focus the expected ethical behavior on the immediate project or program.

Periodic follow-on ethics training, in the absence of an assignment to advance contract planning or proposal evaluation teams, is recommended because awareness of the agency's ethical policies is likely to diminish over time. Simply because an official or employee is not expected to serve on an advance contract planning or proposal evaluation team in the immediate future does not ensure that he or she will not be placed in a situation that requires a decision regarding the agency's ethics policies. Numerous situations exist outside of advance contract planning and proposal evaluation in which a government representative might be offered a gratuity. Examples of other situations when employees or officials might be offered a gratuity are during sales or marketing visits from prospective contractors, participation in trade shows or professional association meetings, evaluation of an invoice for approval, determination of the acceptability of completed contract work, or during holiday seasons.

Personalization of ethics training with case studies involving convicted or plead-out public employees is likely to make the training more pertinent and better allow those attending the training to relate to the training materials. Cases such as those involving Duke Cunningham, who resigned from Congress and was sentenced to prison for corruption, and Mr. Riechers, who died of an apparent suicide while under investigation, seem appropriate for ethics training to discourage the practice of corruption. Cases unique to the agency, if available, may help class attendees relate to the subject matter. For example, in the situation discussed earlier wherein department personnel were invited to an all-expenses-paid visit to a contractor's facility, the trainer might personalize the training by discussing the propriety of the contractor facility visit and highlighting the fact that acceptance of such trips violates agency policy.

Ethics training conducted for UN members might be personalized by including a discussion of the bribery and money laundering case involving Alexander Yakovlev, who admitted to three charges that carried the possibility of sixty years in prison. Yakovlev, however, testified against Vladimir Kuznetsov, a Russian diplomat, who was subsequently convicted of money laundering but was turned over to Russian authorities for return to Russia to serve sixteen months in jail.

Training in financial reporting normally addresses the nature of finances that need be reported, the value of finances that need be reported, and the frequency of reporting. It is recommended that accuracy of reporting be stressed, and that cases such as Mr. Safavian's conviction for failure to report a gift be discussed.

Employees who become aware of ethics violations on the part of others may be uninformed regarding what events require reporting and how to report ethics violations. The relatively high incidence of ethical transgressions translates to the likelihood that a government representative in a responsible position will at some point in her or his career become aware of an ethical transgression. Therefore, it is imperative that such employees be knowledgeable regarding their responsibilities when confronted with deviations from the agency's ethics policies. The recommended topics for inclusion in training on ethics violation reporting are listed below:

■ What ethics violations are reportable
■ How and where to report violations
■ The duty to report actual or suspected violations
■ Whistleblower protection

Training on the personal consequences of violating agency ethics standards is most effective when presented in a straightforward manner. This topic is best timed to follow the discussion of actual case studies and the fate of those ethics violators who received fines, imprisonment, termination of their government position, devastation of their families, ruination of their reputations, and in certain cases where the employee committed suicide.

When there is a violation, or suspected violation, of an agency's ethics policy, it may be best to delay interviewing the violator or suspected violator because such an interview is likely to hinder an investigation. In addition to delaying the interview of the suspected offender, the agency is advised to establish a protocol regarding who within the organization is notified of the suspected violation and the decision to notify law enforcement officials. The top elected or appointed official as well as in-house legal counsel are likely candidates for notification when a suspected ethics violation is to be reported to a law enforcement agency. Some agencies may also wish to coordinate such activities with human resources. The possible consequences to the organization with a reputation for corruption are also recommended for inclusion in ethics training programs.

Although an organizational zero tolerance policy (prohibition against accepting any gift from a private-sector contractor) is difficult to enforce, individual government representatives are encouraged to establish a personal zero tolerance ethical standard. Low thresholds or zero tolerance policies are difficult to enforce and are not likely to receive leadership support. An organizational zero tolerance policy that is not enforced at the zero value threshold has questionable validity at any level; therefore, it is more appropriate to establish the agency threshold at some value where the standard is enforced. A personal zero tolerance ethical standard, however, as opposed to organizational standards, is highly recommended for the reasons outlined below. Personal zero tolerance ethical standards are practical to regulate because they are self-enforced. Examples of the numerous benefits for an individual public official who establishes a personal zero tolerance policy are provided here:

■ One can never feel indebted to a contractor.
■ One never needs to distinguish between the acceptable value and the unacceptable value for a contractor-offered gift.
■ The public official may develop a standard statement for declining gifts that is an appropriate response to any offer of a gratuity.
■ There is no fear of a threat to one's career, finances, or freedom that are expected when a public official unintentionally accepts a gratuity that exceeds the threshold for acceptance or fails to provide required financial reporting.
■ There is no fear of being drawn into acceptance of unacceptable gifts by initially accepting low-value gifts and then being offered higher and even higher valued gifts until one finds that gifts exceeding the threshold have been accepted.
■ One need never publicly disclose gifts received from contractors, because none are ever accepted.

The inclusion of whistleblower protection, compliance monitoring, and reporting requirements improve the effectiveness of agency ethical standards. Whistleblower protection requires sound protection and appropriate rewards for honest employees who report deviations from the agency's ethical standards by government officials or employees. Failure to provide sound protection for whistleblowers may result in the perception by employees who courageously performed their responsibility to report wrongdoing that the whistleblower protection program is merely a sham. A well-planned whistleblower protection program is recommended because corrupt officials who are reported by subordinates may attempt to use their position to discredit or ruin the career of a whistleblower who was dutifully meeting her or his responsibilities.

3.4.5 Periodic Review and Update of Ethics Standards

Periodic reviews of ethics standards are used to determine the updates required as a result of changes in policies or statutes relating to gifts and gratuities. Agencies might also wish to revisit their thresholds for acceptance of gifts to determine whether the policy is overly generous. Certain organizations establish a relatively high gift threshold, such as $250 or more, which does not require refusal or reporting of the gift. Organizations with such relatively high gift thresholds further compromise the integrity of their employees' ethical behavior by permitting multiple gifts that do not exceed this threshold during any given year. Therefore, it is advisable to periodically review agency standards to ensure that they conform to current statutes and policies, threshold levels are not excessively high, multiple gifts up to the threshold are not permitted during the year, and reporting requirements are sufficient to detect gifts and gratuities that have the potential for influencing the decisions of agency officials or employees.

3.4.6 Difficulty in Enforcement of Zero Tolerance Policy

The difficulty of enforcing zero tolerance gratuity policies was discussed previously. It is appropriate to consider the difficulty of enforcing zero tolerance policies when writing and reviewing ethical behavior standards. Employers must establish some gift threshold for reporting and rejecting gifts to place limits on what employees and officials may accept. Although an agency zero tolerance policy is not practical, the agency's policy might include a recommendation to officials and employees to establish a personal zero tolerance policy.

3.4.7 Agency Representatives with Relatives and Friends Who Represent Contractors

It is likely that a number of agency officials or employees have friends or family members that represent contractors or prospective contractors. Generally included in policies with respect to relatives or friends representing contractors or prospective contractors is a definition of immediate family. The definition is an important distinction because agencies may struggle with a contractor's enrichment of a relative not included in the agency's overly narrow definition of relatives considered as immediate family. Defining the policy with respect to the exchange of gifts between agency officials and employees and their friends who happen to be representatives of a contractor or prospective contractor is also appropriate for inclusion in the agency's written ethical behavior policy. An extreme example of a government representative with relatives employed by a contractor with ongoing contracts and being considered for future contracts is Ms. Druyun, the former top Air Force procurement official. As discussed in Chapter 1, Ms. Druyun pleaded guilty to favoring Boeing in numerous contract negotiations because she felt indebted to Boeing for giving jobs to her daughter and her son-in-law. The reports of Ms. Druyun's confession also indicated that she felt indebted to Boeing because they also gave her a job.

3.4.8 Ethical Standards for Government Contractors

The establishment of ethical standards is highly recommended for government contractors. The potential of severe consequences for government contractors that fail to establish an effective ethical contracting program justifies implementation of an ethics program. Although contractors might consider establishing standards that forbid gratuities exceeding their customers' gratuity thresholds, this is likely to be confusing because different customers will likely have differing thresholds. Additionally, public servants may be offended by a gift that is offered merely because of the public official's job. Rather than attempting to establish a policy that permits gifts up to the value of varying customer thresholds and risking the embarrassment of the customer refusing or returning the gift, it is recommended that government contractors establish a policy prohibiting their employees from offering any gifts to government officials or employees. This recommendation for a government contractor policy also includes refraining from other activities or discussions that might constitute or appear to constitute a conflict of interest. For example, it is recommended that such ethical standards include the prohibition of discussions with government employees regarding future employment with the contractor as well as the actual employment of ex-government employees for two years following their government employment. This recommendation also includes widespread publication of the contractor's zero tolerance policy to ensure that it is understood by contractor employees and government representatives alike. Publication of the government contractor's ethics program is recommended for prominent locations within contractor facilities, contractor websites, advertising materials, and all proposals, bids, or quotations sent to government contractors or potential government contractors.

Implementing an effective ethical contracting program as described here is certain to benefit both agency personnel and the agency itself. The agency as well as officials and employees benefit from informed agency representatives who understand the agency's policies regarding gifts and gratuities. This recommendation is summarized in Table 3.4.

3.4.9 Solicitation and Contract Provisions to Encourage Contractors' Ethical Behavior

Ethical behavior for government contractors can be furthered by discouraging conflicts of interests through provisions in government solicitations and contracts. The CD accompanying this book contains a solicitation and a model contract that include provisions intended to discourage conflicts of interest. The solicitation (in this case, an RFP) and the contract were developed through a best practices research project in which participating government entities provided copies of their RFPs and contracts. The documents provided in support of the research project were subjected to a document review to select the best features to include in the solicitation and contract. The CD also includes a description of the research project and a discussion of all the best practices that were identified during this project. The features for discouraging practices associated with corruption are included in the solicitation and contract provided on the CD. The terms and conditions in the model contract are not intended as substitutes for FAR provisions required for federal contracts and subcontracts.

The provisions of the solicitation and contract documents on the CD are comprehensive; they may be overly comprehensive for all but high-value, high-risk contracts. In recognition of the fact that less-comprehensive provisions may be appropriate for low-value, low-risk contracts, alternative RFP and contract documents included on the CD provide less extensive risk avoidance provisions. The less comprehensive provisions can be found on the CD in the file entitled "Short Form RFP with Short Form Contract."

3.5 Conclusion

Implementation of the preceding recommendations in government and contractor ethics programs does not guarantee the prevention of fraudulent activities such as reported by FBI Director Robert S. Mueller, III.[16] Director Mueller, in his 2007 congressional testimony, stated that the FBI had 640 special agents dedicated to more than 2,400 pending public corruption cases. The 640 cases represented an increase of 42% from 2001. His testimony included the conservative estimate that fraudulent health care costs ranged from 3 to 5% of total health care costs. If fraudulent health care equals the low end of the range (3%), then actual fraudulent health care costs would equal $68 billion. The tremendous loss of funds to fraud combined with the personal tragedies for affected individuals demand concentrated efforts to implement processes to improve ethical behavior on the part of government and private-sector contractor representatives alike.

Notes

1. From welcoming remarks in "Fighting Bribery in Public Procurement in Asia and the Pacific," 7th Regional Seminar on Making International Anti-Corruption Standards Operational, Bali, Indonesia, 5–7 November 2007. Hosted by the Corruption Eradication Commission (KPK), Indonesia.
2. "Report on the Activities of the Office of the Inspector General Fiscal Year 1999," Charles C. Maddox, Esq., Inspector General of the Government of the District of Columbia, Office of the Inspector General.

3. "Proposed Report of the Special Investigative Committee," State of Illinois, 95th General Assembly, House of Representatives, Special Investigative Committee, undated.

4. Based on an article in *The Independent*, "President's Aides Convicted on Corruption Charges," Alex Duval Smith, October 27, 2005, and an article posted on guardian. co.uk, "Sleaze Trial Swirls around Chirac," Jon Henley, March 21, 2005.

5. The details of Mr. Safavian's conviction were reported in a U.S. Department of Justice media release, "Former GSA Chief of Staff David Safavian Convicted of Obstruction, Making False Statements," December 19, 2008. He was reportedly convicted of several counts, including lying on his financial disclosure report. The media release stated "the jury also found that Safavian filed a false statement on his 2002 financial disclosure form."

6. Refraining from the use of auctioneering techniques does not imply that the fairly recent practice of reverse auctioneering should be discouraged.

7. Miguel Bustillo, "Louisiana Tires of Its Rogues," *Los Angeles Times*, January 27, 2006, in-print edition, A-1.

8. New charges were included in the Department of Justice press release by Jim Letten, U.S. attorney, Department of Justice, Eastern district of Louisiana, August 11, 2006.

9. The guilty plea was announced in the Department of Justice press release by Jim Letten, U.S. attorney, U.S. Attorney's Office, Eastern district of Louisiana, April 3, 2008.

10. Although this is often quoted as indicated here, some reports have suggested that Speaker Unruh's language has been sanitized in this version.

11. Details of the Oracle Corporation contract were reported in the *Los Angeles Times*, "Top Davis Aides Say They Were Misled on Oracle," Dan Morain and Nancy Vogel, May 22, 2002.

12. The information on the GSA settlement with NetApp, Inc., is based on a Department of Justice media release, "GSA Contractor NetApp Agrees to Pay U.S. $128 Million to Resolve Contract Fraud Allegations," April 15, 2009.

13. The sentencing was announced in the Department of Justice media release by Alice H. Martin, U.S. attorney, Northern district of Alabama, "Former Executive Director of Alabama Fire College Sentenced to 125 Months in Prison," October 29, 2008.

14. Numerous disadvantages for government contractors relate to the criminalization of activities that would be unethical, at worst, in public sector business activities. Although unethical behavior is deplorable, it does not approach the consequences of criminal behavior. For example, the government contractor NetApp settled with the U.S. government by agreeing to pay $128 million to resolve contract fraud allegations relating to allegedly false statements regarding the failure to disclose discounts to commercial customers that were greater than NetApp disclosed to the General Services Administration. It is inconceivable that there would be consequences approaching this severity had such a failure to disclose discounts to other customers occurred during business-to-business negotiations. Other known disadvantages for government contractors include greater customer oversight and profit limitations.

15. Jonathan P. West and Evan M. Berman. (2004) "Ethics Training in U.S. Cities: Content, Pedagogy, and Impact," *Public Integrity*, vol. 6, no. 3, pp. 189–206.

16. The testimony by FBI Director Mueller was made before the House Judiciary Committee on July 26, 2007.

Chapter 4

Sole Source or Competition?

> The price of monopoly is upon every occasion the highest which can be got. The natural price, or the price of free competition, on the contrary, is the lowest which can be taken, not upon every occasion, indeed, but for any considerable time together.
>
> **Adam Smith**

4.1 Appeal of Competitive Contracting

This chapter provides readers with the fundamentals of competition in contracting, the disadvantages of sole source contracts, the challenges to and benefits from embracing competition, the rationale for establishing a dollar threshold where sole source justifications are required as well as situations that do and do not justify sole source contracts. This chapter, like Chapters 3 and 5, does not represent phases of the contracting cycle. However, the significance of ethics, competition, and social contracting justifies an entire chapter dedicated to each topic. These three chapters were positioned following Chapter 2 (Processes and Issues in Contracting), featuring a discussion of advance contract planning, and prior to Chapter 6 (Solicitations and Pre-Proposal Communications). The advance contract planning team normally determines the approach to ethics, competition, and social contracting that will affect the content of the solicitation. Therefore, the logical placement for the chapters on ethics, competition, and social contracting is following the chapter that describes advance contract planning and prior to the chapter on preparation of the solicitation.

Elected and appointed officials, as well as the constituency, normally insist on competitive procurements to ensure that excessive amounts are not paid from tax revenues and that favoritism is not a factor in the selection of contractors. Advance contract planning ideally establishes a contracting environment wherein full and open competition is prescribed.

Government entities have a reputation for purchasing through the use of IFBs, wherein the lowest priced responsible contractor or supplier providing a responsive bid is selected. This approach leads to the selection of contractors often referred to as "the low bidder." However, the IFB-type solicitation is normally reserved for the purchase of commodities that can be specified distinctly or for traditional construction contracts. In rare cases, state or federal grants require competition through the use of an IFB for service contracts. Granting agencies, in such cases, normally provide an IFB template and guidelines for use of the IFB by the contracting agency. Because the use of IFBs is fairly well understood and not controversial, discussion of IFBs in this book is limited to their distinctive features. The distinctive features of IFBs, other than the selection of the contractor based on low bid, are that the responses from prospective contractors are referred to as "bids." IFBs are used in a competitive environment, must be rejected if received after the time established by the agency for receipt of bids, are opened publicly and read aloud, and are not subject to negotiations. Certain agencies refer to IFBs as RFBs. However, the RFBs that have been reviewed by this author appear to be the same type of solicitation as an IFB but with a different name.

The type of solicitation known as an RFQ is similar to an IFB; however, it is an informal method of soliciting prices from prospective contractors when the resultant contract price is expected to be below the price for which use of the more formal IFB is mandated. Responses to an RFQ from prospective contractors are referred to as "quotations" or occasionally as "quotes." Agencies normally establish guidelines for handling quotations, and it is recommended that those guidelines be included in their RFQ documents to inform prospective contractors of the process for handling quotations. One guideline recommended for inclusion is that quotes may be accepted if received late. However, whenever prospective contractors are advised that their responses to RFQs or RFPs may be accepted if received late, it is further recommended that they also be advised that quotations may be rejected if received late and, therefore, they are urged to submit the quotations by the due date.

The RFCQ is used to determine the qualifications of contractors with the objective of establishing a list of qualified contractors. The RFCQ is normally the first step of a two-step process to obtain proposals only from pre-qualified contractors. Three problems with this two-step solicitation process are that it is time consuming, the agency incurs added work in that the agency must evaluate the statement of qualifications received in response to their RFCQ, and prospective contractors that are not discovered until after the initial firms were solicited likely do not have time to participate in the contractor qualification process. Because the RFCQ is not suitable for selecting a contractor, it is necessary to prepare and release an RFP to the contractors that were qualified during the first step of the process. Therefore, additional time and work is required to select a contractor through this two-step process.

The solicitation type referred to as RFP is appropriate for use for most service contracts, design/build construction contracts, and commodity contracts when either the needed commodities cannot be described sufficiently to permit solicitation by an IFB or the contractor is selected on the basis of price and other factors. The use of IFBs by government is declining whereas the use of RFPs is increasing due to the growing popularity of selecting contractors on the basis of price and other factors and design/build construction contracts. Sole source justifications are most frequently written for service contracts, occasionally for commodity contracts, and rarely for construction contracts. Government entities often establish a relatively high value threshold for award of service contracts that may be awarded without competition or with limited competition. However, it is recommended that service contracts be awarded in full and open competition whenever possible to obtain the full benefits available through competitive procurements. Full and open competition limits opportunities for unethical contracting practices and permits the contracting agency to select the contractor that is proposing the optimal combination of price, quality, and timeliness.

Full and open competition means involvement of all competitors that wish to compete for a particular contract and treating all prospective contractors equally. The Dallas Independent School District (DISD) case involved two lucrative contracts with a cumulative value of approximately $120 million, and all prospective contractors were not treated equally.[1] Ruben Bohuchot, DISD Chief Technology Officer, provided Frankie Wong and his company, Micro Systems Engineering, Inc. (MSE), with inside information that enabled MSE, partnered with Hewlett Packard (HP), to obtain the two contracts mentioned above. William Frederick Coleman III, a friend of Bohuchot and former DISD employee who had previously been in charge of DISD's purchasing department, assisted MSE as a consultant. However, Coleman was not eligible to consult for MSE because of his past DISD employment and the fact that he was paid on a contingency fee basis. Wong established and became president of Statewide Marketing, LLC. During the trial, the government provided evidence that Wong made available a 46′ Post motor sport fishing yacht for Bohuchot's use. A second, larger, 58′ Viking yacht was purchased by MSE, through Statewide Marketing, and was used by Bohuchot 80% of the time that the yacht was in use. All of the expenses and operating costs of the two yachts, including the boat captain's salary, were paid by Statewide Marketing and MSE at the direction of Wong. Bohuchot and Wong were found guilty of bribery and money laundering. Coleman pled guilty to one count of attempting to influence a grand jury and testified for the government.

The necessity to provide equal opportunities for all parties to compete for government contracts, which was absent in the DISD case, has its origins in the U.S.

Constitution.[2] Some state constitutions have similar provisions that extend equal contracting opportunities to the state and local government level. However, the absence of such provisions in state constitutions does not diminish their applicability to states and local governments subject to the U.S. Constitution provisions for competitive procurement.

There are situations, however, wherein there is just one contractor qualified for certain contracts. When there are absolutely no opportunities for obtaining competitive proposals, documenting the justification for award of a sole source contract is recommended. A form to document the justification and approval of sole source contracts, "Sole Source Justification/Approval" form, is provided on the CD provided with this book.

4.2 Establishing a Favorable Environment for Competitive Procurement

The recommendations for discouraging ethical problems in government procurement presented in Chapters 1–3 do not require technical processes. However, proactive measures needed to minimize the impact of corruption on government procurement do require the implementation of technical approaches. The recommendations beginning in Chapter 4 introduce more technical processes to combat procurement corruption. Readers are spared some of the technical details here; detailed descriptions of the more technical processes appear on the CD accompanying this book. Individuals interested in greater detail are encouraged to read the expanded competitive processes on the CD. Although the recommendations in this chapter begin to include more technical processes, the proposal evaluation techniques described in Chapter 7 include the most technical recommendations in this book. The proposal evaluation recommendations provided on the CD are more technical than those presented in Chapter 7.

A questionnaire sent to government entities for a best practices research project in the United States included a question designed to determine the dollar threshold at which it was necessary to obtain sole source justification for contracts. The emphasis in this chapter is on the importance of obtaining competition when selecting a contractor, and the introduction of a form that can be used to justify and approve sole source contracts when competition is not available. The questionnaire responses are summarized in Table 4.1.

4.2.1 Justification for Sole Source Contracts

Agency departments that manage contracts often research available contractors and develop a favored contractor well before the solicitation is released and proposal evaluation has begun. Department personnel, in this situation, often prepare a misguided sole source justification based on their favored contractor as the "best"

Table 4.1   Response to: At What Dollar Threshold Are Sole Source Justifications Required?

States	Local Agencies	Response
0	1	No dollar amount, but sole source must be proven
1	1	$1,000
2	0	$2,500
3	1	$3,000 to $3,100
3	2	$5,000
0	1	$10,000
2	0	$50,000
1	0	$62,600

qualified company or individual to provide the service or commodities. However, the solicitation and proposal evaluation processes are the best means to identify the contractor best suited to perform under the government contract. Sole source justifications are intended to justify sole source contracts when there is but one qualified contractor. Writing a sole source justification for the contractor perceived as the "best" by the individual writing it denies the government an opportunity to choose the best contractor through an established, well-planned process designed to select the best of the contractors competing for the agency's business.

Although there were no known ethical violations involved, the Swiss Federal Bureau for Building and Logistics reportedly awarded a 14 million Swiss Franc noncompetitive contract to Microsoft for Windows desktops and applications with support and maintenance.[3] Red Hat, a Linux provider, and seventeen other contractors protested the noncompetitive contract award to Microsoft. The Red Hat dispute will be referred to the Swiss Federal Administrative Court. (OSOR.ev news items, "CH: No settlement between Swiss government and open source suppliers," posted December 9, 2009.) Sole source contracts to Microsoft are reportedly commonplace in Europe while considerable savings have been achieved through use of alternative open source software.

In recognition of the fact that there are cases when there is but one contractor that can provide the required service or product, provisions for approval of sole source contracts are recommended for inclusion in government contracting policies. Development of a form similar to the "Sole Source Justification/Approval" form on the CD can be an effective tool to document the decision to approve a sole source contract. Ideally, a limited number of agency officials are authorized to approve sole source procurements, and such approvals are based on a determination that the recommended sole source contractor is the only contractor that can provide the needed service or product. Two reasons that are not normally considered as justification for sole source contracting are determinations that the recommended contractor is the lowest price contractor or that there is insufficient time to award the contract on a competitive basis.

Lowest price is not considered as justification for a sole source contract. Market pricing can normally be determined only through the competitive process. Therefore, it is necessary to conduct a competitive procurement to determine the market pricing from qualified contractors. Departments that attempt to justify sole source contracting based on lowest pricing generally base their justification on a previous competitive procurement. However, previously unsuccessful contractors are likely to propose more competitive pricing during subsequent competitive procurements. Contractors presently performing services or providing products for the contracting agency may be more inclined to increase pricing for follow-on procurements. This inclination to increase pricing for follow-on contracts is more likely if the present contractor is aware that its previous pricing was significantly lower than the competitors' pricing. Therefore, follow-on competitive procurements are likely to result in a closer alignment of proposed pricing between the competitors.

Insufficient time to conduct a competitive procurement also does not constitute justification to contract on a sole source basis. Although it is tempting to criticize departments for failing to plan their work when they base sole source justifications on insufficient time, there are even more constructive arguments against reliance on insufficient time to justify sole source procurements. If there is sufficient time to obtain pricing and a proposal from one company, then there is normally time to obtain pricing and a proposal from numerous contractors on a concurrent basis. The proposals may also reveal that one or more of the competing contractors, that may not have been permitted to submit a proposal in a sole source environment, is capable of ramping up faster and beginning the delivery of products sooner than the company that was being considered for the sole source contract. In the event that the contract in question is a follow-on contract, departments may have a stronger argument for calling out insufficient time as justification to forego competition. The temptation to criticize departments for failure to plan to obtain competitive proposals for continuation of ongoing contracts is even greater. However, it is usually preferable to have a policy and mechanism in place to extend current contracts for a limited time period to allow sufficient time to conduct a competitive procurement for the follow-on contract.

Government entities are invited to adapt the "Sole Source Justification/Approval" form, and any other materials on the CD, for their own contracting or academic program. The sole source form is designed for completion on a computer or typewriter or by hand. Detailed sole source justification and approval instructions for completing the "Sole Source Justification/Approval" form are provided on the CD along with a copy of the form.

As an alternative to preparing the solicitation and evaluating bids or proposals, numerous government entities participate in cooperative purchasing agreements.

The U.S. Communities™ is a nonprofit organization that provides cities or counties an opportunity to participate in competitive procurements that were conducted by other government entities. One city or county agrees to take the lead in soliciting bids or proposals on a nationwide basis for a product or product class. The U.S. Communities alliance assigns an advisory group to help the local agency with the solicitation. Once the local contract is awarded, it is reviewed by U.S. Communities to determine whether it can be used nationally. If the contract is accepted on a national basis, then any public agency participating in the U.S. Communities program can make purchases based on the terms of the lead agency's contract.

The U.S. General Services Administration (GSA) also provides an opportunity to take advantage of volume discount pricing for over 11 million products or services from commercial companies. GSA provides the option of ordering directly from GSA contractors or GSA's online shopping and ordering system. Federal, state, and local government agencies may be able to obtain lower prices and shorter lead times by purchasing through the GSA Schedules (also called Multiple Award Schedules and Federal Supply Schedules).

Government entities that wish to participate in cooperative purchasing arrangements, such as those offered by U.S. Communities or the U.S. General Services Administration, may require a change to their purchasing regulations to establish their authority to participate in such cooperative purchasing arrangements. Agencies participating in cooperative purchasing arrangements may also wish to periodically verify that they are receiving preferred pricing or expedited delivery by comparing the pricing and delivery offered through the cooperative purchasing arrangement to pricing and delivery offered in response to a locally conducted competitive solicitation for like products or services.

4.2.2 Recommendations for Competition by Government Contractors

Government contractors may wish to establish a position as the government's sole provider of certain products or services. Such a goal may prove fruitful because contracts that are obtained through the normal competitive process tend to require commitments for lower profits, higher quality levels for service or products, and expedited deliveries. A sole source position is established through innovative products or services required by the government that cannot be matched by potential competitors. As evidenced by the cases cited in Chapters 1–3, however, employing unethical practices such as those included in Table 1.1, to gain a sole source position is likely to result in government sanctions that culminate in fines, forfeiture of assets, imprisonment of corporate executives or personnel, termination of employment, or other perils that far exceed the benefits of any temporary advantage gained through unethical or illegal business practices.

Maximization of competition in subcontracting efforts by government contractors is also recommended. As discussed in Chapter 10, federal government agencies conduct contractor purchasing system reviews (CPSRs) for the subcontracting function of prime contractors. Three key indicators included in CPSRs are the level of competition achieved, price analyses, and justification of subcontractor selection. Acceptable or commendable performance with respect to all three indicators is maximized through competitive subcontracting.

4.3 Failed Competition Fosters Corruption and Diminishes Budgets

The earlier discussion indicated that contractors aware of their status as the sole source provider for a particular service or commodity tend to charge higher prices, provide less than optimal quality, and tend to be less concerned with timely performance. Noncompetitive contracting also provides opportunities for procurement corruption. Corrupt or lackluster contractors negatively impact government entities that condone noncompetitive contracting and the constituency that provides the agency's financial resources. The increased funding required due to corrupt or sole source contractors naturally results in decreased funding available to support the agency's mission. When the timeliness and quality of contracted commodities or services are compromised, the agency and its constituency both suffer the consequences of paying premium prices while receiving delayed delivery of poor-quality goods or services.

Competition contributes to discouraging corruption; however, competition does not eliminate the possibility of procurement corruption. Learned individuals argue that competition may be correlated with procurement corruption in certain markets.[4] The conclusions reached by Celentani and Ganuza regarding the growth of corruption and competition in certain markets are not challenged here. However, the multitude of procurement corruption cases associated with noncompetitive contracting verifies the fact that many instances of procurement corruption can be attributed to sole source contracting. Noncompetitive procurement establishes a business environment that includes the unwelcome specter of gratuities or other inducements to foster continued limitation or elimination of competition with the objective of corrupting the agency, its officials, and its employees. Most government contractors are represented by honest employees who do not seek to unjustly enrich their companies or themselves; however, a minority of contractor personnel is willing to engage in illegal activities for an opportunity to achieve inflated prices for inferior products or services that are delivered late. Such illegal activities usually necessitate locating a corrupt agency official or corrupting an otherwise honest agency representative. Contracts awarded in an environment of full and open competition significantly reduce opportunities for corruption in contracting. Sole source contracting, however, offers abundant opportunities for dishonest contractor and agency personnel to collaborate, thus causing the government to pay extravagant prices for inferior products or services that are not provided when needed. Therefore, in addition to receiving overpriced, inferior goods that are delivered late, sole source contracting increases opportunities for the scourge of public corruption.

The UN Convention against Corruption, conducted in Vienna, Austria, developed the "Compendium of International Legal Instrument on Corruption," which relies heavily on competition in procurement to prevent corruption. Paragraph 1 of Article 9, "Public Procurement and Management of Public Finances," appears below in its entirety:

> 1. Each State Party shall, in accordance with the fundamental principles of its legal system, take the necessary steps to establish appropriate systems of procurement, based on transparency, competition and objective criteria in decision making, that are effective, inter alia, in preventing corruption. Such systems, which may take into account appropriate threshold values in their application shall address, inter alia:
>
> The public distribution of information relating to procurement procedures and contracts, including information on invitations to tender and relevant or pertinent information on the award of contracts, allowing potential tenderers sufficient time to prepare and submit their tenders;
>
> The establishment, in advance, of conditions for participation, including selection and award criteria and tendering rules, and their publication;
>
> The use of objective and predetermined criteria for public procurement decisions, in order to facilitate the subsequent verification of the correct application of the rules and procedures;
>
> An effective system of domestic review, including an effective system of appeal, to ensure loyal recourse and remedies in the event that the rules or procedures established pursuant to this paragraph are not followed;
>
> Where appropriate, measures to regulate matters regarding personnel responsible for procurement, such as declaration of interest in particular public procurements, screening procedures and training requirements.

Contracting terminology in use by the UN and many countries varies from standard U.S. usage. Although the meaning of these contracting terms is likely familiar to public servants and government contractors globally, several contracting terms common to U.S. usage is compared, in Table 4.2, to contracting terminology in common usage in the UN and in other countries.

The above provisions of the "Compendium of International Legal Instrument on Corruption" are commendable and consistent with corruption prevention measures

Table 4.2 Comparison between Contracting Terms in the U.S. and Other Countries

U.S. Contracting Terminology	Terminology in Certain Other Countries
"Solicitation" or, specifically, "request for proposals"	Invitations to tender
Prospective contractor or offeror	Tenderer
Proposal preparation instructions	Tendering rules
"Proposal" as the response to an RFP (or responses such as "bid" to IFBs or "quotation" to RFQs)	Tender

professed by most organizations advocating against corruption in public procurement. The provisions of Article 9 of this compendium are quoted in subsequent chapters where they coincide with the recommendations in this book and with the best practices RFP contained on the CD that accompanies this book. Based on the continuing media accounts regarding procurement corruption by UN officials, however, it appears that the UN has not effectively implemented these commendable provisions in all UN procurement practices.

The results from maximizing competitive subcontracting, as opposed to minimal competitive subcontracting, are so favorable to government prime contractors that any tendency toward noncompetitive versus competitive subcontracting is an indicator of unethical or illegal practices. A higher than expected level of sole source subcontracting, though in the absence of unethical or illegal activity, strains the prime contractor's ability to perform well with respect to CPSR indicators regarding the level of competition achieved, price analyses, and source justifications. Poor performance during a CPSR can result in withholding approval of the contractor's previously approved purchasing system, leading to the necessity for obtaining advance government approval of high-value subcontracts and lower scores for contractor management criteria during competition for government prime contracts. Failure to maintain an approved purchasing system can also result in the negotiation of lower profits.

4.4 Multiple Benefits of Full and Open Competition

There are occasions when there is truly just one contractor that is qualified and willing to perform the required service or provide the needed products for the government. There are also occasions when one contractor's qualifications and skills are unique or far exceed any other competitor's qualifications, and a case can be made for contracting with that company on a sole source basis. However, specific recommendations cannot be made here regarding justification for every sole source decision, because such decisions are made on a case-by-case basis. As discussed in Chapter 3, department personnel oftentimes discover a favored contractor early in the contracting cycle. The skills and qualifications of many favored contractors are oftentimes not sufficiently unique to justify a sole source contract. Public servants throughout the world are faced with amiable yet aggressive contractor representatives who strive to become the preferred (or favored) contractor despite the existence of well-qualified competitors. One opportunity for contractors to achieve preferred customer status is when government personnel planning to contract for unfamiliar products or services seek advice from one known provider of those products or services. An aggressive contractor representative who is approached under these circumstances may offer to assist the agency personnel by providing a draft of the solicitation, specifications, contract, and even drafting the justification for a sole source contract in exchange for assurance that the contract is awarded to the helpful contractor on a noncompetitive basis. This pattern has been followed repeatedly on a worldwide basis and has, too frequently, proved successful. Agencies can address this problem by training personnel involved in the development of specifications and advance contract planning to obtain contracting advice solely from the agency's contracting staff. When it continues to be necessary to obtain input from the private sector, however, restrictions to competitive contracting can be avoided by advising the helpful contractor that the only possible consideration for their assistance is inclusion on the list of solicited firms. In this scenario it is essential that specifications prepared with contractor assistance do not exclude the helpful contractor's competitors. A preferred alternative under these circumstances is for the agency to develop a draft solicitation, specifications, and contract that are sent to all prospective contractors for comment in advance of the formal solicitation. The feedback from all prospective contractors can then be used to finalize the contracting documents.

Sole source contractors occasionally lobby elected and appointed officials to pressure contracting professionals to continue awarding, extending, or renewing the contract on a sole source basis. When these lobbying efforts are successful, the contracting professional feels considerable resistance to her or his efforts to solicit proposals through full and open competition.

The existence of a favored contractor creates a significant challenge to agency officials, employees, and contracting professionals who are committed to achieving the benefits available through full and open competition. Seeking competition is especially challenging when a favored contractor has traditionally been selected on a sole source basis. The contracting staff's insistence on awarding follow-on contracts on a competitive basis is often a source of great tension between the program staff and the contracting staff. This is understandable when the contracting staff is required to award contracts competitively whenever possible and the program staff has confidence in the present contractor. When competing contractors are available, the government's policy normally provides the contracting staff no option but to award the contract through the competitive process. The program staff's concern is often based on the belief that the contract will be placed with a marginally qualified company that offers the lowest pricing. Assurances by the contracting staff that the contractor will be selected on the basis of price and other factors, with program staff participating on the proposal evaluation team, is often sufficient to dislodge the program staff's objection to the competitive process. The contracting staff might also explain that introduction of competition in an environment that previously excluded competing contractors is expected to result in not only lower pricing, but improved quality and improved on-time delivery as well.

Government's reputation for concentrating on lowest pricing, above all other considerations, leads instinctively to the correlation between competition and low pricing. Not so intuitive, however, is the correlation between competition and improved quality as well as between competition and timely delivery. Three attributes for measuring the success of contractors and programs are price, quality, and schedule compliance. Certain contractor personnel that are comfortable with the assurance that they will obtain a contract or contracts on a sole source basis have not only less motivation to provide competitive pricing, but may feel less committed to providing excellent quality and timely contract completion. The program staff, therefore, is likely to benefit from competitive procurements when competition is introduced into a previously sole source environment, thereby resulting in improvements in the key performance parameters of price, quality, and schedule.

Enactment of legislation and adoption of a contracting policy and procedure requiring competition over a specified value threshold are highly recommended. The existence of such legislation as well as a policy and procedure requiring competitive procurements are essential to ensure that the contracting professional has support for her or his decision to proceed on a competitive basis. This support is essential when there is pressure to proceed on a noncompetitive basis. Competition provides a significant incentive for contractors to deliver their services or products for economical pricing, to produce high-quality products or services, and to adhere to their schedule commitments. It is conceivable to routinely award service contracts employing competitive proposals just as commodity or traditional construction contracts are routinely placed on the basis of competitive bids.

Approval of a justification for a sole source contract based on the assertion that the presumptive contractor offers the lowest pricing is based on fallacious reasoning because the lowest pricing can accurately be determined only in a competitive procurement. Although the present contractor may have proposed or bid the lowest pricing when the present contract was awarded, that present contractor is likely to seek a price increase for a follow-on contract. A contractor that competed for the present contract but was unsuccessful because their pricing was not competitive is likely to propose more competitive pricing for the follow-on contract. Therefore, it is not possible to justify sole source to the existing contractor based on low pricing.

In addition to the benefits of full and open competition discussed above, agencies also reduce opportunities for corruption during the contracting process, earn respect from the constituency for compliance with their expectations, and avoid the tragedies associated with public servants who get entangled in corruption scandals. Objections of departmental personnel who argue against contracting on a competitive basis are normally feeble in comparison with the advantages of competitive contracting.

Just as with government contracting, subcontracting by prime contractors allows government contractors to obtain the optimal combination of price, performance, and timeliness for subcontracted products and services. Achievement of attractive pricing, performance, and timeliness makes the proposals or bids that include subcontracted products or services more attractive to the prime contractors' government customers. In addition to providing more competitive bids and proposals, maximizing subcontracting competition assists federal prime contractors when they are subjected to CPSRs conducted by the federal government. Achieving a high level of competitive contracting is looked upon favorably by government personnel conducting the CPSR. Because competitive subcontracting also simplifies price analysis and source justification, the prime contractors maximizing competitive subcontracting are likely to perform well in the price analyses and source selection justification area of the CPSR. As discussed in more detail in Chapter 10, favorable CPSR results lead to an approved purchasing system for prime contractors. The maintenance of an approved purchasing system simplifies the prime contractor's approval of high-value subcontracts, favors prime contractors in price negotiations with government representatives, and can result in an improved competitive posture when prime contractor management is a criterion in the government's source selection.

4.5 Conclusion

Competition is recognized globally as an approach to government procurement that guards against collusion and incorporates fairness in government's processes for acquiring products, services, and capital projects from the private sector. The quote below, from *A Handbook on Fighting Corruption*,[5] published by the U.S. Agency for International Development, is representative of the recognition globally of the effectiveness of competition in combating procurement collusion:

> Competitive procurement limits the authority of government officials thereby guarding against corruption. Competitive procurement removes personal discretion from the selection of government suppliers

and contractors by prescribing an open bidding process and laying out clear procedures and criteria for selection. Because a corrupt procurement process can derail their development efforts, donors are making procurement reform a priority. For example, as an outcome of the 1997 Global Coalition for Africa's Policy Forum on Corruption, the World Bank is assisting the governments of Benin, Ethiopia, Malawi, Mali, Tanzania, and Uganda reform their procurement procedures. Yet, absent such government leadership, private firms may foster a competitive process. Through anti-bribery pacts such as Transparency International's "islands of integrity" approach, bidders agree not to pay bribes for a government contract and post sizable bonds that are subject to forfeiture in the event of non-compliance.

Full and open competition is considered one of the most, if not the most, significant mechanisms for fighting procurement corruption. Other recommended actions, such as "laying out clear procedures and criteria for selection," included in the above quote, strengthen the effectiveness of competition in curbing procurement corruption.

Notes

1. Information on the Dallas Independent School District (DISD) case was obtained from a U.S. Department of Justice media release, "Former Dallas Independent School District (DISD) Executive and Houston Businessman Convicted in Federal Corruption Trial," July 10, 2008.
2. The specific clauses in the U.S. Constitution that provide equal opportunities for all parties to compete for government contracts are the privileges and immunities clause, the commerce clause, and the equal protection clause.
3. eWeekEurope, "Red Hat Sues Switzerland Over Microsoft Monopoly," Peter Judge, May 22, 2009.
4. Marco Celentani, Universidad Carlos III de Madrid, and Juan-José Ganuza, Universitat Pompeu Fabra, present a case for the possibility of increased corruption in a competitive procurement environment in their paper, "Corruption and Competition in Procurement," January 2001.
5. *A Handbook on Fighting Corruption*, Center for Democracy and Governance, Bureau for Global Programs, Field Support, and Research, U.S. Agency for International Development, Washington, DC, February 1999.

Chapter 5

Social Objectives through Government Contracting

I have a dream that my four little children will one day live in a nation where they will not be judged by the color of their skin, but by the content of their character. I have a dream today!

Martin Luther King, Jr.

5.1 Social Contracting Fundamentals

This chapter introduces readers to social contracting programs including affirmative action, equal opportunity, and green contracting. Equal opportunity and green contracting techniques for developing a successful social contracting program are explored. The equal opportunity techniques discussed include establishment of an incentive awards program, training for contracting professionals, encouragement by managers to use targeted companies, agency participation in a supportive organization, establishment of rapport with targeted companies, provision of direct assistance to targeted companies, promotion of internal networking, and incorporation of program support as a part of employee job responsibility.

Social contracting includes both socioeconomic programs, wherein equal opportunity or affirmative action programs are employed to expand contracting opportunities with targeted companies, and green contracting to avoid an adverse impact on the environment. In both cases governments pursue social or economic goals through the award of contracts that support achievement of these objectives. *Targeted company* is the generic term used for companies that are agency targets for increased contracting opportunities through the agency's socioeconomic contracting program. Examples of targeted companies include small business, minority-owned small business, woman-owned business, veteran-owned business, and disabled veteran-owned business.

Socioeconomic contracting programs encourage the award of contracts to contractors that fit certain criteria, such as a maximum number of employees or ownership of and management by a person or persons fitting one of the classifications mentioned in the preceding paragraph. Equal opportunity programs involve outreach efforts to discover prospective contractors in targeted groups that historically have had less than full access to government contracts. The outreach programs involve efforts to identify such companies and offer them the chance to compete with traditional contractors, but do not afford any competitive advantage with respect to price, quality, or schedule adherence. Equal opportunity programs are normally established on the assumption that the management of small, minority-owned, woman-owned, or other targeted contractors is not inherently less qualified to compete with more traditional contractors in a capitalistic environment. Therefore, to succeed as government contractors they need only be given the opportunity to compete. They do not require a competitive advantage, which is considered unfair by traditional contractors and the constituency. Providing a competitive advantage to a class of contractors provides opportunities for unethical contracting practices by firms that incorrectly affirm that their company is a targeted company or the establishment of a targeted firm as a front for a large business to obtain government contracts with limited or no competition. Affirmative action programs, like equal opportunity programs, involve outreach. Affirmative action programs are differentiated from equal opportunity programs in that contractors targeted for affirmative action may be awarded a contract despite the fact that competing non-targeted companies have proposed lower pricing, higher quality services or products, or earlier project completion or delivery. Constituents, as well as government representatives, may object to the prospect of expending more government funds for products or services that may be inferior and not made available in a timely manner.

Contracting to promote less adverse impacts on the environment is often referred to as green contracting, green procurement, or green purchasing. Criteria considered in green contracting include higher proposal evaluation scores for contractors that provide commodities or construction projects that minimize harmful or non-recyclable products or materials; minimize environmental impacts through their internal operations; maximize recycling of waste material such as rubbish collection or in building demolition projects; minimize environmental impacts from transportation operations; practice energy conservation; use alternative energy production; or provide janitorial, pest control, or landscaping services that minimize the use of hazardous chemical products. Establishing environmentally friendly practices as one of the proposal evaluation criteria is effective in meeting green contracting goals for contracting agencies that foster business operations designed to avoid harming the environment.

A company that embodies environmentally friendly practices and would rank highly with respect to environmentally friendly proposal evaluation criteria is

Sierra Nevada Brewing Co. in Chico, California. This company brews premium beer, operates a restaurant and gift shop, and provides an acoustically optimized music room. Phase one of their solar energy installation consists of photovoltaic cells, which are installed over a large parking lot. The photovoltaic cells track the path of the sun and provide 503 kW of power to the plant. Phase two of their solar installation is a rooftop photovoltaic project that provides an additional 1.42 MW of power to the plant. Combining this power with the on-site fuel cells, Sierra Nevada is able to produce roughly 90% of their power needs on-site. Other environmentally friendly practices include heat and carbon dioxide recovery, energy efficiency, water conservation, emissions reporting, and an environmentally friendly transportation system. Additionally, mash created from the brewing process is fed to farm animals at the local university to produce meat products served in the restaurant and natural fertilizer used to feed the hops that are grown on their premises.

Social contracting programs are normally enacted by law or administrative procedures to institute the furtherance of goals for expanding contracting opportunities to targeted companies or to meet other social objectives. In addition to the targeted companies and green contracting practices discussed above, government entities occasionally provide similar advantages to companies based within their jurisdiction. States and local government agencies, however, might consider suspending such local preference programs for contracts that are funded either fully or partially through the federal government because local preference programs are prohibited when federal funding is used.[1]

The research project discussed in Chapter 1 included a document review on twenty-two RFPs submitted by states and local government agencies. Four of those twenty-two RFPs (18%) included a preference for local contractors in the proposal evaluation process. The previous paragraph discussed the prohibition against providing local preferences when federal funding is included in the project budget. Although it may be permissible to provide local preferences when federal funding is not involved, states and local government agencies may wish to reconsider the inclusion of local preferences in their standard solicitation templates because they are not acceptable for projects that are partially or fully funded by the federal government.

The research project also revealed that eight of the RFPs (36%) submitted by participating agencies included social preferences for targeted companies other than local contractors. The best practices RFP does not include any socioeconomic preferences employed in the selection process. However, it does include a preference for companies that promote environmentally friendly practices. This chapter describes a proven methodology for establishing outreach programs, based on one that was employed for nine years by a government prime contractor. During that nine-year period, contracting participation from targeted contractors increased significantly while the cost of materials declined, purchased product quality improved, and late deliveries were reduced. Although that program was used primarily for outreach to minority-owned and woman-owned companies, the techniques employed are equally applicable for contractors that target other historically underrepresented companies or companies that implement environmentally friendly practices.

Socioeconomic contracting programs that employ solely equal opportunity measures and do not include affirmative action techniques have met and surpassed their socioeconomic contracting goals. Affirmative action-based socioeconomic contracting programs may experience higher goal achievement; however, reliance on affirmative action measures is likely to result in higher pricing, lesser quality, and delinquent deliveries, and provide more opportunities for unethical contracting practices. Equal opportunity socioeconomic contracting programs may establish outreach programs to targeted companies and may offer assistance to targeted companies if such assistance does not provide the targeted companies with a competitive advantage over the companies that are not targeted. This limited assistance may be considered by some targeted company advocates as a minimal effort; however, this chapter outlines a program that relied solely on equal opportunity measures and proved to be highly successful in significantly increasing the participation of targeted companies. Table 5.1 provides a summary of the differences between equal opportunity and affirmative action approaches to meeting diversity goals. The differences are discussed briefly above and more thoroughly near the end of this chapter.

Research suggests that minority set-aside programs, an affirmative action tool that prohibits non-targeted companies from competing for procurements that have been set aside, may not be as effective as expected in increasing the success rate of minority-owned companies. One would assume intuitively that when certain procurements are limited to minority-owned companies, their success rate would improve. However, a statistical analysis of racial discrimination in the State of New Jersey[2] indicated that not only did the success rate of minority-owned companies fail to increase following the reinstitution of a minority set-aside program, there was actually a decline in the success rate of minority-owned companies after the set-aside program was reinstituted.

Another affirmative action tool is to provide targeted companies with a 5–10% monetary advantage over non-targeted companies. Intuitively, this would increase the cost of government programs in pursuit of the objective to increase the probability of awarding government contracts to targeted companies. Justin Marion, in his study including 4,136 highway construction contracts awarded in California,[3] found that a 5% monetary preference for small businesses resulted in a 3.8% increase in procurement costs. In addition to the disadvantage of the government paying a premium for government programs, the monetary advantage also provides an opportunity for procurement fraud. One opportunity for fraud is for a non-targeted company to use a targeted company as a front. One example of just such a front company is described in a U.S. Department of Defense, Office of the Inspector General, report,[4] revealing that a front company earned $135,000 while providing no added value. An additional opportunity for fraudulently taking advantage of preference programs, that has since been restricted, is to falsely represent a non-targeted company as a targeted company. The U.S. government's small disadvantaged business (SDB) program formerly

Table 5.1   Contrasts between Equal Opportunity and Affirmativ Programs

Program Characteristics	Equal Opportunity	Affirmative Acti.
Ease of meeting goals	Meeting goals is challenging but achievable	Meeting goals is greatly simplified
Pricing	Increased competition is likely to result in favorable pricing variances	Reduced competition is likely to result in higher pricing
Quality	Increased competition tends to improve quality of materials and services	Reduced competition is likely to adversely impact quality of materials and services
Timeliness	Improved on-time deliveries are likely to result from increased competition	Reduced on-time deliveries are likely to result from lesser dependence on competition
Exposure to corruption	Exposure to corruption is unlikely to change because of continued reliance on full and open competition	Exclusion of entire categories of companies from competitive base results in more corruption due to excluded companies misrepresenting their classification and the use of contractors meeting category definition as front companies

permitted companies to self-certify their SDB status. Beginning on October 1, 1998, companies claiming SDB status were required to be certified by the Small Business Administration (SBA). Based on the number of SDB companies that had previously been self-certified, the SBA expected 30,000 firms to be SDB certified by the SBA.[5] As of August 24, 2000, however, just 9,034 were certified by the SBA as SDBs. SBA officials provided numerous reasons why the numbers dropped so significantly. The last reason, in the bulleted list below, for companies failing to request SDB certification by the SBA, implies that a number of firms had previously been self-certified even though they did not meet the SDB criteria:

- Unlikely to obtain a government contract
- Expected to receive government contracts regardless of SDB certification
- Certification process is an administrative and financial burden
- Previously SDB self-certified companies not SDB qualified or no longer SDB qualified

Arguing in favor of affirmative action programs that provide for award of government contracts to companies owned and managed by disabled persons, women, veterans, or members of minority groups despite the fact that they might have proposed higher pricing, have a poor history of product or service quality, and cannot complete the project within the requested schedule is difficult unless one suggests that their owners and managers are less capable than their competitors. However, companies cannot be judged as having lesser qualifications based on ownership and management by disabled persons, women, veterans, or members of minority groups. Certainly, government entities do not consider their own employees to be less capable because they may belong to one of these groups. Therefore, there is a strong argument to design socioeconomic contracting programs around equal opportunity measures rather than affirmative action.

5.2 Failed Social Contracting Creates Exposure to Corruption

Existing legislation permits the noncompetitive award of contracts to companies owned and operated by members of historically underrepresented groups and to companies that design and install alternative energy and energy efficiency systems. Social contracting programs that waive competitive contracting rules create numerous risks for government. Noncompetitive contracting introduces unwelcomed opportunities for corruption in contracting that contribute to the corruption of public officials and private-sector company representatives.

The Sphinx case, discussed in Chapter 3, described a major corruption incident that was facilitated by waiving the requirement for competitive contracting, regardless of the contract value, with a Native American tribally owned business. In this case, a public official directed contracts to the tribally owned business. The tribally owned company kept a portion of the proceeds, but sent the majority of the funds to Sphinx. Millions of dollars in government contracts were directed to Sphinx after a public servant and two of his accomplices were given a 75% interest in that company. The penalties assessed against the seven individuals found guilty or pleading guilty in the Sphinx case, including one perpetrator's son who accepted a payment from a contractor on behalf of his father, included imprisonment, supervised release, community service, restitution, and forfeiture of assets.

Although the Sphinx case was presented in the chapter on contracting ethics, it is reintroduced here for a different reason. Socioeconomic contracting programs that provide equal contracting opportunities to historically underrepresented groups help correct an injustice that existed over an extensive period of time. Correcting such injustices, however, by providing for the award of contracts to targeted groups without competition creates unnecessary opportunities for corruption in contracting. The Sphinx case is representative of the approach wherein the targeted company is used as a front to obtain the noncompetitive contract and the primary beneficiary is a company that is not targeted and is normally required to compete for contracts. Another reprehensible approach to the illegitimate receipt of non-competitive contracts intended for targeted companies is for a company owner who is not a member of a targeted group to misrepresent her or his ethnicity, gender, geographic location, disability, veteran or economic status, or other attribute, thus characterizing her or his company as a member of a targeted group.

A report prepared by the Office of the Inspector General of the U.S. Small Business Administration[6] stated that a large business "or an affiliated company obtained a total of 39 contracts that were set aside for small businesses even though the bidder may not have met SBA's criteria to be considered a small business." The allegation was that personnel hired by the large business were employees of the large business and not independent contractors, as represented. Although there was no determination, in this case, that the large business misrepresented its size, the report illustrates the possibility that a large business could represent its employees as independent contractors as yet another possible approach to garner the benefits intended for targeted companies.

The City of Chicago was plagued by contractors that fraudulently claimed to be minority business enterprises (MBEs) to such an extent that this problem contributed to the resignation of two chiefs of procurement in about a one-year period.[7] To combat this problem, the City of Chicago found it necessary to add staff charged with monitoring the MBE purchasing program and to require the disclosure of tax returns, lease agreements, and distributor agreements prior to permitting MBEs to submit bids or proposals for city contracts. In an unrelated California case, the competitor of a company that self-certified its business as a woman-owned MBE advised the purchasing office that the self-certification was fraudulent. The purchasing office asked the alleged woman-owned MBE for a copy of its business license and for a meeting with the majority owner of the company, who was supposedly a Native American woman. When the majority owner failed to appear for two meetings and the business license reflected a company name that did not match the name used by the company, the matter was turned over to a government investigative agency. The investigation verified the fraudulent self-certification and resulted in termination of the government subcontracts and prosecution of the company's owner.

All the approaches discussed here regarding contractors that misrepresented their status as a targeted company also involved an absence of competition or limited competition. In all such cases the government not only is faced with a procurement corruption case but also is burdened with higher prices, lower quality, and untimely performance characteristic of sole source contracts. When contract awards to legitimately targeted companies are made in the absence of full and open competition, there is a great likelihood of price, quality, and delivery problems.

Risks associated with the failure to establish an effective green contracting program include noncompliance penalties imposed on government entities by higher levels of government, increased costs associated with hazardous waste disposal, lack of protection from increasing costs associated with petro-fueled energy generation,

ie ecology, and associated health problems as well as increased costs for
e and legal actions.

.l and income taxes paid to federal governments by residents in states,
counties, cities, or other regional or local government entities are often partially
allocated to states and local government agencies for specific projects. The federal
government is able to impose strict rules for the expenditure of such funds. States
and local government agencies that fail to comply with environmental laws may find
that federal funds for certain classes of projects, such as highway construction funds,
are withheld. States may also withhold funding from counties, cities, and other local
government entities that fail to conform to state environmental regulations.

Protection of the environment is a global concern. Despite its laissez-faire reputation for environmental concerns, the People's Republic of China (PRC) is moving forward in efforts to protect the environment. A media release on February 25,
2008, from the Ministry of Environmental Protection (formerly known as the State
Environmental Protection Administration), entitled "The Third Environmental
Economic Policy — Guide to Green Securities — Unveiled," outlined environmental administrative penalties for companies that significantly exceeded dis-
charge standards or pollutant caps leading to major pollution accidents and severe
violation of environmental regulations. This action by the PRC to protect their
environment was apparently taken when the government realized the full extent
of environmental damage experienced during the accelerated growth of industrial
activity within the PRC. Although not all the environmental damage within the
PRC resulted from contracting activities, the extensive damage to the country's
atmosphere, waters, and soil demonstrates how failure to protect the environment
leads to disastrous health implications for the citizenry and threatens the capability to provide nutritious food, potable water, and continued industrial production.
Media reports of the environmental damage within the PRC provide a lesson to
all other countries regarding this most significant of all perils resulting from the
failure to protect the environment.

Government contractors that fail to comply with contract provisions requiring
implementation of a socioeconomic contracting program, risk the consequences of
defaulting on or breaching their contract. Limiting competition for certain subcontracts to targeted firms also introduces the risk of awarding a subcontract to a firm
that misrepresented its ownership status and, in fact, did not meet the criteria for a
targeted company. Misrepresentation of companies as belonging to a targeted class
is not uncommon. A firm known as Windy City Maintenance in Chicago, Illinois,
was misrepresented as a minority-owned and woman-owned company.[8] Windy City
Maintenance's misrepresentation earned it more than $100 million in city contracts.
After this scheme was discovered, a member of a mob-connected (organized crime)
family received a sentence of nearly ten years in federal prison. Two co-defendants
received sentences of nearly six years and slightly less than two years.

The personal and corporate consequences stemming from the Siemens Medical
Systems and Faustech Industries case, discussed in Chapter 2, impacted both

companies as well as personnel from both companies. Two officials from Siemens Medical Systems were sentenced to a year of home confinement and four years of probation. Siemens Medical Systems was ordered to pay more than $2.5 million. Faust Villazan, owner of now-defunct Faustech Industries, suffered more significant consequences. In pleading for sentencing leniency, Mr. Villazan said that he had lost his company and personal investments. He also said that he feared losing his residence and custody of his son if sentenced to prison. The judge sentenced Villazan to thirty-three months in prison.

Prime government contractors that are noncompliant or in minimal compliance with socioeconomic subcontracting requirements are at a disadvantage when competing for government contracts with fully compliant competitors. Additionally, an ineffective socioeconomic subcontracting program may lead to negotiation of lower than standard pricing[9] on their federal prime contracts.

5.3 Establishing an Effective Social Contracting Program

Reference was made in Section 5.1 to a social contracting program that significantly increased the participation of targeted companies solely through equal opportunity measures. The balance of this section, with the exception of the material on green contracting, is dedicated to the discussion of recommended methods for facilitating success in the implementation of social contracting programs by government while relying solely on equal opportunity measures.

There are eight equal opportunity measures that, when applied simultaneously, have proven to significantly increase the number of contracts and value of contracts awarded to targeted companies. Certain individuals argue that social contracting programs are inconsistent with traditional procurement goals involving low pricing, high quality, and on-time delivery. However, the program to be described here was implemented in a company that achieved significantly greater contracting participation from targeted companies while also achieving cost savings, improved quality, and a higher percentage of on-time deliveries. Implementation of six or seven of these measures may prove successful. However, when all eight of the measures presented in this chapter were employed by a government contractor to increase awards to minority-owned businesses and woman-owned businesses, significant and continuous improvement was measured over the program's nine-year duration. The measures are all categorized as equal opportunity tools because they do not provide price, quality, or schedule advantages to targeted companies. The company[10] where this socioeconomic contracting program was implemented had historically awarded 2% of contracted dollars to minority-owned companies and 1% of contracted dollars to woman-owned companies. The value of awards to minority-owned companies increased from 2% to greater than 15%. This represents an increase of more than 600% in the value of contracts awarded to minority-owned contractors. The value of awards to woman-owned businesses increased from 1% to greater than 6%. This represents an increase of more than 500% in the value of contracts awarded to woman-owned companies.

Not all government agencies have social contracting programs that specifically target, as in this example, woman-owned and minority-owned companies. However, all eight of these measures are applicable to any category of targeted companies as well as to green contracting programs. Although this example is from a government contractor, it is applicable to all government entities because the government contractor is a prime contractor of the federal government and, as such, operates its subcontracting and purchasing function essentially as a government contracting and purchasing office. An additional significant difference between the government contractor used for this example and government entities is that the contracts in the example were primarily for the procurement of parts and assemblies used in a manufacturing process with a significantly lesser percentage for service contracts. However, despite these differences, the measures described in this section are readily transferable to government entities that contract for services or commodities.

The company that developed the program described here had the option of using both affirmative action and equal opportunity tools. However, they elected to use only the available tools that fit in the definition of equal opportunity measures. Despite the fact that the affirmative action measures, including price advantages for targeted companies and set-asides, were not employed, impressive results were achieved. Set-asides is the term used to describe procurements for which solicitations are sent only to a targeted class of contractors (such as small businesses or disabled veteran-owned businesses) and responses to the solicitation are not considered unless the responding companies are members of the targeted class of contractors. The targeted companies in this example, in fact, were required to compete with traditional contractors on an equal basis without set-asides or other advantages. In addition to competing equally with respect to competitive pricing, the targeted companies were also required to meet the same high-quality and on-time delivery standards required of traditional contractors.

Certain government entities may be required to rely on self-certification by contractors that their company qualifies as a targeted company. However, nontargeted companies may inappropriately self-certify as targeted companies. When government is not prevented by law from requesting documentation to establish a company's status as a targeted company, it is recommended that such documentation be requested. The City of Chicago requires the submittal of tax returns, lease agreements, and distributorship agreements before permitting targeted companies to bid or propose on city contracts as a targeted company.[11]

At the onset of the socioeconomic contracting program used as this example, there was considerable concern that higher prices would be paid for inferior products that might also be delivered late. To guard against the possibility of such abhorrent results accompanying increased procurement from targeted companies, all of the contractors that were historically solicited remained on the solicitation lists, but at least one targeted company was added to each list of contractors solicited. This practice ensured that the targeted company would not be selected unless their pricing was lower than the traditional contractors, the number of traditional companies competing for contracts would not be reduced, and other selection factors for the targeted companies were required to be equal or better than the selection factors for traditional contractors. Pricing, schedule performance, and quality had been measured for numerous years prior to implementing this socioeconomic contracting program. The historical price, schedule, and quality measuring process remained in place for the entire nine years that the equal opportunity socioeconomic subcontracting program was in place. The continued reporting indicated not only that the worst fears did not occur, but also that there was actually a slow but continuous improvement in pricing, on-time project completion, and product quality throughout the duration of the program. Such outstanding results are not surprising, because minorities and women who are employed by government require no special compensation to compete in the workplace with non-minority males. The results of this program demonstrate that minority-owned and woman-owned companies, when provided an equal opportunity, are capable of successfully competing with non-minority male-owned companies.

Affirmative action programs, such as providing a price advantage to targeted companies or establishing set-asides wherein only targeted companies may compete for contracts, increase the cost of materials and possibly result in lesser quality products and late deliveries, all of which have an adverse impact on profit for the federal contractor. The increases in price occur as the result of lessened reliance on full and open competition. The increased chance of receiving lesser quality and slower deliveries is based on the tendency for companies operating in less than a fully competitive environment to take their future market share for granted and relax their efforts to meet or exceed quality and delivery standards.

Although government entities need not be concerned with profit, the same disadvantages to private-sector companies that employ affirmative action measures are likely to also affect government contracting agencies. Constituents who contribute the revenue for government operations expect that such tax revenues are expended in a fair and rational manner without providing unnecessary opportunities for unethical contracting practices. It is difficult to justify higher expenditures to the public for purchase of inferior products or services that are not provided on time. This is especially true when most targeted companies, such as those in this example, can compete with historical contractors on an equal basis.

5.3.1 Sample Affirmative Action Measures

The eight measures employed to obtain the results in the above example are described below.

5.3.1.1 Incentive Awards

Rewarding employees who excel in their work performance is recognized as a successful method for motivating certain employees. Meeting goals for discovering targeted companies and developing them to the point where they can compete with historical contractors is readily measurable. An incentive awards program for government representatives who excel in their efforts to discover and develop targeted companies is recommended for contracting agencies that wish to have a successful social contracting program.

Measurable activities that lead to a successful social contracting program include attendance at trade shows where targeted companies demonstrate their capabilities, providing targeted companies with opportunities to compete for agency contracts, first-time contract awards to targeted companies, the number of or percentage of contracts awarded to targeted companies, and the value or percentage of dollars awarded to targeted companies. Certain agency employees may specialize in contracting for products or services for which there are fewer opportunities to develop targeted companies; therefore, adjustments may be made to the recognition criteria to ensure fairness to employees competing for incentive awards. Another measure for ensuring that more agency employees have an opportunity to be recognized for their social contracting support is to limit the frequency with which employees may be recognized. In the example from the private sector, the award was presented twice each year and employees were not eligible to receive the award more than once in any two-year period. This prevented multiple awards to the same individual and provided an opportunity for more agency employees to compete for the incentive awards.

The types of recognition provided to agency employees for outstanding support of the social contracting program might include one, or any combination, of cash, government bonds, a plaque, favorable mention in the employee's performance evaluation, a letter or certificate placed in the personnel files, an article in the agency's newsletter, lunch or dinner in a local restaurant, or any other recognition deemed appropriate by the contracting agency.

5.3.1.2 Training

Whereas certain employees are predisposed to wholeheartedly embracing the implementation of a social contracting program, other employees are inclined to remain neutral or even hostile to supporting such programs. Agency employees who first excel in discovering and developing new targeted companies are generally those who embraced the program from the beginning. Appropriate recognition of those early achievers is an excellent tool that can be combined with training to encourage their continued success as well as success by other motivated employees. Combining the reward program with training may encourage program support by those employees who are more neutral or even hostile toward the social contracting program.

Combining the recognition program with training in a forum that permits the contracting professional who received the most recent award an opportunity to describe how the targeted contractor or contractors were discovered and developed is an effective method for reaching more employees. Public recognition of employees who excel in meeting social subcontracting goals and the positive impact on their careers helps motivate the more neutral and hostile employees to more actively participate in the social contracting program. Employees who had exceeded their social contracting objectives should be given the opportunity to share their successful techniques with their colleagues. This sharing approach encourages the adoption of successful employee-developed techniques by the previously less successful agency representatives and thus improves their social contracting performance.

5.3.1.3 Encourage Use of Targeted Companies

Agency representatives in leadership roles control the assignment of projects to their direct reports. When the assignments include contracting opportunities, the leader might suggest names of targeted contractors that could be included in the list of firms to be solicited for bids or proposals. When assigning projects or contracting efforts to subordinates, the manager has an excellent opportunity to identify targeted firms that appear qualified to perform the contracted services or deliver the needed products. This identification of targeted companies to contracting professionals at the time of project assignment is highly recommended.

Agency leaders who elect to follow this recommendation obviously need to be familiar with targeted companies and their capabilities. One advantage leaders have in this respect is that, by reviewing the work of all their direct reports, they become aware of targeted companies that have been awarded contracts by other agency employees. More importantly, agency representatives in leadership positions become aware of targeted companies that have performed well on contracts awarded by other agency employees. Agency representatives who give contracting assignments to their direct reports can also become familiar with the capabilities of targeted companies through trade show attendance. Particularly valuable trade shows for familiarizing leaders with target company capabilities are those trade shows provided by the supportive organizations described below.

5.3.1.4 Supportive Organizations

Social contracting program development can be an overwhelming task for one government organization, which may be using virtually all of its resources just to perform its primary public service mission. However, if such an agency joins with similar organizations to develop an entity that facilitates development of a social contracting program, all member agencies benefit from the combined effort to develop a program that requires less labor yet is superior to the program they might develop on their own. An excellent organization[12] of this type was formed in the San Francisco Bay Area and could be used as a model for government entities striving to develop a world-class social contracting program without overextending their resources.

The original founders of this model organization are all private-sector companies with federal government contracts requiring the establishment of socioeconomic subcontracting programs. Targeted companies and government entities were permitted to join as nonvoting associate members. The membership of the entity established for this purpose has since grown to include private-sector companies that are not required to develop socioeconomic subcontracting programs as a condition of federal contracts, but wish to provide the same historically underrepresented companies with improved opportunities to compete for contracts. The model organization holds monthly luncheons that afford a venue for the large corporations, targeted businesses, and government entities to network. The model organization also holds periodic procurement fairs where organization members and government entities proclaim the products and services they acquire from private-sector companies and where targeted companies exhibit their capabilities.

Regardless of whether the government's participation in a social contracting program is mandatory or voluntary, a cooperative arrangement such as the model organization discussed above is worthy of consideration. It is likely that following the initial, extensive efforts to form such a cooperative organization, the participating contracting agencies achieve a superior social contracting program while expending fewer resources than required for a less successful individual program.

5.3.1.5 Rapport with Targeted Companies

The initial meeting between an agency official or employee with a management or sales representative from a targeted company may be the only opportunity the agency has to establish a business relationship with that targeted company. Whereas agency personnel who deal with sales representatives may feel that the sales representatives persistently pursue them, the pursuit by targeted company sales representatives may be less persistent. Targeted companies are often smaller than the average small business and may be classified as microbusinesses. As microbusinesses, they likely have limited sales representation. Companies with limited sales representation, yet are in demand by government, may be relatively inaccessible. Therefore, failure to establish rapport at the initial meeting may result in a lost opportunity for any future business relationship. The other extreme, involving eagerness of the targeted company to establish a business relationship with the government, when combined with the possibility that the sales representative is not yet familiar with ethical contracting restrictions, may lead to an inappropriate gratuity offer. Just as when dealing with any contractor management or sales representative, public servants need be alert to inappropriate business practices on the part of targeted companies and the need to explain their agency's policies with respect to ethical procurement practices, and to caution management or sales representatives from targeted companies to refrain from improper offers of gratuities to government representatives.

Government representatives are accustomed to dealing with sales representatives who are aggressive and persistent. Although there is no shortage of aggressive, persistent sales representatives from targeted companies, those sales representatives may blame an unproductive sales contact on their perceived impression that the government representative is prejudiced, chauvinistic, or even dedicated solely to the existing contractor base. The targeted company representatives may suspect that the business relationship between the government and their traditional contractors is unscrupulous. One reason for placing blame for a failed meeting on unethical government representatives is that the minority of government personnel who are dishonest are the ones who are more likely to have their exploits broadcast by the media. It is not considered newsworthy to report on the immense majority of government contracting professionals who perform their day-to-day work in conformance with the law and their organizations' policies and procedures. When a government contracting professional is convicted or found guilty of procurement fraud, however, the story is normally carried nationally or globally. The miniscule percentage of dishonest government contracting representatives, therefore, gives the more typical honest government representatives an undeserved reputation for corrupt contracting practices.

Suggestions for establishing rapport with targeted company representatives are provided here for government employees and officials who wish to consider alternative approaches for establishing a meaningful business relationship with targeted companies. First, a friendly, personal relationship is not required. Professional sales representatives, just as with professional government representatives, are normally interested in developing a business relationship rather than a personal relationship. The preferred approach to establishing meaningful rapport is demonstrating a genuine interest in the targeted company's resources and capabilities. If this is not successful and the sales representative is inexperienced, leading questions will help reveal a possible match between the targeted company's capabilities and the needs of the government. Asking the sales representative to explain the targeted company's capabilities, disclose projects performed for other government organizations, or describe what the contractor can do to support the government helps establish whether there is a basis for an ongoing business relationship. Additional questions along these lines expressing an interest in the company and the government representative's willingness to learn about the company's strengths and how they can contribute to the contracting agency's objectives may reveal a match between the targeted company and the government.

Targeted companies are often in great demand by other contracting agencies. Missing an opportunity to discover a match between the needs of the public agency and the capabilities of a targeted company during the initial contact could result in missing the agency's only opportunity to develop that targeted company as a commodity supplier, service provider, or construction contractor. This is especially true if another contracting agency makes a connection, recognizes the ability of that particular targeted company to contribute to its agency's success, and provides a sufficient quantity of work to cause the targeted company to scale back its sales and marketing efforts.

5.3.1.6 Direct Assistance

As discussed earlier, providing a price advantage, forgiving poor quality, or tolerating late performance is not advocated. Likewise, set-asides for targeted companies are not advocated. Assistance, short of such affirmative action measures, may prove to be acceptable for targeted companies. Examples of direct assistance that can be provided include critically reviewing the targeted company's sales or marketing literature, suggesting venues (such as trade shows) where targeted companies can contact government representatives from other government organizations, and referring the targeted company representative to a government entity thought to have requirements for the services or products provided by the targeted company.

5.3.1.7 Internal Networking

Sharing information on challenges and successes in social contracting between government representatives within a particular government organization is the nature of networking advocated in this book. Internal networking provides an opportunity for government employees who have succeeded in meeting social contracting goals to share their methodology with others. Successful employees are also able to describe the capabilities of the firms they developed, thus permitting other agency personnel to determine whether the targeted companies may be qualified to compete for upcoming contracts. Government employees who find it challenging to meet their social contracting goals have an opportunity to learn of successful techniques for developing targeted companies, and to learn about the capabilities of targeted companies that have been developed by other government representatives.

Internal networking is introduced by government department heads and other government representatives in leadership positions during periodic interdepartmental meetings or other venues. One opportune venue for promoting such networking is during the announcement of the award of a significant contract to a targeted company or completion of a successful project by a targeted company. In addition to recognizing the targeted company, this venue presents an occasion for recognizing government representatives who participated in the successful project.

5.3.1.8 Support for Program as Part of Job Responsibility

Contracting professionals as well as project managers and project specialists are typically evaluated with respect to job performance on the basis of conformance to their project budget, performance of the contractor or completed project, and adherence to project schedules. When the success or failure of goal achievement is directly influenced by the performance of employees, agencies routinely include progress toward such goal performance as an integral part of their job responsibility. Therefore, when it is essential to garner support for goal achievement from contracting professionals or project personnel, it is appropriate to evaluate their performance with respect to meeting social contracting goals along with budgetary, quality, and timeliness goals. Although the incentive program discussed earlier in this chapter encourages certain government representatives to support these programs, evaluating employee performance regarding achievement of social contracting goals garners the attention of all employees.

5.3.2 Development of Proposal Evaluation Criteria for Social Contracting

In addition to the eight measures discussed above, certain agencies may wish to consider the expected contribution to social contracting goals among competing proposals when selecting the contactor for a particular project. This can best be accomplished by including social contracting as one of the proposal evaluation criteria. Establishing one criterion solely for green contracting and one solely for socioeconomic contracting, or separate criteria for green and for socioeconomic contracting, or a single criterion for the combination of green and socioeconomic contracting are possible alternatives for evaluating the social contracting aspects of proposals. Examples of an RFP and the evaluation of proposals incorporating green contracting proposal evaluation criteria are included on the CD that accompanies this book.

Government officials and employees may harbor strong feelings against the benefits of certain social contracting programs. Public service professionals may provide rationale and recommendations against adoption of a proposed social program based on the fact that such programs may not comply with their expectations for full and open competition, may not be constitutional, may not be in the best interests of the public, may result in higher costs than services or products available from other companies, or that services or products from targeted companies will likely be delivered late and with lesser quality than products or services offered by non-targeted competitors. However, once a particular social contracting program has been adopted by their agency, true professionals are expected to support successful program implementation regardless of their personal feelings.

Agencies may provide for a mixture of tools to achieve socioeconomic contracting goals. In the event those tools are optional and include a mix of affirmative action and equal opportunity tools, the contracting professional who is adverse to the use of affirmative action tools (because he or she feels that such tools may not be in the best interests of the constituency) may be in a position to meet the agency's goals while implementing solely those tools that are considered as equal opportunity measures.

The above recommendations do not afford targeted companies with any undue advantage over non-targeted companies. However, numerous government entities have implemented social contracting programs that do provide targeted companies with extraordinary advantages such as set-asides, price advantages, and waiving of quality and on-time delivery requirements. Caution is recommended for government entities involved in social contracting when the advantages afforded targeted companies are sufficient to motivate certain companies to collude in order to inappropriately obtain contracts. As reported by the *Chicago Tribune*,[13] the former owner of a company used as a minority front, Faustech Industries, pleaded guilty to mail and wire fraud and paying $20,000 to influence a county official. Siemens Medical Systems paid Faust Villazan, sole owner of his now defunct company, a fee of $500,000 for use of Faustech Industries as a front company in order to win a $49 million contract. The scheme was discovered following a challenge to the contract award by GE Medical Systems, a competitor of Siemens Medical Systems.

A summary of the recommendations for an effective social contracting program is provided in Table 5.2.

5.3.3 Recommendations for Government Contractors' Socioeconomic Procurement Program

The above recommendations for government entities implementing a socioeconomic contracting program are also appropriate for prime contractor socioeconomic subcontracting plans. The recommended program, in fact, is based on a highly successful socioeconomic subcontracting program that was developed by a federal government prime contractor. The prime contractor had traditionally solicited four prospective contractors for each procurement action. When the revised subcontracting program was implemented, the four traditional contractors continued to be solicited; however, at least one targeted company was added to the list of firms solicited.

Government contractors are cautioned against developing a relationship with a targeted company that represents, or appears to represent, an arrangement wherein government contracts are awarded to the targeted company based on exceptions to competitive contracting requirements, but where the majority of the work is performed by a large business or otherwise non-targeted company. Large corporations entering into such illegitimate business relationships are subject to, or their employees are subject to, significant federal penalties.

Table 5.2   Recommended Components of an Effective Social Contracting Program

Social Contracting Program Components	Social Contracting Program Acceptability
Permit noncompetitive contracts to targeted companies	Not recommended: Targeted companies are capable of competing against non-targeted companies without such advantages, which are not in the best interests of the government or the constituency. Unnecessary advantages for targeted companies provide for the possibility of paying a premium for lower quality products or services that are not available in a timely manner. Providing such advantages also encourages non-targeted companies to misrepresent their companies as targeted, establish sham targeted companies, and other corrupt practices to obtain targeted company advantages.
Establish set-asides to permit competition solely by targeted companies	
Provide a price advantage for targeted companies	
Provide a waiver to targeted companies for untimely delivery	
Provide a waiver to targeted companies for substandard quality	
Establish proposal evaluation criteria for targeted companies	Not recommended for targeted companies for reasons stated above. However, proposal evaluation criteria are appropriate for green contracting programs.
Establish incentive awards program for supporting social contracting	Recommended: The listed social contracting program components have proven to significantly increase the participation of targeted companies in government contracting without subjecting the agency to payment of premium prices for substandard quality products or services that may not be provided in a timely manner. Because no class of contractors is provided a competitive advantage over other contractors, there is no incentive for them to fraudulently represent their status as a targeted company, establish a sham targeted company, or commit any other fraudulent acts to participate in agency contracting programs.
Encourage use of targeted companies when making procurement assignments	
Encourage membership in organizations that promote targeted companies	
Establish rapport with representatives of targeted companies	
Provide direct assistance, short of providing a competitive advantage, to targeted companies	
Provide for internal networking within the agency to share successful approaches to contracting with targeted companies	
Establish support for social contracting program as a part of agency employees' job responsibilities	

5.4 Government Goal Achievement and Improved Contractor Profitability through Successful Social Contracting

Social contracting programs may rightfully be perceived by skeptics as expensive and wasteful. Skeptics are likely accurate when social contracting programs are not intelligently designed. However, well-designed programs, such as a program incorporating the eight equal opportunity contracting strategies described in Section 5.3, can provide significant benefits for government. These benefits include an increase in contracting opportunities for targeted companies while reducing costs, increasing quality, and improving on-time delivery. Supplementing the existing base of contractors and suppliers by adding previously underrepresented companies increases competition in contracting, thereby leading to the need for contractors to offer more competitive pricing, superior quality, and improved on-time performance to remain competitive. The need to be competitive following the introduction of traditionally underrepresented contractors pertains to both the traditional contractors and those contractors recently added to the contractor base. Traditional contractors that lose business to new suppliers selected on the basis of price, quality, and on-time performance are forced to become more competitive in all three respects to maintain an acceptable market share. The historically underrepresented companies realize that they do not receive repeat orders unless they too are highly competitive with respect to price, quality, and on-time performance.

Environmentally conscious government entities with access to the necessary resources provide incentives for the installation of alternative energy systems. Although most government entities do not have the resources needed to offer such incentives, most agencies can obtain or supplement their own electrical energy requirements through alternative energy projects. One example of such an alternative energy project is the 400-kW-power photovoltaic system installed on the roof of the Court of Justice of the European Communities in Luxembourg. The photovoltaic cells are compatible with the architecture of the building in that they complement the aesthetics in aerial views but are not visible from ground level. The system, consisting of 2,262 photovoltaic modules manufactured by the Kyocera Corporation of Kyoto, Japan, was completed in December 2008.

Green contracting programs can likewise be effectively implemented through the eight contracting strategies described in Section 5.3. Although green contracting does not lead to lower pricing, improved contracting, and superior on-time performance from contractors, it does have benefits. These include reduced energy costs, reduced cost of hazardous waste disposal, less harmful impact on the environment, and improved reputation for the government entity that promotes a greener environment. Reduced energy costs can be achieved through alternative energy projects such as solar or fuel cell installations to provide energy to the government. Although these projects often require a significant upfront capital expenditure, selection of contractors on a competitive basis and taking advantage of incentive programs help control the initial cost and shorten the time required to recoup the upfront costs and realize the savings from reduced energy costs. Reducing the hazardous material content in purchased products and construction projects eventually leads to reduced costs associated with the disposal of hazardous materials. There is necessarily a delay in payback from reduced hazardous materials disposal for construction projects that are not realized until the green building is remodeled or demolished. However, the payback from the purchase of other green products is realized at the end of their shorter useful lives. The beneficial impact on the environment is obvious when one considers that fewer hazardous materials are included in products and buildings obtained through green contracting; however, a greater benefit is realized through the reduction of hazardous atmospheric emissions associated with alternative energy projects. The generation of electricity through photovoltaic cells in lieu of natural gas significantly reduces the emissions of carbon dioxide, sulfur dioxide, and nitrogen oxides. Government entities that pursue social contracting also receive recognition from their constituency and advocates who support environmental responsibility.

Implementation of an effective social contracting program, for both socioeconomic and green contracting, is consistent with law and policy applicable to most government entities. Compliance with social contracting laws and policies protects government resources, including the availability of time devoted to regular public agency functions for elected and appointed officials, as well as agency employees, by avoiding the need to respond to actions required when government entities are found to be noncompliant.

One primary benefit to prime contractors that implement an effective socioeconomic subcontracting program is that this action conforms to prime government contract provisions. The federal prime contractor that added at least one targeted company to each of its lists of firms solicited, as described above, introduced a greater level of competition into its subcontracting program, which resulted in significantly lower material costs, higher quality purchased parts, improved on-time delivery, and a lessened opportunity for unethical contracting practices. Lowering subcontracting costs through lower pricing and improved quality favored the company's profitability. Additionally, an outstanding rating on the prime contractor's socioeconomic subcontracting program, as reflected in the subcontracting plan, was used as a tie-breaker, resulting in the award of a government contract to the prime contractor based on its outstanding socioeconomic subcontracting program, and resulted in higher prices[14] for most negotiated government contracts.

5.5 Conclusion

Implementing the eight equal opportunity measures recommended in this chapter is certain to improve the participation of historically underrepresented groups of contractors while treating traditional contractors fairly and without degrading the government's record for cost control, on-time delivery, or the quality of purchased products and services. The need to be especially alert to fraud is paramount when a social contracting program is in place. The recommendations in this chapter help guard against numerous schemes for engaging in procurement fraud. The problem with disadvantaged business enterprise (DBE) front companies, where DBEs are controlled by non-minorities, is especially difficult to resolve. The following extract from a U.S. Department of Transportation (DOT), Office of the Inspector General (OIG), backgrounder[15] is representative of this problem as it was discovered, primarily at Federal Aviation Administration (FAA) facilities, in the aftermath of Hurricanes Katrina and Rita:

> The investigation disclosed instances of significant programmatic deficiencies and violations in key areas with the DBE programs of the Louis Armstrong International Airport, New Orleans Rapid Transit Authority, and the New Orleans Levee District (which operates New Orleans Lakefront Airport). OIG investigators found DBE firms that were controlled by non-minorities, and, in some cases, we uncovered potential DBE fraud — namely fronts. It is important to note that the period covered by this investigation preceded the election of New Orleans Mayor Ray Nagin.
>
> The report recommended that DOT's Operating Administrations, FAA in particular, need to strengthen the effectiveness of their stewardship of the DBE program beyond the status quo, which largely consists of limited, historical documentary reviews conducted periodically within local agency DBE program offices.

Holding meetings at company facilities and reviewing documents submitted by companies claiming targeted company status are likely to reveal the existence of front companies. Following through with an investigation of a company's claimed targeted status based on complaints from other targeted companies is highly recommended. Investigation into possible criminal activities, however, is best referred to investigative agencies.

Notes

1. One such restriction against local preferences in evaluating bids or proposals is contained in the *Code of Federal Regulations* (CFR), Title 24, Part 85, Section 36, which states, "Grantees and subgrantees will conduct procurements in a manner that prohibits the use of statutorily or administratively imposed in-State or local geographical preferences in the evaluation of bids or proposals, except in those cases where applicable Federal statutes expressly mandate or encourage geographic preference."
2. Samuel L. Myers, Jr., and Tsze Chan. (1996) "Who Benefits from Minority Business Set-Asides? The Case of New Jersey," *Journal of Policy Analysis and Management*, vol. 15, no. 2, pp. 202–226.

3. Justin Marion, "Are Bid Preferences Benign? The Effect of Small Bus: Highway Procurement Auctions," December 2006 version, Departme University of California, Santa Cruz.

4. Department of Defense, Office of the Inspector General, "Acquisitioi Administration Section 8(a) Program Contracting Procedures at the Defense Supply Center, Columbus," Report number D-2004-070, April 12, 2004.

5. U.S. Government Accountability Office, "Status of Small Disadvantaged Business Certifications," Report number GAO-01-273, January 2001.

6. "Review of Blackwater Worldwide Compliance with Small Business Laws as Requested by Cong. Waxman," Office of the Inspector General, U.S. Small Business Administration, July 25, 2008.

7. "The Set-Aside Syndrome," Zach Patton, *Governing* magazine, July 2005.

8. www.chicagotribune.com, "City Bars Duff for Just 3 Years: Contract Cheat Eludes a Life Ban," Todd Lightly and Laurie Cohen, March 20, 2008.

9. FAR 15.404(d)(1)(iii), which permits favorable profit consideration for companies that support federal socioeconomic programs, also permits unfavorable profit consideration for companies that do not support federal socioeconomic programs.

10. The socioeconomic contracting program in this example was implemented at the Electron Devices Division of Litton Industries in San Carlos, California. The program was implemented in 1986, and the increased percentage of dollars awarded to minority-owned and woman-owned companies steadily increased until the referenced increases were achieved in 1995. As a result of the success of this program, Litton Electron Devices Division was awarded the Dwight D. Eisenhower Award for Excellence by the U.S. Small Business Administration. The Electron Devices Division of Litton Industries has since been acquired by L-3 Communications.

11. See note 7 above.

12. The Industry Council for Small Business Development (ICSBD) in Sunnyvale, California, was formed by federal government private-sector contractors that were required to establish socioeconomic subcontracting programs as a condition of one or more of their federal contracts. The ICSBD maintains a website at www.icsbd.org.

13. The account of the collusion between the employees of a Siemens AG subsidiary and minority contractor Faustech Industries relies on a posting by www.chicagotribune.com, "Man Gets Prison for Bribery in Cook Deal: Minority Bid a Sham; Official Is Identified," Michael Higgins, February 29, 2008.

14. FAR 15.404(d)(1)(iii) permits favorable consideration in profit negotiations for contractors that support federal socioeconomic programs.

15. Office of the Inspector General, U.S. Department of Transportation, Office of the Secretary of Transportation, "OIG Oversight of Hurricane Response and Recovery Activities," October 2005.

Chapter 6

Solicitations and Pre-Proposal Communications

This chapter provides an introduction to and recommendations for preparing solicitation documents and managing pre-proposal communications. The resultant benefits of effective documentation and management as well as the problems associated with deficient documentation and ineffective pre-proposal communications management are described. Government entities are advised of the potential for ethical lapses during the pre-proposal phase of the contracting cycle and how to guard against such ethical lapses. Government contractors are provided with recommendations for preparing solicitation documents and managing pre-proposal communications with respect to their subcontracting process.

6.1 Solicitation Fundamentals

Solicitation is the generic term for the various types of documents, such as request for proposals (RFP) and invitation for bids (IFB), prepared by government entities seeking proposals from prospective contractors for providing the agency with services, commodities, or construction projects. It is important for readers to understand the differences between the various types of solicitations because selection of the incorrect solicitation type may distort the contractor selection process, thus resulting in selection of the wrong contractor. For example, using an IFB to select a contractor on the basis of price and other factors will force the government to select the contract primarily on the basis of the lowest price. In the research project mentioned earlier, the document review of RFPs submitted by participating governments indicated that numerous contracting personnel do not have a basic understanding of the differences between the various types of solicitation documents. This discussion of the basic components of solicitation documents begins with an overview of the various types of solicitations commonly used in government procurement. Understanding the differences between the various types of solicitations helps government representatives select the type of solicitation document best suited for their project.

6.1.1 Types of Solicitations

The types of solicitation documents traditionally used in government contracting are RFPs, requests for contractor qualifications (RFCQs), requests for quotations (RFQs), and IFBs. There has been a trend toward use of a request for bids (RFB) by some agencies; however, review of RFB documents from several agencies indicates that RFBs are basically IFBs with a different name.

The type of solicitation used primarily to solicit private-sector companies for proposals to provide services to government entities is the RFP. RFPs are, in some cases, used to solicit proposals for providing commodities when the agency intends to select the contractor on the basis of pricing and other factors. Government entities normally use an RFP to solicit private-sector responses for design/build construction projects as well. An RFP typically includes a short introduction of the government entity soliciting the proposals; background for the services or products to be contracted, to include the present manner in which the services or products are being provided; a description of the services or products to be provided; evaluation criteria to be used in selecting the successful contractor; rights reserved by the contracting agency; format for contractor-prepared proposals along with page limitations, when appropriate; and a copy of a model contract that includes the government's terms and conditions, required contractor insurance coverage, and a scope of work.

This chapter includes an extensive discussion of the RFP designed through a national best practices research project. A Microsoft Word version of this best practices RFP is provided on the CD that accompanies this book, to facilitate adaptation of the RFP by government entities or government contractors. Although there were serious deficiencies in many of the RFPs submitted by government entities participating in the best practices research project, virtually all the features in the resultant best practices RFP were contained in one or more of the originally submitted RFPs. The RFP on the CD contains features that will likely prove valuable to all government entities; however, the RFP provisions and the terms and conditions of the model contract attached to the RFP are not intended to replace the U.S. *Federal Acquisition Regulation* (FAR) provisions that are mandatory for

U.S. federal agencies and federal government contractors, nor are they intended to replace mandatory provisions for any other government entities.

The expected response to an RFP from prospective contractors is a proposal. Proposals describe the approach that contractors intend to employ to meet the service or product needs of the government organization that released the RFP. Proposals typically describe the prospective contractor's experience and qualifications to perform such services or provide the products as well as their proposed pricing and any other information requested in the RFP. Proposals in response to RFPs, unlike bids in response to IFBs, are not opened publicly, are treated confidentially until the contract is awarded or recommended for award, and are subject to negotiation and change. Whereas bids in response to an IFB are rejected for being nonresponsive or delivered after the due date and time, proposals in response to an RFP are not normally rejected summarily for these reasons. Proposals deemed to be nonresponsive may be modified through negotiations to render them responsive. If the agency states in their RFP that it may elect to consider proposals received after the due date and time, the agency may consider late proposals if in the best interests of the agency. However, some jurisdictions are prevented, by law, from accepting late proposals.

A type of solicitation similar to the RFP is the RFCQ; however, the RFCQ is limited to obtaining information on the qualifications of various private-sector entities that may be qualified to deliver the required products or services. The contractors' response to the government organization that released the RFCQ is a statement of qualifications. The contracting agency evaluates statements of qualifications submitted by the contractors to determine which firms or individuals are qualified to receive an RFP. An RFP is then prepared and sent to all the firms that were determined to be qualified through the RFCQ process. The RFCQ, therefore, is actually the first step in a two-step solicitation process. When the contracting agency is familiar with prospective contractors, the RFCQ process can be avoided. The two-step RFCQ/RFP process requires approximately twice the time needed for a one-step RFP process. Therefore, RFCQs are normally not used when time is of the essence for placing the services or products under contract. Certain agencies refer to RFCQs merely as requests for qualifications (RFQs) or requests for information (RFIs). However, use of the term RFQ can lead to confusion between requests for quotations and requests for qualifications, and RFI is not sufficiently descriptive of the nature of this solicitation type. The agency preparing the RFCQ normally specifies the information to be included in the statement of qualifications prepared by the prospective contractors. The government normally requests only the information needed to determine the qualifications of the prospective contractors. However, this is not necessarily limited to technical issues; the contracting agency could request information on the contractors' financial statements to evaluate their financial strength, references to evaluate their reputation, or any other information needed to evaluate their qualifications. The statement of qualifications, however, does not normally include pricing and does not normally result in the award of a contract unless the RFCQ is followed up by an RFP to all the qualified contractors.

The most informal type of solicitation is the RFQ. RFQs are normally used to solicit quotes for low-value commodities that are easily described, and when the successful contractor is selected primarily based on price or life cycle cost. Because of the informality of RFQs, additional selection factors, such as promised delivery date, may also be used in selecting the contractor. RFQs are normally not used to solicit quotations for services. The responses to RFQs received from prospective contractors are referred to as quotes or quotations. RFQs are typically prepared on standard templates designed to permit prospective contractors to merely fill in the blank spaces of the RFQ form that is sent to contractors by mail, facsimile, or e-mail. The blank spaces are normally limited to pricing, promised delivery date, payment terms, identifying company information, and the signature of a contractor representative. Because the RFQ is an informal document, the contracting agency may establish the rules for handling responses from contractors. The government may permit quotes to be submitted via facsimile or in a sealed envelope, late quotes may be summarily rejected or accepted if in the best interests of the agency, contract award may be made without negotiations, or negotiations may be conducted at the option of the contracting agency. Attaching a document to the RFQ that describes how the quotes are handled and how the contractor is selected is recommended to ensure that all the prospective contractors are treated equally.

The most formal of the types of solicitations is the IFB. Use of an IFB to solicit prospective contractors is occasionally referred to as formal bidding. IFBs are normally used to solicit bids for high-value commodities, capital equipment, or construction projects. They are normally not used to solicit bids for service contracts. Certain agencies that make grants to other government entities, however, occasionally require solicitation by IFB for contracts that use their grant funds. When the granting agency requires the solicitation of prospective contractors via IFB, it normally provides a template to be used by the contracting agency. The contracting agency has no choice but to solicit prospective contractors with an IFB. The contracting agency may request a waiver to use an RFP; however, it may be difficult to justify use of an RFP in this situation. Bids received in response to an IFB are opened publicly and result in award of a contract to the responsive and responsible contractor with the lowest price. Just as with quotations or quotes, bids are typically prepared by contractors that complete information in spaces on a government-prepared bid form. Information provided by the prospective contractors on the bid form is similar to that provided for quotations or quotes. However, the bid form is likely to require more information than the quote form because IFBs are customarily used for high-value projects that require a greater amount of information than what is required for low-value contracts.

The fact that IFBs are normally used for high-value procurements makes this type of solicitation document a candidate for a "Prospective Contractor Certification" (for IFB), provided on the CD that accompanies this book. The recommended certification guards against corruption in that it requires prospective contractors to list company officials that have been found guilty or pleaded guilty to bribery, or had contracts terminated for default, and to certify that no public officials benefit from the award of a contract to their company.

The formality of the IFB is most evident in the treatment of bids in response to it. There is normally no flexibility in the evaluation of bids in response to an IFB. Bids that are not received by the due date and time are rejected. Bids are opened publicly and read aloud for the benefit of anyone interested in the offered pricing. The bids are recorded on a spreadsheet that is considered public information, and copies of the spreadsheet are available to the public and competing contractors. Bids in response to an IFB are awarded to the responsible contractor that submitted the lowest priced responsive bid. A summary of the various types of solicitations is provided in Table 6.1.

Addendum is the term used to describe the document used to make changes to an RFP or any other type of solicitation after the solicitation has been sent to prospective contractors and before contractor responses are due.

Research into solicitations in preparation for writing this book revealed that numerous states and local government agencies in the United States incorrectly use terms synonymously when such terms are intended to differentiate between the various types of solicitations. Examples of such incorrect usage of terms are in an RFP where the responses from contractors are referred to as "bids" rather than "proposals" or when the prospective contractors are referred to as "bidders." Consistent use of correct terminology is encouraged to ensure that prospective contractors or unsuccessful contractors do not file protests or lawsuits based on misunderstandings regarding the handling of proposals or bids created by such incorrect usage of terminology. Using "bid" and "proposal" interchangeably may lead to misunderstandings because each type of solicitation is unique and contractor responses to RFPs are treated differently from contractor responses to IFBs.

Responses to each unique type of solicitation from prospective contractors are dependent on the type of solicitation selected. Proposals are the only appropriate response to an RFP, bids are the only appropriate response to an IFB, and quotes or quotations are the only acceptable responses to RFQs. If the text of an RFP states incorrectly that bids are due at a time and date certain, then prospective contractors may expect a public bid opening. However, proposals, which are the correct contractor response to an RFP, are not normally opened publicly. Proposals are treated initially as confidential and are subject to negotiation. Bids in response to an IFB are opened publicly, immediately become public information, and are not subject to negotiation.

There are numerous alternative types of solicitations used in government contracting. The characteristics of RFPs, RFCQs, RFQs, and IFBs were described earlier; however, IFBs and RFPs are the only types of solicitations that normally lead to high-value contracts. When awarding a contract based on the lowest price in response to an IFB, there is little latitude for selecting other than the contractor

Table 6.1 Comparison between Types of Solicitations

Type of Solicitation	Acquisition of Services or Property	Contractor Response	Public Opening	Late Responses Acceptable	Basis of Evaluation	Subject to Negotiation
Request for proposals (RFP)	Normally used for acquisition of services. However, may be used for acquisition of property or a combination of services and property.	Proposal	No	Yes, but only if in the best interests of the contracting agency.	Proposals are evaluated on the basis of criteria identified in the RFP. The criteria normally include the contract price or life cycle costs.	Yes
Request for contractor qualifications (RFCQ)	Normally used for acquisition of services. However, may be used for acquisition of property or a combination of services and property.	Statement of qualifications (SOQ)	No	Yes, but only if in the best interests of the contracting agency.	SOQs are evaluated on the basis of criteria identified in the RFCQ. The criteria do not include the contract price or life cycle costs.	Negotiation is not applicable. SOQ normally does not result in contract award primarily because it does not include pricing.
Request for quotations (RFQ)	Normally used for purchase of relatively low-value property.	Quote or quotation	No	Yes, but only if in the best interests of the contracting agency.	Quotes or quotations are evaluated primarily on the basis of price.	Yes

| Invitation for bids (IFB) | Normally used for purchase of relatively high-value capital equipment, construction, or commodities. However, an IFB is occasionally used for the acquisition of services when price is the primary factor affecting contractor selection. | Bid | Yes | No | Bids are evaluated solely on the basis of price if the bid is responsive and the contractor is responsible. | No |

that submitted the lowest price. The evaluation of proposals in response to an RFP according to price and *other factors* creates more risks for government. The subjective nature of *other factors* permits more latitude in contractor selection and the accompanying risk of experiencing the unsavory consequences listed in Table 1.1. To provide government with recommendations to guard against the greatest risks of procurement corruption associated with the evaluation of proposals, the balance of this book is concentrated on RFPs rather than the other types of solicitations.

6.2 Failed Management of Pre-Proposal Communications and Protest Vulnerability

Failure to implement an effective pre-proposal communications management plan hinders the contracting agency's ability to respond to legitimate questions in a timely manner while treating all prospective contractors equally. When one contractor receives more favored treatment from the government than the treatment provided its competitors, the agency does not reap the benefits available through full and open competition. More favorable treatment to one contractor can, in fact, skew the contractor selection process in favor of the contractor proposing less value, higher pricing, or less value for a higher price. This skewing of the selection process to favor a particular contractor constitutes an aberration of the contractor selection process that could result in selection of a contractor that is not in the best interests of the contracting agency. This places the contractors that did not receive favorable treatment at a competitive disadvantage. A significant percentage of protests that have been upheld were based, at least partially, on more favorable treatment afforded one contractor at the expense of its competitors. Such unequal treatment of contractors, if permitted by the contracting agency, is likely to result in an excessively high rate of protests and provide opportunities for procurement fraud.

Legitimate protests damage an agency's reputation, delay programs, increase costs, and drain agency resources. The consequences of these adverse impacts on the agency were discussed earlier in this book. Therefore, it is merely reiterated at this point that protests have the propensity to cause the public and agency employees to lose confidence in the government's competence and ethics, create delays in the award of contracts and commencement of programs, and require agency employees to devote considerable time responding to protests when that time might have been more efficiently devoted to other agency responsibilities.

Procurement fraud also damages an agency's reputation, delays programs, increases costs, and drains agency resources. However, the degree of damage from fraud is monumental when compared to protests. This is understandable because procurement fraud constitutes a serious crime, whereas protests, although occasionally revealing fraud, are oftentimes frivolous and frequently based on alleged minor administrative irregularities. Although protests occasionally have a significant impact on the agency's reputation, program schedules, costs, and resources, such impacts are rarely as significant as the damage resulting from procurement fraud.

6.3 Content of the Best Practices RFP

A comprehensive discussion of the recommendations for a best practices RFP is available on the CD that accompanies this book. Two versions of a best practices RFP are provided on the CD. The full-length version is identified as the "Best Practices RFP"; it is intended for high-value, high-risk contracts and includes all conceivable provisions to avoid the risks associated with such contracts. The "Model Contract" on the CD is recommended as an attachment to accompany the best practices RFP. A shorter version of the RFP and model contract are identified on the CD as the "Short Form RFP with Short Form Contract"; they are intended for lower value, lower risk contracts. The definitions for high value and high risk are generally dependent on the budget size for each government entity; therefore, no attempt is made here to recommend the value or level of risk that determines use of the long version or the short version of the RFP and the model contract. The documents provided on the CD are in Microsoft Word to permit modification by agencies to conform to local policy. As previously mentioned, the provisions of the best practices RFP and terms and conditions for the best practices contracts are not intended as replacements for mandatory FAR provisions or mandatory provisions applicable to any government organization.

The best practices RFP was developed by incorporating the best features from all the RFPs provided by government entities participating in the research project undertaken in preparation for writing *Contracting for Services in State and Local Government Agencies*. Certain government entities participating in the research project did not use the title "request for proposals" for their solicitation document. However, in virtually all cases, the solicitation documents met the characteristics of RFPs better than any other type of solicitation document. Each provision of the best practices RFP is described in detail on the CD. An abridged discussion of the best practices RFP provisions is provided in this section.

When RFPs are sent to prospective contractors without a copy of the government's template for the contract they intend to award, prospective contractors often propose their standard contract. This presents a problem because contractors' standard contract formats often include provisions that favor the contractors' interests over the government's interests. To avoid this problem, it is recommended that a copy of the agency's standard contract template be designated as a "model contract" and included with every RFP. It is further recommended that the RFP include a statement indicating that the agency intends to award a contract essentially in the form of the attached model contract.

The model contract included on the CD, like the RFP, was developed by incorporating the best features of the contract documents provided by government entities participating in the above-referenced research project.

The best practices RFP on the CD consists of the basic RFP document, certifications to be completed by prospective contractors, and a model contract. The "Prospective Contractor Certification" in the best practices RFP requires prospective contractors to certify that their company is in conformance with the government's ethical standards. The model contract also has three attachments: contract insurance requirements, scope of work, and the government contract terms and conditions. The features of the best practices RFP and the model contract, and attachments to both documents, are described here.

Cover page: The information included on the cover page normally includes the phrase "request for proposals," an RFP number, government entity name, project name, solicitation date, and the name of the agency's contracting representative or project manager and his or her contact information. Placing all variable information, except for the scope of work, on the cover page simplifies preparation of the RFP. Provisions such as "All questions regarding this RFP shall be referred to the agency's Project Manager at the e-mail address indicated on the RFP cover page" make it unnecessary to insert variable information such as the project manager's name and e-mail address in the text of the RFP.

Table of contents: A table of contents is recommended for relatively lengthy RFPs. Including it in the agency's RFP template also reminds department personnel preparing the RFP to insert page numbers in the document and to consider including information on all the topics included in the agency's RFP template table of contents.

Accommodations: Regarding accommodations, the best practices RFP provided on the CD refers only to the provision of solicitation material in an alternative format, such as a larger font for persons with vision impairment.

Notice to prospective contractors: The notice to prospective contractors cautions contractors to carefully read the RFP and to submit all comments via e-mail by the established deadline. Designating e-mail as the only method for posing questions is recommended to facilitate handling questions and providing feedback to all prospective contractors, create a uniform and rapid method of communications, and provide the capability to prepare a paper or electronic trail of the pre-proposal activities.

Confidentiality of proposals: Unlike bids in response to an IFB that become public documents when opened by the agency, proposals in response to an RFP are treated as confidential because they are subject to negotiations. When competing contractors become familiar with the content of their competitors' proposals, the negotiations are compromised.

Contact information: Contractors that are not on the agency's list of firms solicited may learn of the solicitation from the agency's website or from some other source. To ensure that such prospective contractors become known to agency personnel, such contractors are advised to contact the agency's project manager to advise him or her that they wish to be considered as a prospective contractor.

Address and due date for proposals: The provisions of the best practices RFP include the date and time when proposals are due. It may be necessary to indicate separate addresses for proposals sent via the U.S. Postal Service (that may be addressed to a post office box) and for proposals sent via courier services, which require a street address.

No public opening: The contractor response to the best practices RFP is a proposal that is not opened publicly. Prospective contractors are advised of this fact in the best practices RFP to ensure that there is no misunderstanding regarding the absence of a public opening.

Contractors without e-mail access: The best practices RFP includes provisions for participation in the contracting process by contractors that do not have e-mail access.

RFP addenda: When it is determined necessary to modify an RFP that has been released, the customary document to make such a change is an addendum.

Questions and responses posted on website: The best practices RFP includes instructions for prospective contractors to pose all questions concerning the RFP to the project manager via e-mail.

Introduction: The introduction identifies the contracting agency and announces the agency's intent to enter into a contract for the applicable project.

Background: A clear description of the project background permits prospective contractors to determine whether this is a contract that they wish to pursue, assign the appropriate contractor project manager, and prepare their proposal.

Scope of work: This section of the best practices RFP refers prospective contractors to the scope of work in the model contract for a complete description of the contractor's responsibilities.

Contractor selection process: It is essential that prospective contractors understand the contractor selection process. The description of the contractor selection process in the best practices RFP includes information on the release of the RFP, the government's method for responding to contractor questions regarding the RFP, the number of copies of the proposal that contractors need to provide, due date for proposals, confidential opening of proposals, method for evaluating proposals, weighting of proposal evaluation criteria, and the government's right to request contractor presentations and to conduct negotiations. Also included in the contractor selection description are the prospective contractors' right to request a debriefing regarding the government's selection of a competing contractor and the unsuccessful contractors' right to protest the selection of a competitor.

The provisions of the best practices RFP for offering debriefings to unsuccessful contractors and explaining the process for filing protests is consistent with the UN's *Compendium of International Legal Instruments on Corruption,* where it is stated that procurement systems should include: "An effective system of domestic review, including an effective system of appeal, to ensure legal recourse and remedies in the event that the rules or procedures established pursuant to this paragraph are not followed."

The description of the contractor selection process in the best practices RFP also includes a lengthy list of agency rights to include the right to reject any or all submittals, waive informalities or irregularities, not select any firm, conduct negotiations, request added information from prospective contractors, and award more than one contract if that is in the government's best interests.

Proposal requirements: The proposal format instructions in the RFP advise prospective contractors of the rules for preparing and assembling proposals in conformance with the agency's requirements. Requiring prospective contractors to include topics in the proposals that have a direct relationship to the evaluation criteria simplifies the work of the proposal evaluation team and helps ensure that the prospective contractors are treated equally. The requirement to prepare the proposal in a certain format, sequence, and maximum length greatly simplifies the agency's task when comparing the competing proposals to determine which proposal best meets the agency's requirements.

The best practices RFP prescribes specific information for inclusion in the contractors' proposal cover letters and the requirement to organize the proposal in six sections. Establishing a format wherein there is a proposal section for each of the proposal evaluation criteria greatly simplifies the effort involved in evaluating proposals. The proposal selection criteria and section titles and content specified for the contractors' proposals are past performance, environmental considerations, risk assessment, project plan, outsourcing, and life cycle cost.

Contractor certifications: Five certifications for completion by prospective contractors are included in the best practices RFP. However, three of the certifications are not applicable if the project has no federal funding. The certification of price or cost information is not applicable unless the agency anticipates award of a cost reimbursement contract or a fixed-price contract that was not competitively awarded. Agencies are advised to avoid cost reimbursement contracts if at all possible. When the agency expects to competitively award a fixed-price contract without any federal funding, it need only include the prospective contractor certification.

Prospective Contractor Certification: The Prospective Contractor Certification, which is included in the RFP, includes a large number of individual certifications including the certification that

- all work is performed by United States citizens or to comply with applicable immigration laws
- the employee or representative signing the proposal for the prospective contractor is authorized to commit the company
- the company is the prime contractor
- the contractor will furnish the insurance certificate within ten calendar days of the notice of award
- the contractor is in compliance with the agency's ethical standards including specific certification that proposal pricing was developed independently and without collusion

- the contractor has not made any arrangement with any elected or appointed official or agency employee to benefit financially or materially from the award of the contract
- no attempt has been made to induce any other person or firm to submit or not submit a proposal
- contractor agrees not to discuss or otherwise reveal the contents of the proposal to any source outside the contracting agency until after contract award
- none of the company officials directly involved in obtaining the contract have been convicted, have had probation before judgment, or have pleaded *nolo contendere* to a charge of bribery, attempted bribery, or conspiracy to bribe in violation of any state or federal law

One of the most memorable *nolo contendere* pleas was made by then-Vice President Spiro Agnew, who pleaded *nolo contendere* to income tax evasion while being investigated for routinely soliciting and accepting bribes while serving as a county executive and governor of Maryland prior to becoming vice president of the United States. Agnew resigned from office as vice president.

This certification specifies the period of time when the proposal remains valid. The agency enters the applicable period of time prior to release of the RFP to provide the agency with sufficient time to evaluate proposals and award the contract. The certification also indicates the proposed total cost or not-to-exceed contract price. The contract price differs from the life cycle cost in that the contract price does not include incremental agency costs to be incurred through execution of the resultant contract.

The prospective contractor certification also requires prospective contractors to reveal all instances of bribery, attempted bribery, or conspiracy to bribe in violation of any applicable law, to indicate whether it has attached a description of potential instances of collusion or other violations, and if the contractor attached a list of exceptions to the RFP.

The certifications required for contracts that are fully or partially federally funded, as referenced earlier, are the Certification Regarding Lobbying; Certification of Compliance with Pro-Children Act of 1994; and Certification Regarding Debarment, Suspension, Ineligibility and Voluntary Exclusion — Lower Tier Covered Transactions. These certifications too are provided on the CD that accompanies this book. To ensure that the current versions of the federal certifications are in the RFP, agencies can access the online version of the FAR and paste the versions of the FAR certifications over the certifications on the CD.

Debarment, suspension, and ineligibility are not unique to organizations subject to the FAR. A Russian firm reportedly paid $700,000 in "consulting fees" to a UN procurement officer.[1] Although the Russian firm, Volga-Dnepr, had not been suspended as of March 15, 2007, when the story was reported, the UN did suspend Volga-Dnepr and the Italian-based firm, Corimec Italiana SPA, by May 16,

2007.[2] Two other firms, Italian-based Cogim SPA and Avicos Insurance Company of Russia, were also reportedly removed from the list of UN contractors.

Proposal preparation and submittal instructions: A comprehensive explanation of the proposal preparation and submittal instructions is included in the best practices RFP to guide prospective contractors. Readers can access the proposal preparation explanation by opening the best practices RFP on the CD that accompanies this book. However, a brief introduction to proposal preparation and submittal instructions is provided here.

The exceptions provision advises prospective contractors that the agency intends to award a contract substantially in the format of the model contract attached to the RFP. Prospective contractors are cautioned that exceptions to any provisions in the RFP must be fully disclosed in their proposals and that exceptions to the agency's terms and conditions could render their proposals nonresponsive.

Model contract: The best practices RFP provides for attachment of the agency's model contract immediately following the proposal preparation and submittal instructions. The model contract was developed during the best practices research project and consists of the best practices found in the contracts provided by the government entities participating in the research project conducted in preparation for writing *Contracting for Services in State and Local Government Agencies*. The model contract is discussed earlier in this section, and there is a more detailed discussion in the "Characteristics of the Model Contract" on the CD. The attachments to the model contract are the insurance provisions, the scope of work, and the terms and conditions.

Government contractor RFPs: The recommendations for government RFPs are also appropriate for the subcontracting efforts by government contractors. Because the value of subcontracts is expected to be considerably lower than the value of their prime contract, government contractors may wish to consider the short-form RFP and model contract on the CD that accompanies this book for all but their high-value RFPs. Government entities frequently identify provisions of their proposal or contract that must be included in contractor solicitations and subcontracts. Such mandatory flow-down provisions normally are applicable solely to subcontracts over established threshold values. A careful review of the prime contract is needed to reveal all mandatory subcontract flow-down provisions. Government entities occasionally include requirements for contractors to award contracts according to their corporate procurement procedures. When permitted by the terms of their government contract and company policies, low-value or low-risk subcontracting activities may be conducted through a less formal process such as the use of RFQs as the solicitation documents and purchase orders in lieu of subcontracts. Whenever contractors expect to award subcontracts for significant products or services, however, consideration of the above RFP process for government is highly recommended for government contractors as well.

The features of the best practices RFP are summarized in Table 6.2.

Table 6.2   Features of a Best Practices Request for Proposals (RFP)

Feature	Content
Cover page	An RFP cover page that includes the agency name and project identification is fairly standard for government entities. The best practices RFP includes most information that varies for individual RFPs on the cover page to avoid the need to change information imbedded in the RFP boilerplate.
Table of contents	A table of contents is recommended for lengthy documents to facilitate lookup of specific information.
Accommodations	An offer to provide the RFP in larger font is recommended to accommodate individuals with vision impairment. However, other accommodations are normally not required unless the agency's facilities are not ADA compliant.
Notice to prospective contractors	This is a lengthy section of the RFP that includes information on the confidentiality of proposals, need for contact information from prospective contractors, RFP addenda, due date for proposals, the lack of a public opening of the RFPs, contact information for contractors without e-mail access, a space to list addenda received by prospective contractors, and information on prospective contractor questions and agency responses posted on the agency's website.
Introduction	The introduction identifies the contracting agency and announces the agency's intent to enter into a contract for the applicable project. This section also makes reference to the scope of work and the agency's intent to award a contract essentially in the format of the attached model contract.
Background	This section includes the project background to permit prospective contractors to decide if this is a contract that they wish to pursue, to assign the appropriate contractor project manager, and prepare their proposal.
Scope of work	The scope of work section on the RFP merely refers prospective contractors to the scope of work attached to the RFP for a description of the work to be performed by the successful contractor.

(continued)

Table 6.2 Features of a Best Practices Request for Proposals (RFP) (Continued)

Feature	Content
Contractor selection process	The contractor selection process is fully explained to include release of the RFP; posing questions regarding the RFP; required number of copies and a CD version of proposals; due date for proposals; method of evaluating proposals; the agency's option to require presentations, discussions, or negotiations; process for requesting a debriefing or filing a protest; and an enumeration of the agency's rights.
Proposal requirements	The requirements for preparing proposals is fully described to include sections of the proposal that coincide with the selection criteria for past performance, environmental considerations, risk assessment, a project plan, outsourcing, and life cycle costs.
Contractor certifications	The best practices RFP includes a prospective contractor certification. Federal certifications are included in the RFP but may be deleted if no federal funds are involved. A certification of cost or pricing data is also included, but may be deleted if a fixed-price contract is to be awarded based on full and open competition.

6.4 Superior Contractor Selection and Protest Avoidance with Best Practices RFP

Following the preceding recommendations in this book, government may achieve a well-planned RFP based on the best practices of government entities throughout the United States. Specific dividends resulting from such a well-planned RFP include the many benefits of full and open competition, prudent management of pre-proposal communications, a standardized format for proposals, assurances that the contractor is in compliance with the agency's ethical standards, and establishment of the agency's model contract as the contract that is awarded to the successful contractor.

6.4.1 Full and Open Competition

Full and open competition not only provides a greater opportunity for contractors to compete for agency contracts, but also provides the government with a broad choice of contractors, thus increasing its opportunities to consider proposals from excellent contractors. An additional benefit results from contractors that realize they are participating in a full and open competitive environment. Prospective contractors tend to offer lower pricing in full and open competition than under limited competition or sole source contracting. Full and open competition also minimizes opportunities for corrupt government officials to award overpriced contracts to companies that were not selected in the agency's best interests.

The effect of competition in reducing opportunities for procurement corruption is substantiated in the UN's *Compendium of International Legal Instruments on Corruption*, which includes provisions for state parties to "take the necessary steps to establish appropriate systems of procurement, based on transparency, competition and objective decision making, that are effective, inter alia, in preventing corruption."

6.4.2 Prudent Management of Pre-Proposal Communications

Implementation of the recommendations for developing an RFP based on best practices results in government having the tools needed to manage pre-proposal communications, thus promoting equal treatment of prospective contractors and preventing protests from contractors that would otherwise have recognized the unequal treatment.

6.4.3 Standardized Format for Proposals

Homogenous contractor proposals that are organized in sections with standard titles, page limitations for each section, and content directly related to the proposal evaluation criteria greatly simplify the proposal evaluation process and facilitate the evaluation of proposals according to the criteria in the RFP. Standardized proposal formats also contribute to equal treatment and, as with full and open competition, assist in the prevention of protests from aggrieved contractors.

6.4.4 Assurances That the Contractor Is in Compliance with the Agency's Ethical Standards

The prospective contractor certification format requires contractors responding to agency solicitations to certify that they are in compliance with numerous enumerated agency ethical standards. The recommendation to include this certification in solicitations that are expected to result in moderate- to high-value contracts is intended to help agencies avoid experiencing the lapses included in Table 1.1.

6.4.5 Agency Model Contract

Advising prospective contractors that the agency intends to award a contract substantially in the form of the model contract attached to the RFP guards against the possibility that contractors propose their own standard contract format. The model contract provided on the CD accompanying this book minimizes the risks faced by the agency while providing contract provisions that are well balanced between the agency and the contractor. Because all the prospective contractors are subject to identical contract provisions if selected for award of the contract, the agency's intention to award the model contract to the winning contractor further contributes to equal treatment of all prospective contractors.

6.4.6 Benefits to Government Contractors from Use of Well-Structured RFPs

The benefits to government contractors that use well-structured RFPs, as described in Section 6.3, parallel the benefits to government entities. Full and open competition advances achievement of the optimal combination of price, performance, and timeliness, thus leading to opportunities for increasing profitability. Effective management of pre-proposal communications assists government contractors in their efforts to treat prospective subcontractors equally; however, prospective subcontractors rarely protest the solicitation process or selection of subcontractors. The standardized format for proposals does minimize the effort required to evaluate proposals and assists government contractors in their selection of the best-qualified subcontractors. Including a copy of the government contractor's model subcontract in the solicitation package, along with a statement that the contractor intends to award a subcontract essentially in the form of the model subcontract, discourages prospective subcontractors from proposing their subcontract format. Subcontract formats proposed by prospective subcontractors are likely to have provisions favoring the subcontractor over the prime contractor and contribute to the difficulty of treating all prospective subcontractors equally.

6.5 Errant Contractor Selection and Corruption Exposure with Deficient RFP

Failure to follow the preceding recommendations could lead government to release a poorly planned RFP that fails to include the best practices of government entities throughout the United States. Specific consequences resulting from the release of a poorly planned RFP include exposure to protests from aggrieved contractors, exposure to procurement corruption, added work and expense required to evaluate proposals, delays in the award of contracts, and a lesser number of contracts awarded through full and open competition.

6.5.1 Exposure to Protests from Aggrieved Contractors

Government entities that fail to properly manage pre-proposal communications have greater exposure to the possibility of providing one contractor with favorable treatment in comparison to competing contractors. An example of mismanaged pre-proposal communications became known after protests were filed and it was learned that a top Air Force procurement official admitted to giving Boeing favorable treatment with respect to several procurement actions. A former Boeing executive discussed the possibility of providing a high-level position with his company to the Air Force official. Boeing also provided employment for the Air Force official's daughter and son-in-law. The former Air Force procurement official did secure the high-level position with Boeing. Eventually she admitted to giving Boeing favored treatment in numerous contracting actions. However, she and the former Boeing executive were subsequently fired, fined, and sentenced to prison. Numerous protests are filed based on the government's failure to evaluate proposals according to the criteria stated in its RFPs. The inclusion of instructions in RFPs for prospective contractors to organize their proposals in a standard format that correlates the proposal information to the proposal evaluation criteria is recommended to minimize this problem. The correlation of proposal sections to the proposal evaluation criteria simplifies the evaluation of proposals and avoids inadvertent failure to evaluate proposals according to the evaluation criteria. When the investigation into the merits of a protest reveals that the government is at fault, it is not unusual for the government to reimburse the contractor for the cost of filing and pursuing the protest. In complex cases, the reimbursed costs are substantial. Protests delay contract award and program commencement, and may result in program cancellation. In the Boeing/Air Force case, Congress approved replacement of the aging air refueling tanker fleet in 2001. A series of protests and the investigation into procurement corruption have delayed replacement of the air refueling tanker fleet to the extent that as of early 2010 the contractor for this program has yet to be selected.

6.5.2 Exposure to Procurement Corruption

Failure to obtain full and open competition exposes the government to opportunities for procurement fraud. The U.S. Central Intelligence Agency (CIA) is not exempt from ethical lapses leading to imprisonment and ruined careers involving noncompetitive contracts. A former high-ranking CIA official who was the CIA's executive director, Kyle "Dusty" Foggo, was given a thirty-seven-month prison sentence for steering a contract to a contractor who was a close friend.[3] Prosecutors claimed that Mr. Foggo received tens of thousands of dollars in gifts and vacations in return for helping the contractor obtain sole source contracts, meals at exclusive restaurants, and a job offer following his retirement. Other reports of the sentencing of Mr. Foggo indicated that prosecutors claimed that Mr. Foggo also attempted to have the CIA hire his mistress for a high-paying position for which she was not qualified. In *quid pro quo* political corruption cases, a favored method for rewarding contractors or consultants is the award of a sole source contract. Government entities can avoid such exposure to procurement corruption by requiring all contracts to proceed through all the phases of the contracting cycle described in Chapter 2.

6.5.3 Added Work and Expense to Evaluate Proposals and Delayed Contract Awards

Failure to construct RFPs according to the recommendations in this book is likely to result in contractors proposing their standard contract format and dissimilar proposals that are not readily evaluated according to proposal evaluation criteria. Review and approval of contracts based on the agency's standard contract format is a well understood process because the contract provisions were developed with input from those involved in the contract review and approval process. The proposal to use a contractor's standard contract format necessitates added time to review and comment on the unfamiliar provisions and time to negotiate changes to provisions that favor the contractor over the agency. Following the recommendations in this book for planning and constructing the RFP helps avoid protests, which require considerable time and expense to investigate and make a determination. The resultant protests also result in additional time and expense for government.

6.5.4 Fewer Contracts Awarded through Full and Open Competition

In addition to the greater exposure to opportunities for procurement corruption, sole source and limited competition lead to higher contract prices, lower quality, and less timely deliveries. Higher contract prices are one obvious result of limited competition. The lower quality of contractor-provided products and services and less timely service and product delivery are not as apparent. However, government representatives who have experience administering contracts often observe a pattern of declining quality and timeliness of deliveries from contractors that have their contracts continually renewed on a sole source basis.

6.5.5 Consequences for Government Contractors That Use Poorly Structured RFPs

Although the risk of protests regarding subcontracting is not so significant for government contractors as the risk of protests regarding contracting actions by government, prospective contractors that recognize a poorly structured RFP and perceive an unfair subcontractor selection process are likely to be reluctant to undertake the task of preparing a proposal. Such reluctance to prepare proposals limits the level of competition and may eliminate the possibility of awarding a subcontract to the best qualified provider for the required products or services. Just as with government, failure to obtain full and open competition in subcontracting subjects government contractors to added exposure to the possibility of procurement corruption. The fact that procurement corruption occurs at the subcontracting level does not diminish the severity of the crime. Federal contractors that suspect fraud in their subcontracting program are required to notify the government, according to FAR 52.203-7, Anti-Kickback, and FAR 52.203-13, Contractor Code of Business Ethics and Conduct. Federal contractors are required to display hotline posters for their employees to report contract fraud to the government per FAR 52.203-24, Display of Hotline Poster. FAR clause 52.203-7 is required to flow down to subcontracts exceeding $100,000. FAR clauses 52.203-13 and 52.203-14 are required to flow down to subcontracts exceeding $5,000,000. Dissimilar proposals from prospective subcontractors are likely for government contractors that fail to specify the format for proposals. Dissimilar proposals contribute to difficulty in evaluating proposals and in correlating proposals with the evaluation criteria.

6.6 Promises of Well-Managed Pre-Proposal Communications

The contracting cycle phase, beginning with the release of the RFP through the date when proposals are received by the contracting agency, is a particularly critical period of time. Uncontrolled communications between the prospective contractors and the agency during this time period can result in opportunities for procurement fraud and in protests from competing contractors. Protests are frequently based on contractors' perception of unequal treatment afforded contractors by government representatives. The discussion in Section 6.5 addressed the negative impacts, including the need for added government effort to investigate the merits of protests, expenses associated with the added effort, and the possibility of reimbursing contractors for their costs associated with filing and pursuing protests. The discussion in Section 6.5 also addressed costs associated with the need to terminate inappropriately awarded contracts, and delays in the award of contracts and program commencement. Alternative methods for managing pre-proposal communications include conducting a pre-proposal conference; questions posed verbally; questions posed via letter, overnight courier, and e-mail; submitting questions via e-mail; and the agency posting questions and responses to the website. The merits and weaknesses of the various alternatives for managing pre-proposal communications discussed above are compared below, and one approach is recommended.

6.6.1 Pre-Proposal Conference

Pre-proposal conferences appear to be an excellent tool for ensuring that all prospective contractors hear the same questions and responses from the contracting agency. The contracting agency, however, may wish to avoid holding a pre-proposal conference because such a conference affords the prospective contractors the opportunity to evaluate the competitive environment. Prospective contractors may be reluctant to pose questions regarding the proprietary elements of their proposals in a forum attended by their competitors. Conducting a pre-proposal conference does not guarantee that no questions are posed following the conference. Additional questions that are subject to communications management can be expected subsequent to the pre-proposal conference. Therefore, pre-proposal conferences are not recommended for managing pre-proposal communications.

6.6.2 Questions Posed Verbally

To maintain equal treatment of contractors, questions posed by telephone or during a contractor visit necessitate the transcription of the questions and agency responses for transmittal to all prospective contractors. Although this could be a burdensome task, there is also a risk that the formal questions are followed up by informal questions that are helpful to the prospective contractor but seemingly unimportant to the government employee who responded to the questions. In the event that the questions did not seem important to the agency employee, he or she may fail to advise the other contractors of those questions and the agency responses. One-on-one meetings between government and prospective contractor representatives during this sensitive period of the contracting cycle also provide an unwelcomed opportunity for violating the agency's ethics standards. Inviting or permitting prospective contractors to pose questions via telephone or during contractor visits is discouraged.

Discussions between prospective contractors and government representatives are common occurrences in procurement corruption cases. In one such case, Diana

Bakir Demilta pleaded guilty to one count of wire fraud in connection with a scheme involving insider information she received regarding a contract about to be awarded for 540 bulletproof vests.[4] The vests were for the Civilian Police Assistance Training Team in Baghdad, Iraq. The government representative who collaborated with Ms. Demilta advised her via e-mail to obtain three bids for the vests. Demilta then sent an e-mail to a Kuwaiti firm instructing the owner to prepare three bids. One bid was to be inflated by 60% of the retail price and another was to be inflated by 80%. The lowest bid was from the Kuwaiti firm. Demilta arranged for delivery of the vests and collected payment of $202,500 in cash. Court documents indicated that the DoD paid $70,000 excess due to the scheme.

6.6.3 Letter, Overnight Courier, and E-Mail

Questions submitted via letter, overnight courier, or e-mail and answered by one of the same methods provide an excellent paper trail, and all are superior to the earlier alternatives: a pre-proposal conference, receipt of questions via telephone, or questions posed during contractor visits. The superiority of written questions is based on the ability to guard against overlooking seemingly minor questions or making errors transcribing the questions. However, questions submitted via letter result in unacceptable delays, whereas questions submitted via overnight courier are more costly than warranted by the slightly shorter delay. E-mailed questions from prospective contractors and e-mailed responses from the contracting agency comprise the preferred choice among the alternative methods for submitting written questions and providing written responses. However, this is not the recommended method for handling pre-proposal communications.

6.6.4 Providing a Website for Posing Questions and Posting Agency Responses

Establishing a website, or use of an existing website, where all questions are posed by prospective contractors and answers are posted by the agency, does effectively manage pre-proposal communications. Employing this method does overcome the deficiencies of the methods discussed earlier. However, some agencies may not wish to implement a method that permits parties other than agency employees to enter information on its website.

6.6.5 Submitting Questions via E-Mail and Posting Questions and Responses to the Website

A process wherein prospective contractors submit questions to the agency via e-mail and the agency posts both the questions and responses to the website facilitates equal treatment of all prospective contractors. Because the agency posts both the questions and responses to the agency's website, it avoids the possibility of non-agency personnel posting information on the agency's website. This is the recommended method for managing pre-proposal communications.

The agency requires time to read the questions, prepare the responses, and post the questions and responses to the website in time for all prospective contractors to consider the agency responses prior to finalizing their proposals. Agencies normally establish a final date for submittal of questions to provide the agency with the time required to complete these actions.

6.7 Protest and Fraud Avoidance through Well-Managed Pre-Proposal Communications

Implementation of an effective pre-proposal communications management process facilitates equal treatment of prospective contractors, discourages protests, and minimizes opportunities for procurement fraud.

The primary objective of a pre-proposal communications management plan is to respond to legitimate questions in a timely manner while treating all prospective contractors equally. The numerous benefits forthcoming from full and open competition can be achieved only when this objective is met. Equal treatment of all competing contractors is not only fair to all prospective contractors and consistent with existing legislation and policy for most government contracting agencies, but it also facilitates selection of the contractor expected to provide the optimal combination of contract price, product or service quality, and timely availability of the product or service.

Treating contractors equally defeats one of the principal justifications for filing a protest. When equal treatment of all competitors is demonstrated to prospective contractors, previously unacceptable rates of protest filings are likely to decrease to an acceptable level. Government entities that legitimately discourage contractor protests are more likely to award contracts in a timely manner; have more resources available to provide essential services rather than react to protests; and realize increased financial resources by avoiding expenditures associated with investigating the merits of protests, terminating inappropriately awarded contracts, and reimbursing contractors for the costs of filing and pursuing protests.

The equal treatment of prospective contractors resulting from an effective pre-proposal communications management process also minimizes opportunities for procurement fraud. The existence of full and open competition combined with processes that promote equal treatment of prospective contractors maximizes the propensity for an honest contracting process. An honest contracting process results in the procurement of products and services minus the costs associated with the illegitimate enrichment of individuals and inflated contract costs.

6.8 Conclusion

Including the features recommended in this chapter for government RFPs avoids numerous preventable problems. Including provisions for requiring debriefings prior to filing a protest, managing pre-proposal communications, describing the method for evaluating proposals and the proposal evaluation criteria, specifying the format for proposals to simplify the proposal evaluation process, and measures to discourage corruption in the contractor selection process all contribute to treating prospective contractors equally, discouraging the filing of protests, and selecting the best qualified contractor. Implementation of the recommendation to include a model contract in the RFP with a statement indicating that the government intends to award a contract essentially in the form of the model contract also avoids a potential problem. An example of a potential problem is provided in a U.S. Department of Agriculture report from its Office of Inspector General.[5] The audit was conducted to evaluate the administration of the National School Lunch Program (NSLP) by the U.S. Department of Agriculture's (USDA) Food and Nutrition Service (FNS). FNS has written agreements with state agencies that administer the NSLP statewide. The state agencies provide program oversight by monitoring and assisting school food authorities (SFAs) that provide meals to children who meet certain requirements. The SFAs solicit management companies through RFPs for award contracts for operation of their nonprofit food service operations. One audit finding was that FNS had not provided any specific contract language or procedures for state agencies and SFAs to follow. In their responses to the RFPs, some management agencies inserted contract provisions that conflicted with federal regulations, thus allowing management companies to retain benefits intended for the SFAs. This finding demonstrates the efficacy of following the recommendation in this book for including a model contract in RFPs and a statement indicating that the government intends to award a contract essentially in the form of the model contract.

Notes

1. FoxNews.com, "Russian Firm That Paid $700G to Crooked U.N. Official Still on Approved Vendor List," George Russell and Claudia Rosett, March 15, 2007.
2. Reuters, "UN Strikes Russian, Italian Firms from Vendor List," James Pethokoukis, March 16, 2007.
3. *New York Times*, "Ex-C.I.A. Official Sentenced to Prison for Defrauding Government," David Johnston, February 26, 2009.
4. Federal News Radio, "Defense Contractor Pleads Guilty in Bribery Case," May 27, 2009.
5. "Food and Nutrition Service National School Lunch Program Food Service Management Companies," Report number 17601-0027-CH, U.S. Department of Agriculture, Office of Inspector General, Midwest Region, April 2002.

Chapter 7

Proposal Evaluation

7.1 Process for Selecting the Best Contractor

7.1.1 Background

Previous chapters discussed the characteristics, described the potential promises, and cautioned the readers about ineffective versus effective implementation of advance contract planning, ethical contracting, competition, social contracting, development of a request for proposals (RFP), and management of pre-proposal communications. A truly effective evaluation process is contingent upon effective implementation of the earlier processes in the contracting cycle, which are intended to result in a well-planned RFP to solicit proposals from qualified contractors in a full and open competitive environment.

A well-structured RFP requires contractors to submit proposals in a standard format that is correlated with the proposal evaluation criteria to simplify the evaluation of proposals in accordance with the criteria stated in the RFP. Finally, communications between the prospective contractors are managed to promote equal treatment of all companies competing for the contract. Competent implementation of the recommendations for proceeding through the earlier phases of the contracting cycle facilitates an effective proposal evaluation process and helps protect the government against the perils listed in Table 1.1.

A proposal evaluation team is customarily assembled to evaluate the proposals received in response to the government's RFP. The minimum number of government representatives recommended for assignment to a proposal evaluation team is two, and that recommendation is contingent on the expectation that competition for the contract is not contentious and the resultant contract is relatively low priced. High-value contracts for complex procurements may have a hundred or more proposal evaluation team members. Team membership for evaluating proposals for complex procurements likely consists of evaluators with expertise matching the various disciplines required to complete the contractor's work. Those disciplines might include manufacturing; electronic, mechanical, chemical, or aeronautical engineering; quality assurance; subcontracting; or other disciplines applicable to the scope of work. Additionally, the government may assign cost and pricing analysts to review the contractors' proposed pricing or life cycle costs. The reference to life cycle costs does not imply that the agency intends to award a cost reimbursement contract. As recommended in Chapter 6, cost reimbursement contracts are not recommended because greater contract risks are assumed by the government when awarding them.

Written guidance and training covering the agency's proposal evaluation policies is recommended for proposal evaluation team members. This combination minimizes the possibility of misunderstandings and errors by team members. Recommended evaluation team guidelines include the evaluation of proposals in strict conformance with the agency's policies and procedures and with the evaluation criteria described in the RFP. A confidentiality statement, signed by each evaluation team member, committing each team member to comply with the agency's proposal evaluation practices and confidentiality policy is also recommended. The act of signing a confidentiality statement reinforces the team members' comprehension of the need to maintain confidentiality. Confidentiality statements are more pertinent when they include a certification that the proposal evaluation team member has no financial relationship that can be affected by the selection of any of the prospective contractors.

The requirements for proposal evaluation team members to be trained, to be provided with guidance for evaluating proposals, and to sign a confidentiality statement are consistent with the provisions of the UN's *Compendium of International Legal Instruments on Corruption*, which includes the establishment of procurement systems that include provisions, including, "Where appropriate, measures to regulate matters regarding personnel responsible for procurement, such as declaration of interest in particular public procurement, screening procedures and training requirements."

Added topics recommended for inclusion in the written guidance for proposal evaluation team members includes team member responsibilities and tasks, a definition of and procedures for protecting proprietary or trade secret information, avoidance of undue influence from certain members of the proposal evaluation team, the application of independent versus consensus evaluations or the combination of independent and consensus evaluations, rules for conducting negotiations, the importance of meeting schedules, templates for evaluating proposals, the need to protect the confidentiality of all proposals until the contract is awarded or recommended for award, procedures for responding to requests for debriefings, and responding to potential or actual protests.

Virtually all government entities are prohibited from accepting bids that are not delivered by the due date indicated in the invitation for bids (IFB). However, most government entities are not prohibited from accepting late proposals in response to an RFP. The provisions of IFBs normally indicate that late bids are rejected. For a more comprehensive description of IFBs and RFPs, readers are referred to Section 6.1.1 and Table 6.1. The provisions of RFPs normally indicate either that late proposals are accepted if such acceptance is in the best interests of the agency, or that late proposals are rejected. If the agency's practice is to reject late proposals, all proposals received after the closing date and time indicated in the RFP must be rejected. However, exceptions may be made if a proposal was delivered to the correct address on time, but through mishandling by government personnel, it was not delivered on time to the government official designated to receive proposals.

Prior to conducting a detailed evaluation of the proposals, agencies are likely to determine whether the contractors that submitted proposals are responsible. Responsibility is defined by the contracting agency and may consist of considerations such as a reasonable expectation that the contractor has the management, technical, financial, equipment, and human resources available to ensure adequate performance of the work described in the solicitation; previous compliance with ethical contracting and environmental laws; and successful completion of previous contracts as measured by evaluating the particulars of contracts that were terminated for default in the past several years.

Although environmental protection is a commendable activity, contractors involved in environmental operations are not inherently responsible or immune from criminal activities. Government officials in New Orleans, Louisiana, blamed Veolia Environmental[1] and another French firm for repeatedly discharging sewage into the Mississippi River. The president of a subsidiary of Veolia was convicted of bribing a New Orleans, Louisiana, member of the sewer board to gain his support in the renewal of its contract.

The definition of responsibility may also exclude companies that have been debarred or suspended, or convicted of certain offenses within certain specified time periods. Debarred refers to contractors that have been excluded from government contracting and government-approved subcontracting, usually for unethical or criminal acts, for a specified time period. Suspended refers to contractors that have been proposed for debarment, debarred, excluded, or otherwise disqualified from government contracting and government-approved subcontracting. It may also be possible in a cursory review to determine whether the proposals are responsive to the requirements outlined in the RFP. However, in certain cases the failure to be responsive cannot be determined until the proposals are comprehensively evaluated. When it is determined that a contractor could make changes to its proposal that render it responsive, government entities normally initiate discussions with the contractor to effect those modifications.

A government contracting maxim establishes the need for a contractor to be responsible and for the proposal to be responsive as prerequisites for award of a contract. Proposals from contractors that are not responsible are subject to summary rejection. Negotiations are normally conducted, however, to initiate contractor changes needed to make proposals responsive.

Prior to proceeding to the description of the recommended proposal evaluation process, it is important to differentiate between proposals prepared by contractors in response to an RFP and bids prepared in response to an IFB. This chapter is dedicated to the evaluation solely of proposals in response to an RFP. Bids in response to an IFB, resulting in the award of a contract to the responsible contractor that submitted the lowest priced responsive bid, are not included in the following discussion on the evaluation of proposals.

Selection criteria for evaluating proposals typically include price, or life cycle cost, and other factors. Depending on the complexity of the work to be performed by the contractor, criteria for evaluating proposals can be numerous and complex or relatively simple. The source selection team evaluating proposals for a large systems contract likely consists of teams assigned to evaluate one or a group of related evaluation criteria. A large number of such teams, whose scores are combined with the scores of other teams to calculate a combined score for each of the competing contractors, is a typical approach for large systems contracts. The proposal evaluation process is relatively complex in comparison to the evaluation of bids in response to an IFB. Price or life cycle costs, and occasionally technical criteria, are normally the only criteria that can be measured objectively. All other criteria are relatively subjective. This complexity and subjectivity with respect to the evaluation of proposals in response to an RFP make the contractor selection process more susceptible to protests than for bids in response to an IFB.

Protests that are sustained, following the investigation of their merits, are often viewed as a poor reflection of the competency or honesty of the government contracting agency. In recognition of the complexity involved in the evaluation of proposals and the detrimental effects of sustained protests, the material in this chapter is concentrated primarily on selecting the best contractor, but also relies on an approach to evaluating proposals that instills confidence in the proposal evaluation team and minimizes the probability of protests filed by aggrieved contractors. Elements of the recommended approach include selecting a method for the proposal evaluation team members to score the proposals, ensuring that proposals are evaluated solely according to the criteria stated in the RFP, evaluating proposals with weighted evaluation criteria, and including guidelines for conducting negotiations.

An example of a sustained protest involving evaluation of proposals using criteria that differed from that indicated in the solicitation is provided in the matter of Sikorsky Aircraft Company and Lockheed Martin Systems Integration-Owego (LMSI), which protested the Air Force's award of a contract to The Boeing Company for the Combat Search and Rescue Replacement Vehicle (CSAR-X). The Government Accountability Office (GAO) sustained the protest,[2] where the solicitation for the CSAR-X provided for calculation of cost/price data on the basis of most probable life cycle cost, to include both contract costs and operations and support costs. The solicitation required information from the prospective contractors, quantifying the maintenance required for their proposed CSAR-X. However, the agency normalized maintenance cost when calculating operations and support costs, thereby disregarding the low maintenance effort claimed for the competing CSAR-Xs. The protest was sustained because agencies are required to adhere to the proposal evaluation criteria disclosed in the solicitation.

As mentioned in Chapter 4, certain recommendations for curbing corruption are necessarily technical in nature. Opportunities for procurement fraud during the proposal evaluation process are abundant. The evaluation of proposals, especially for high-value or technical projects, involves technical processes for evaluating the proposals according to the criteria established by the contracting agency. The following recommended proposal evaluation processes involve technical calculations. Alternative proposal evaluation techniques may be as technical or essentially as technical as the recommended approach; however, alternative processes may be prone to failure through deficient design or failure to limit opportunities for procurement fraud. The processes recommended here, however, are designed to inhibit technical deficiencies and procurement fraud opportunities while permitting the government to select the superior contractor from the field of competitors.

Proposal evaluation teams for medium to large programs routinely spend hundreds or thousands of hours evaluating proposals from competing contractors. When there are numerous proposal evaluation team members, the proposal evaluation effort represents a significant cost. The results of the proposal evaluation effort are normally documented by the head of the proposal evaluation team and presented to the person designated to select the contractor to be awarded the contract. The person designated to select the successful contractor is referred to as the source selection authority (SSA). Because the proposals are normally evaluated on the basis of price, or life cycle cost, and other factors, the SSA is oftentimes presented with two or more numbers reflecting the evaluation for each proposal. When those numbers appear contradictory, as in the Table 7.1 example, the enormous amount of time and expense attributed to the evaluation of the proposals was futile. If the SSA selects one contractor for award of a contract based on the seemingly contradictory information shown in Table 7.1, there is a fairly high probability that a protest will be filed by one of the unsuccessful contractors.

Table 7.1 Conflicting Information Provided to Source Selection Authority

		Contractors		
Criteria	Weight	A	B	C
Technical	25	85	83	79
Management	20	86	80	88
Past performance	20	81	80	82
Life cycle cost ($ billions)	35	$9.2	$9.4	$9.0

Table 7.2   Nonconflicting Single Score Provided to Source Selection Authority

Criteria	Weight	Contractors		
		A	B	C
Technical	25	21.3	20.8	19.8
Management	20	17.2	16.0	17.6
Past performance	20	20.3	16.0	16.4
Life cycle cost ($ billions)	35	34.2	33.5	35.0
TOTALS		93.0	86.3	88.8

The SSA presented with the information provided in Table 7.1 faces a difficult choice. If Contractor A is not selected, that contractor could argue that it had the highest technical score and the second highest score for all the other criteria. If Contractor B is not selected, that contractor does not have credible arguments. However, if Contractor C is not selected, that contractor could argue that it proposed the lowest life cycle cost (which is assigned the highest weight) and also has the highest scores for management and past performance. Had the scoring process provided the SSA with a single score for each contractor, incorporating a life cycle cost score that reflected the weight of that criterion with a high number being favorable, the decision by the SSA would be greatly simplified and the unsuccessful contractors would have little basis for filing a protest. The process recommended in this book yields just such a single score for each contractor, to be presented to the SSA. The recommended proposal process results in information as illustrated in Table 7.2 for the SSA's consideration.

The example in Table 7.2 provides the SSA with comparative scores reflecting the efforts of the proposal evaluation team, incorporating the criteria rating selected by the agency, and recommending contract award to Contractor A based on receipt of the highest rated proposal as reflected in the "TOTALS" row in Table 7.2. The example presented in this chapter describes the technique and provides formulas for calculating the single total score for each contractor, reflecting the results of the proposal evaluation team and weighting of all the criteria including the weighting for price or life cycle cost.

As an illustration of the presentation of proposal evaluation results that do not include a single total score clearly identifying the contractor recommended for award of the contract, Table 7.3 reflects the actual proposal evaluation results provided in a GAO report. Although the price was deleted for two of the three proposals, it is presumed that this deletion was restricted to the GAO report, and that the SSA was provided with the proposed prices for all three proposals. Although government RFPs often reflect a weight for price or life cycle cost, the results of the

Table 7.3 Actual Proposal Evaluation Results Provided in GAO Report

Factor	IAP[a]	AFM[b]	Offeror C[c]
Technical			
Relevant experience	Excellent	Excellent	Very good
Technical approach/methods	Excellent	Excellent	Satisfactory
Management	Excellent	Very good	Satisfactory
Safety	Excellent	Excellent	Satisfactory
Small business subcontracting	Very good	Very good	Very good
Overall	Excellent	Excellent	Excellent
Past performance	Excellent	Very good	Marginal
Price	$186,673,244	$[DELETED]	$[DELETED]

[a] IAP World Services, Inc. of Cape Canaveral, FL
[b] Academy Facilities Management of Gardena, CA
[c] Offeror C's proposal was the lowest-priced proposal received and was considered in the agency's price/technical tradeoff.

From GAO report "Academy Facilities Management — Advisory Opinion," File B-401094.3, May 21, 2009.

proposal evaluation team regularly fail to reflect the weighted score for price or life cycle cost. The proposal evaluation technique recommended in this chapter, unlike the actual proposal evaluation results in Table 7.3, results in weighted ratings for all objective and subjective criteria. The recommended technique also combines all the weighted criteria scores to obtain one overall total score representing the relative ranking of all the competing contractors and clearly indicating, as reflected in Table 7.2, the contractor with the highest total score.

7.1.2 Proposal Scoring Method for Subjective Criteria

Selecting the proposal scoring method for proposal evaluation team members may seem a commonplace decision. However, there are distinct advantages and disadvantages to the alternatives in this seemingly straightforward task. Selecting a scoring method with inherent weaknesses can jeopardize the validity of the agency's proposal evaluation and contractor selection effort. Methods employed by government entities for scoring the subjective criteria include assignment of numerical scores based on predetermined scales, assignment of specific adjectives describing the acceptability of the contractors' proposals, use of color codes to evaluate the contractors' proposals, and the ranking or forced distribution technique. A discussion of the advantages and disadvantages of each of these scoring methods follows.

The recommended process for scoring objective criteria, such as price or life cycle cost, is described in Section 7.2.

7.1.2.1 Predetermined Numerical Scales

One popular method for scoring proposals is by rating individual criterion on a scale of 1 to 10 or 1 to 100. Such predetermined numerical scales have likely been used by team members in other applications and are easily understood. One disadvantage of this scoring method is that the final result is prone to achieving identical or nearly identical final scores for all the proposals or for the highest-rated proposals. Tied scores, or nearly tied scores, negate the results of considerable time and effort expended by proposal evaluation team members. A more questionable characteristic of predetermined numerical scales, however, is that one evaluator's score can negate the score of two or more other evaluators. This unfortunate result may occur if one or more evaluators spread their ratings over the full range of available scores while other evaluators use only the upper range of available scores. Limiting scores to the upper range is common. This practice minimizes the difference between the score assigned to the highest-rated proposal and the score assigned to the lowest-rated proposal. The tendency to spread scores over the entire range of available scores is not as widespread. The differences in spreading scores may result from one person's tendency to compress the scores closely while other evaluators tend to innocently disperse their scores over a wide range. However, it is also possible that an individual evaluator spreads his or her scores over the entire range of available scores to benefit a favored contractor for unethical purposes. Table 7.4 illustrates the possible undue influence of one evaluator over two other evaluators.

As illustrated in Table 7.4, Evaluator MacIntyre used the entire range of numbers from 1 through 10, whereas Evaluators Washington and Rodriguez restricted their ratings to 7 through 10. Proposal C has the highest total score despite the fact that both Washington and Rodriguez assigned higher scores to Proposal B. This undue influence exercised by Evaluator MacIntyre may have resulted from his or her

Table 7.4 Assignment of Scores Based on a Scale of 1 to 10 Permits Undue Influence by One Proposal Evaluation Team Member

Evaluator	Proposal A	Proposal B	Proposal C
MacIntyre	1	4	10
Washington	9	10	7
Rodriguez	7	10	9
TOTALS	17	24	26

Table 7.5 Assignment of Scores Based on Adjectives for Proposal Evaluation Fails to Identify the Successful Contractor

Evaluator	Proposal A	Proposal B	Proposal C
MacIntyre	Average	Good	Good
Washington	Good	Good	Good
Rodriguez	Average	Good	Good
COMBINED	Average+	Good	Good

natural tendency to spread scores throughout the entire available range, or it may have been an intentional effort to favor the contractor that submitted Proposal C.

7.1.2.2 Specific Adjective Scales

Specific adjective scores such as "good," "average," and "poor" are used by other government entities. As with specific numerical scores, an adjective scoring system is simple to use. Another attribute shared with numerical scores, however, is the fact they also are subject to a high probability of tied scores. Highly qualified contractors are likely to receive the highest rating of "good," thereby resulting in tied scores. Specific adjective scoring is not recommended for selecting the successful contractor; however, adjective scores are practical for initial scoring to select finalists from a large number of proposals. The tendency to obtain tied scores with a specific adjective scale, when evaluating proposals from well-qualified companies, is illustrated in Table 7.5. Additionally, as with predetermined numerical scales, certain evaluators are prone to restricting their ratings to average and good whereas others use the entire range of ratings from poor through good. In this event, the evaluators using the entire range of available ratings exert greater influence on the final overall evaluation.

7.1.2.3 Color Coding Scales

Color codes for scoring proposals are also popular with government entities. An example of a color coding scale is the assignment of blue for good proposals, yellow for average proposals, and red for poor proposals. Color codes have the same advantages and disadvantages as specific adjective scales. Professionally prepared proposals from well-qualified contractors are also highly susceptible to tied scores. Just as with the adjective rating system, however, color coding scales may be used to narrow a large number of proposals to the select few finalists that are subsequently evaluated by a more discriminating scoring method. The tendency to obtain tied scores with a color coding scale, when evaluating proposals from well-qualified

Table 7.6 **Assignment of Scores Based on Color Codes for Proposal Evaluation Fails to Identify the Successful Contractor**

Evaluator	Proposal A	Proposal B	Proposal C
MacIntyre	Yellow	Green	Green
Washington	Green	Green	Green
Rodriguez	Yellow	Green	Green
TOTALS	Yellow+	Green	Green

companies, is illustrated in Table 7.6. The problem of undue influence by evaluators who use the entire range of available color codes over those evaluators who restrict their ratings to the upper end of the color scale is another characteristic of color coding scales.

An example of a problem associated with color-coded proposal evaluations is provided in a Department of Defense Office of Inspector General (DoD/OIG) audit. Based on a request from the Office of Undersecretary of Defense for Acquisition, Technology and Logistics, the DoD/OIG performed an audit of the source selection process for an Air Force program.[3] One audit finding relating to problems associated with color ratings is quoted here:

> Evaluation Reporting. AFFARS 5315, Part 5315.304, Air Force Informational Guidance 5315.305, "Proposal Evaluation," July 6, 2000, states that the Proposal Analysis Report narrative assessment of the offerors' proposal evaluations must be precise. However, the CMIS Phase II Proposal Analysis Report and SSAC Addendum to the Proposal Analysis Report included undefined and inconsistently applied color ratings. These types of errors could lead to evaluation interpretation problems and mislead the SSA when making source selection decisions.

7.1.2.4 Narrative Description

The addition of a narrative description associated with each of the scores used in predetermined numerical scales, adjective schemes, and color schemes tends to lessen the possibility of realizing inordinate influence by one evaluator on the total score. The assignment of narrative descriptions to the various scoring methods discussed above is illustrated in Table 7.7.

The detrimental aspects of numerical, adjective, and color scoring methods may also be lessened through extensive training in the assignment of ratings. Holding a consensus meeting following the individual rating sessions also helps ensure that

Table 7.7 Example of Narrative Descriptions

Narrative Description	Numerical	Adjective	Color
Far exceeds all minimum requirements	10	Excellent	Green
Meets minimum requirements and exceeds some	8	Very good	Blue
Meets minimum requirements	5	Good	Yellow
Meets most requirements but fails to meet some	3	Poor	Amber
Fails to meet all or most requirements	1	Inferior	Red

the evaluators are consistent in the assignment of their ratings. These measures, however, may not prevent inordinate influence over the combined ratings by a proposal evaluation team member, influenced by unethical motives, who wishes to intentionally exert more influence than other proposal evaluation team members.

7.1.2.5 Ranking Method

The ranking method has several advantages over other scoring techniques. The possibility of obtaining tied scores is greatly reduced through the forced distribution of scores achieved through the ranking technique. Additionally, one evaluator is prevented from exerting undue influence over the final result because all evaluation team members are required to use the entire range of scores. The ranking method can be difficult to use when there are a large number of proposals. The evaluation of two through five proposals is the preferred range of proposals when using the ranking method. Difficulty in ranking proposals increases proportionally with the number of proposals. When there are a large number of proposals, there is also a greater probability of tied scores. There is an approach to garner the ranking method benefits despite the existence of a large number of proposals to be evaluated. The adjective or color code techniques can be used initially to narrow the field down to two, three, four, or five finalists that are subsequently evaluated by the ranking method. Preventing one team member from exerting undue influence with the ranking method is illustrated in Table 7.8. Team members Washington and Rodriguez have again rated Proposal B the highest whereas evaluator MacIntyre continues to evaluate Proposal C the highest. The use of the full range of scores required with the ranking technique resulted in Proposal B receiving the highest overall total score despite MacIntyre's continued rating of Proposal C as the superior proposal.

Table 7.8 Ranked Scores Prevent Undue Influence by One Evaluator

Evaluator	Proposal A	Proposal B	Proposal C
MacIntyre	1	2	3
Washington	2	3	1
Rodriguez	1	3	2
TOTALS	4	8	6

Note: Assigning scores by ranked proposals is more likely to identify the success-ful contractor and prevents undue influence by one proposal selection team member. In this example, high numbers are assigned as scores for the highest ranked proposals.

The best practices RFP provided on the CD includes advice to prospective contractors that a color scheme is used to reduce a large number of proposals down to five or fewer finalists. The RFP also includes advice to prospective contractors that finalists are evaluated through a ranking process. The recommended proposal scoring method is to use an adjective or color coding scheme to select five or fewer finalists if there are more than five proposals to evaluate. If there are five or fewer proposals to evaluate, or if the field has been narrowed to five or fewer by one of the other scoring techniques, the ranking method is recommended for scoring the subjective criteria.

7.2 Optimizing Contractor Selection with Weighted Proposal Evaluation Criteria

The best practices RFP reflects the use of weighted criteria, as shown in Table 7.9. Weighting the criteria permits government entities to assign more importance to the criteria that are considered most significant for their project. In this example, the agency determined that life cycle cost carries twice the importance of environmental considerations and risk assessment. Disclosing the proposal evaluation criteria and the weighting in the RFP is recommended to fully inform prospective contractors of the agency's proposal evaluation methodology.

With the exception of life cycle cost, all the criteria reflected in Table 7.9 are relatively subjective. In addition to assigning more importance to the more significant criteria, weighted criteria also introduce a greater level of objectivity to subjective criteria. The use of weighted proposal evaluation criteria is recommended for high-value projects and/or for projects wherein the industry is highly competitive or comprised of contentious contractors that are prone to filing a protest when they are not selected for contract award.

Table 7.9 Addition to the RFP Advising Prospective Contractors of the Use of Weighted Criteria[a] in the Proposal Evaluation Process

Criterion	Weight
Past performance	10
Environmental considerations	20
Risk assessment	20
Project plan	5
Outsourcing	5
Life cycle cost	40
TOTAL WEIGHT	100

[a] Weighted criteria: The government has elected to assign weights to the above evaluation criteria. The weights assigned to each of the criteria are indicated in the second column.

Evaluating proposals using weighted criteria can be complex. Therefore, an example of such an evaluation is provided on the CD. Several templates are used in the example to facilitate the evaluation of proposals when weighted criteria have been selected. The templates are also provided on the CD for use by government entities.

7.2.1 Ensuring That Proposals Are Evaluated Solely by Criteria in the RFP

The discussion in the previous section on the evaluation of proposals with weighted criteria included the recommendation to include the proposal evaluation criteria and weighting thereof in the RFP. This recommendation is consistent with ethical contracting practices because it serves to deter the practice of creating criteria or weighting of criteria to correspond to the proposal received from the favored company. This section explains the importance of establishing ground rules for the evaluation team, evaluating proposals solely on the basis of the evaluation criteria in the solicitation, and ensuring that all the evaluation criteria are considered during the proposal evaluation process. Strict adherence to these principles is essential to ensure that prospective contractors are treated equally and fairly, and to minimize the possibility of providing grounds for protests from unsuccessful contractors.

One helpful tool to ensure that all members of the selection team evaluate proposals solely on the criteria in the RFP is a template for scoring the proposals that includes the criteria. An example of such a form is included on the CD that accompanies this book. The proposal evaluation template on the CD includes a column where the exact criteria contained in the "Best Practices Request for Proposals (RFP)" are repeated on the evaluation form. The template also contains a reminder to members of the proposal evaluation team that proposals must be evaluated strictly according to the criteria in the RFP. In the event that the evaluation criteria in the best practices RFP are modified for the actual RFP that is released, it is essential that the proposal evaluation template is modified identically. If not, it is almost certain that proposals will be evaluated using incorrect criteria, the agency will be subject to selecting the incorrect contractor, and the agency will also be subject to the filing of a protest from one or more of the unsuccessful contractors.

An additional protest that was sustained because the agency did not evaluate the proposals according to the criteria in the solicitation is provided in the matter of L-3 Communications Titan Corporation (L-3), which protested the U.S. Army's award of an indefinite delivery indefinite quantity (IDIQ) contract with a not-to-exceed value of $4.65 billion for providing interpretation and translation services for the U.S. armed forces in Iraq.[4] The protest was sustained because the proposal evaluation record failed to reasonably support the agency's determination that the protester's proposed [undisclosed number of] linguists had a higher probability for failing to meet the agency's need to fill 7,217 linguist positions than the awardee's proposed [undisclosed number of] linguists. A second basis for sustaining the protest was the determination that where the "solicitation established specific evaluation benchmarks for evaluation of offerors' experience, and provided for comparative assessments against those benchmarks, an agency may not substitute previously unidentified 'threshold of sufficiency' as an evaluation benchmark against which proposals are evaluated on a pass/fail basis." A third basis for sustaining the protest was not intelligible due to the information that had been redacted from the GAO report.

The proposal evaluation template does not include a space for entering an overall score or spaces for scores assigned to individual criterion. An informal scoring method recorded in an informal format, such as the proposal evaluation form, rather than the more formal proposal evaluation example that is also on the CD, may be entirely acceptable for evaluating straightforward proposals, especially if the contract is for a relatively low value. Formal scoring methods may prove attractive to government entities that award relatively high-value contracts in a highly competitive environment wherein a greater level of sophistication is desired in the selection process. This greater level of sophistication in the proposal evaluation process is also appropriate where contentious competition exists and where there is a greater propensity for protests from aggrieved contractors.

7.2.2 Conducting Negotiations

One of several differences between proposals in response to an RFP and bids in response to an IFB is that proposals are negotiable whereas bids are not negotiable. The selection of contractors submitting proposals in response to RFPs is normally based on price, or life cycle costs, and other factors, as opposed to bids in response to an IFB wherein the lowest price is accepted if the bid is responsive and received from a responsible contractor. Proposal features that may be negotiated include price, delivery, contract provisions, and any other element of the proposal. Detailed information on conducting negotiations is provided on the CD in the "Guidelines for Conducting Negotiations" file.

Numerous recommendations made to this point in this book were intended, at least partially, to avoid protests from aggrieved contractors and to minimize opportunities for unethical behavior. Chapter 3 included recommendations for training agency employees on reporting instances of unethical behavior. Implementation of these recommendations likely minimizes the number of protests received and agency exposure to unethical behavior. However, despite the agency's best efforts to discourage protests, it is likely that not all protests can be prevented. Therefore, the following section includes recommendations for reacting to those protests that were not prevented.

7.3 Effective Reaction to Protests from Aggrieved Contractors

Upon receipt of a protest from an aggrieved contractor, the contracting agency is required to evaluate the merits of the protest and make a determination. Protests that are not filed within the established time period are normally summarily rejected. The recommended actions to take in evaluating the merits of a protest and in making a determination regarding the merits of the protest are: read the protest, notify legal counsel, read the solicitation and initiate the drafting of questions for members of the proposal evaluation team members, read the proposal evaluation team instructions, review the agency's protest policy and procedures and the proposal evaluation record, finalize the questions for the proposal evaluation team members, interview the proposal evaluation team members, synthesize the information, and make the determination.

7.3.1 Read the Protest

The recommended first step upon receipt of a protest from an aggrieved contractor is to carefully read the protest and note all the aggrieved contractor's objections to the contractor selection process or award of the contract. It is expected that the agency official responsible for processing protests investigates the complaints and issues a determination within the agency's standard timeline. A thorough understanding of the extent of the protest is necessary to ensure that the agency's investigation and determination include all applicable issues raised by the contractor. The agency official is normally permitted to contact the aggrieved contractor to clarify any issues that are not entirely understood. Otherwise, the agency's official investigator may make a faulty assumption regarding the nature of the protest.

Written communications, including e-mail, are recommended to establish a paper trail of communications between the agency and the contractor. If there are no options but to contact the contractor by telephone or in person, meticulous documentation of the verbal communications is recommended. A determination that is not favorable to the contractor may result in an appeal or eventually in litigation. In either event, the documentation of verbal communications helps protect the agency's interests. During the thorough reading of the protest, the official investigating the merits of the protest to make a determination is advised to begin drafting questions that need to be answered during subsequent investigative activities. The information obtained during proposal evaluation team member interviews is usually central to the investigation of the facts surrounding the agency's proposal evaluation process. This early start in drafting questions to be posed to members of the proposal evaluation team assists the agency official in conducting meaningful interviews later.

7.3.2 Notify Legal Counsel

Protests may eventually result in litigation. Therefore, advising legal counsel of the receipt of a protest soon after receipt is highly recommended. Legal counsel is normally able to provide valuable advice for reacting to the protest even if the protest is never litigated.

7.3.3 Read the Solicitation

A careful reading of the solicitation provides the agency official with the direction given prospective contractors by the agency. Documentation of all instances where the contractor or the agency did or did not conform to the requirements in the solicitation is also relevant to the investigation. The questions for proposal evaluation team members that were drafted during the previous step may be expanded during this activity. As more facts are discovered during the investigation into the merits of the protest, the questions to be posed to the proposal evaluation team members may be expanded and refined. The availability of a well-considered set of questions assists the responsible official in conducting more meaningful interviews. The agency representative may discover answers to questions drafted while reading the protest, or it may be discovered, at some point, that the earlier questions may require revision or expansion.

7.3.4 Read the Proposal Evaluation Team Instructions

If the proposal evaluation team was provided with written instructions for evaluating proposals, a comparison of the facts determined to that point and the team instructions will likely reveal any inconsistencies pertinent to the investigation. Anomalies between any of the documents reviewed to this point either support or counter the aggrieved contractor's contentions. Further refinement of the questions for proposal evaluation team members is appropriate at this point.

7.3.5 Review the Protest Policy and Procedures

Reviewing the protest policy and procedures is necessary to determine if the source selection process described in the solicitation and instructions provided to the proposal evaluation team members was consistent with the agency's protest policies and procedures.

7.3.6 Review the Proposal Evaluation Record

A review of the completed proposal evaluation forms and any other proposal evaluation team records determine whether the team members complied with the source selection process described in the solicitation, evaluated the proposals according to the criteria in the solicitation, properly applied weighted proposal evaluation criteria (if applicable), used the proper technique for measuring objective data such as the life cycle cost or price, complied with instructions given to team members, and conformed with agency policy and procedures. During this review it is possible to refine the questions that were prepared earlier and draft additional questions for the proposal evaluation team members.

7.3.7 Finalize Questions for Proposal Evaluation Team Members

The questions drafted at every step of the investigation may be edited and organized at this time to place them in a logical sequence for the proposal evaluation team member interviews.

7.3.8 Interview Proposal Evaluation Team Members

Although the review of documents to this point provides the individual investigating the merits of the protest with considerable insight into the proposal evaluation team activities, the interviews invariably provide the best insight into the team's activities. New facts are likely to be discovered while interviewing team members. Personal interviews are valuable because the interviewer gains an opportunity to observe each team member's attitude toward the proposal evaluation effort and get a feel for each team member's determination to select the best contractor. The objective of the interviews is to evaluate the activities of the team members during the proposal evaluation process and their compliance with the ground rules established in the solicitation, instructions given to team members, and agency policy and procedures. Astute interviewers are alert to any indication that proposal evaluation team members may have acted in opposition to the agency's ethical standards during the proposal evaluation process. Although the review of source selection documentation provides meaningful insight into the propriety of the team's activities, the interviews are often the best indicators of the mindset of the team members and the level of their objectivity and sincerity in selecting the best contractor to provide the needed products or services.

7.3.9 Synthesize the Information and Make the Determination

At this point in the process, all the required information has been gathered and the agency official conducting the investigation can synthesize the knowledge she or he acquired through reading the protest, solicitation, and instructions provided to proposal evaluation team members; reviewing the agency's policies and procedures governing protests as well as the records developed by the proposal evaluation team members during the source selection process; and reviewing the results of the proposal evaluation team member interviews. Once this information is synthesized, the official evaluating the protest is prepared to form an opinion with respect to the merits of the protest and to make a determination on the propriety of the proposal evaluation team's decision. The official conducting the investigation might consider the possibility that favoritism was afforded the apparent successful contractor. It is unlikely that procurement fraud was involved in the proposal evaluation process; however, that possibility cannot be dismissed. Reaching a fair and logical determination is essential because the appearance of a determination biased in the agency's favor could unnecessarily lead to an appeal to a higher authority within the agency or litigation to resolve the matter through the court system.

The discovery of errors committed by the proposal evaluation team need not nullify the propriety of the team's decision; for example, if it was determined that the proposal evaluation criteria was taken from a standard template when, in fact, the criteria in the standard RFP template had been modified to suit the project. An error of this nature does not automatically result in a reversal of the contractor selection decision, require termination of the contract award, or require repetition of the solicitation and proposal evaluation process. If it is recognized that the proposal evaluation team would have reached the same conclusion if the error had not been committed, it is appropriate to determine that the award was proper and the contract will remain in place despite certain inconsequential errors.

If the investigation reveals that the proposal evaluation team committed a serious error or errors, but it is not clear that the incorrect contractor was selected, there is a solution that falls short of canceling the solicitation and calling for a new RFP to be sent to all contractors on the original list of solicited contractors. The solution is to request both the originally selected contractor and the aggrieved contractor to submit a best and final offer (BAFO) or a revised proposal. Other responsible contractors that submitted responsive proposals, however, cannot be excluded from the continuing competition. All competitive contractors are normally requested to submit a BAFO or a revised proposal to comply with full and open competition requirements and to ensure that all prospective contractors are treated equally. Documenting agency files with the rationale for not requesting BAFOs or revised proposals from any company that submitted a proposal is highly recommended. Failure to document the exclusion of contractors that submitted a proposal but were not subsequently offered an opportunity to submit a BAFO or a revised proposal may result in yet another protest. The request for BAFOs or revised proposals may include a revision to the original RFP instructions. For example, although the original solicitation may not have specified a structured evaluation procedure or weighted criteria, local procedures may permit refinement of the selection process for evaluating BAFOs or revised proposals to introduce a more structured evaluation process and possibly the use of weighted criteria. If the decision is made to modify the evaluation process, contractors being requested to submit BAFOs or revised proposals need to be advised of the revised evaluation procedures and ground rules.

A protest filed by Global Analytic Information Technology Services, Inc. (GAITS) was sustained[5] because the U.S. Department of Agriculture engaged in discussions solely with the awardee, allowing the awardee to provide the required price escalation rate following the conclusion of its oral presentation despite the agency's instructions to provide such pricing information at the outset of the oral presentations. A second reason for sustaining the protest was the agency's downgrading of GAITS's proposal for failing to include methods for achieving cost or time savings even though this criteria was not listed as a basis for proposal evaluation.

7.3.10 Document the Determination

The final step is to document the determination of the legitimacy of the source selection decision. Memorializing the facts leading to the determination regarding the merits of the protest is essential to preparation of a response to the aggrieved contractor. A memorandum to the record memorializing the legitimacy of the source selection decision plus a letter to the aggrieved contractor constitutes formal documentation. However, in many cases, a file copy of the letter to the aggrieved contractor suffices as the documentation.

Investigation into the legitimacy of the source selection team results usually leads to a determination that the team did follow agency procedures, complied with agency ethics standards, and made the proper source selection decision. The company that expended the time, effort, and expense to prepare a proposal and to follow through with considerable added effort to protest the contractor selection, however, is deserving of a comprehensive written response to their protest. The response to the protesting company is normally in a letter signed by the public agency official making the determination to deny the protest. The letter advising the protesting company of the determination customarily includes details of the fact-finding effort that led to the public official's determination. The letter to the contractor should include instructions for appealing the agency's determination to avoid having an appeal directed to the incorrect official or the aggrieved contractor proceeding directly to litigation. Instructions for filing an appeal customarily include the name and address of the official designated to receive the appeal, the deadline for filing the appeal, and the timeline for the agency's response.

An agency determination that the contractor was selected improperly requires an entirely different course of action. Under these circumstances, the agency has the following alternatives:

■ Terminate the contract and award it to the appropriate company.

■ Request a BAFO or a revised proposal from all the responsible contractors that submitted responsive proposals or proposals that are likely to be made responsive through negotiations. In this event, consideration may be given to providing more structure and objectivity to the source selection process for evaluation of the BAFOs or revised proposals.

■ Cancel the solicitation and release a revised solicitation. Just as with the request for BAFOs or revised proposals, consideration may be given to incorporating greater structure and objectivity into the source selection process for evaluating the new proposals.

Reversal of the source selection decision is required when evaluation of the protest, solicitation, proposal evaluation team instructions, agency policies and procedures, record of the source selection process, and interview of proposal evaluation team members clearly leads to the determination that award of the contract to the aggrieved contractor would be in the government's best interest. If the contract was awarded erroneously, it becomes necessary to review the termination clause in the improperly awarded contract to determine the process and timeline for terminating it.

The first necessary step is to notify the contractor originally awarded the contract. If the determination to reverse the contractor selection decision is made prior to award of the contract to the contractor originally selected, a letter to that contractor normally suffices. Due to the adverse nature of reversing the contractor selection, however, the agency might consider a telephone call alerting the contractor of this unwelcome news before the letter is received. Notification should include full disclosure of the facts leading to the reversal of the selection decision. Such disclosure is the best approach for discouraging yet another protest.

7.4 Overcoming the Perils of a Deficient Proposal Evaluation Process

The recommended method for scoring subjective criteria is the ranking method. As discussed earlier, however, the ranking method tends to be unwieldy when there are more than five proposals to evaluate. Although the adjective and color coding scoring methods are not recommended for making the final contractor selection, either one of these methods are adequate for narrowing a large field of proposals to five or fewer finalists.

The use of weighted proposal evaluation criteria is also recommended because weighting criteria permits government entities to assign more importance to the criteria that are considered most significant for their project. The steps required to evaluate proposals by the ranking method with weighted proposal evaluation criteria are described below. An example of a proposal evaluation using the ranking method of scoring proposals and weighted criteria is included on the CD that accompanies this book.

Proposal evaluation teams may be organized such that all team members evaluate the proposals with respect to all the criteria. This approach is appropriate for relatively low-value contracts that require teams of only two or three members. High-value contracts may have hundreds or even thousands of criteria and a large number of proposal evaluation team members. In this event, two or more evaluation team members are normally assigned to a relatively low number of the criteria. For example, two or three team members may be assigned responsibility to evaluate three or four criteria. Other than the number of team members involved and the number of criteria evaluated, the proposal evaluation process is similar regardless of the contract value. To keep this discussion and the example on the CD workable, the following assumptions are made: there are three proposals, three evaluators, and five criteria, and all the team members evaluate all five criteria.

The objective of the proposal evaluation is to carefully review all the proposals to select the contractor that best meets the criteria and provides the optimal combination of life cycle cost (or price) and the other criteria stated in the RFP. Implementing measures guarding against unethical behavior is imperative to ensure unbiased results from proposal evaluation team members. The end result of the evaluation is the development of single scores for each criterion and a single total score for each proposal. In this case, high scores are more favorable; therefore, the contractor with the highest total weighted score presented in the format provided in Table 7.10 is selected or recommended for contract award. The assignment of scores with the ranking method at the criteria level, when high scores are favorable, results in the proposal with the best rating for each criterion receiving a score that is equal to the number of proposals being considered. The score for the proposal with the next best rated criterion is equal to the number of proposals being considered minus one, and it continues in the same manner to the lowest ranked criterion, which receives a score of 1. If there are three proposals, the proposal with the highest score for each criterion receives a score of 3, the proposal with the second highest score for each criterion receives a score of 2, and the proposal with the lowest ranked criterion receives a score of 1.

A lesser variance between scores may be achieved by assigning a 10 to the best proposal, 9 to the second best proposal, and continuing through 6 for the fifth best proposal, as applicable. The formula to weight the scores work regardless of the scoring method selected. The scoring method should be determined prior to completion of the solicitation to permit its description in the RFP. Use of formats,

Table 7.10 Format for Combined Weighted Scores by All Three Evaluators for All Three Proposals

Combined Weighted Scores Criteria	Proposal A	Proposal B	Proposal C
Past performance			
Environmental considerations			
Risk assessment			
Project plan			
Outsourcing			
Weighted life cycle cost			
TOTAL WEIGHTED SCORES			

such as shown in Table 7.10, that require proposal evaluation team members to score proposals according to the proposal evaluation criteria stated in the RFP is highly recommended to avoid the filing of protests on the basis that the agency evaluated the proposals on criteria that were not specified in the RFP.

Preparing combined weighted scores, for insertion in the Table 7.10 format, begins with proposal scoring sheets prepared by each individual team member. It is not necessary to consider the weighting of criteria until later in the proposal evaluation process. The evaluators record their ranking of each proposal at the criterion level. In this example, with three proposals and three members of the evaluation team, there are three such rating sheets. One rating sheet containing scores for all three proposals is completed by each evaluation team member. The example on the CD includes formats for the various rating sheets used throughout the proposal evaluation process. The scores for the individual team members are then combined on a single form to reflect the combined scores.

All the criteria in this example, with the exception of life cycle cost, are subjective and can be scored by the ranking method. Life cycle cost, however, is represented as a dollar figure. Because monetary values are objective, they cannot be scored by the ranking method. For example, consider the case where there are three proposals with proposed life cycle costs of $1,000,000, $1,200,000, and $2,000,000. To assign scores of 3, 2, and 1, respectively, is not representative of the dollar amounts proposed. In this example, the life cycle cost of $2,000,000 is twice the value of the proposed life cycle cost of $1,000,000, yet the score of 3 is three times the value of the score for $1,000,000. Scores of 3, 2, and 1 are representative for proposed life cycle costs of $1,000,000, $2,000,000, and $3,000,000.

As mentioned earlier in this section, high scores are considered favorable in this discussion. Ranking techniques may use either low scores or high scores to represent the highest ranked proposals. The one caveat is that if low numbers are assigned to the best subjective criteria, then low scores are assigned to the lowest life cycle cost (or lowest price). Likewise, if high numbers are assigned to the best subjective criteria, then high numbers are assigned to the lowest life cycle cost. Representing the lowest cost as a high number and weighting that number to reflect the relative importance of life cycle cost appears to be a challenging task. However, there are two relatively simple calculations required for converting the low life cycle cost to a weighted score where high numbers are favorable. The calculations are described below.

The formulas for converting life cycle cost include weighting of the life cycle cost criterion. The formula for converting proposed life cycle cost to the weighted score where high scores are favorable is

Weighted Score = Lowest Proposed Amount/(Proposed Price/Criterion Weight)

The formula for converting proposed life cycle cost to the weighted score where low scores are favorable is

Weighted Score = Highest Proposed Amount/(Proposed Price/Criterion Weight)

In addition to the use of objective scoring for the weighted life cycle cost, all the evaluators use the same score because all of the evaluation team members have access to the proposed life cycle cost from each of the finalists. Certain agencies may elect to have the life cycle cost (or price) evaluated separately by a different team or individual. The life cycle cost proposed by each of the three finalists is illustrated in Table 7.11.

Calculation of the weighted life cycle cost when high scores are favorable is accomplished as follows:

- Enter the contractor name (or proposal identifier if the contractor names are not revealed to the evaluation team members) in Column A.
- Enter the proposed life cycle cost for each contractor in Column B.

Table 7.11   Calculation of Weighted Life Cycle Cost when High Scores Are Favorable

A	B	C	D
Proposal	Proposed Life Cycle Cost	Proposed LCC/Criterion Weight	Weighted Score = Lowest Proposed Amount/(Proposed LCC/Criterion Weight)
A	5,000,000	125,000	32.0
B	4,000,000	100,000	40.0
C	4,500,000	112,500	35.6

- Calculate the value for Column C by dividing the proposed life cycle cost (LCC) in Column B by the weight assigned to life cycle cost (40), as indicated in Table 7.9.
- The weighted score for the lowest life cycle cost proposal is equal to the weight assigned to life cycle cost (40). To calculate the weighted score for the higher life cycle cost proposals, divide the lowest proposed price ($4,000,000) by the value in Column C.

Table 7.12 Calculation of Weighted Scores for Factors Other than Life Cycle Cost

Weighted Factor Scoring Table			
Weight	Ranking	Multiplier	Weighted Score
5	3	1.67	5.0
5	2	1.67	3.3
5	1	1.67	1.7
10	3	3.33	10.0
10	2	3.33	6.7
10	1	3.33	3.3
20	3	6.67	20.0
20	2	6.67	13.3
20	1	6.67	6.7

The weighting of scores for all criteria other than life cycle cost can be simplified by preparing a matrix as shown in Table 7.12. In keeping with the previous assumptions, the example incorporates the assumption that there are three proposals. Therefore, three possible rankings of 3, 2, and 1 represent the score assigned to the proposals by each of the evaluators. The highest ranked proposal for each factor is assigned a score of 3 and the lowest ranked proposal is assigned a score of 1. There are also three possible weights (the life cycle cost is excluded from this calculation) for each factor. Knowledge of the number of proposals, thus the possible rankings, and the weights, other than life cycle cost, is all the information required to complete the information shown in Table 7.12.

Calculation of weighted scores for factors other than life cycle cost is accomplished as follows:

- Enter the possible weights (other than for life cycle cost) in the weight column while ensuring that the number of rows for each weight equals the number of proposals. In this example there are a total of nine rows. There are three rows (representing the three proposals) for the weight of 5, three rows for the weight of 10, and three rows for the weight of 20.

- The rankings are merely the possible rankings of 3, 2, and 1 resulting from the evaluation of three proposals. These rankings are repeated for each weight.
- The multiplier is calculated by dividing the weight by the highest possible ranking. In this example, the weight of 5 is divided by the ranking of 3 to calculate the multiplier of 1.67. The multiplier of 1.67 is used for all rankings with the corresponding weight of 5. The remaining multipliers are calculated in the same manner, resulting in a multiplier of 3.33 (calculated by dividing 10 by 3) and a multiplier of 6.67 (calculated by dividing 20 by 3).
- The weighted score is calculated by multiplying the ranking by the multiplier.

After the proposal evaluation team has ranked the proposals, calculated the weighted scores for life cycle cost, and completed the table to apply weights to the other criteria, it is prepared to apply weights to the ranking scores. The final result can be displayed in the format shown in Table 7.10. The contractor receiving the highest total weighted score is awarded the contract or recommended for award of the contract. Readers who wish to have more details on the calculations and additional forms used in the proposal evaluation process are invited to review the material on the CD that accompanies this book. Selection of the contractor with the highest combined weighted score is consistent with the agency's intent to select the best qualified contractor, absent unethical bias, based on submittal of a responsive proposal from a responsible contractor that best meets the agency's needs with respect to the evaluation criteria stated in the solicitation.

Although government contractors do not face the same risks from protests as do government entities, the proposal evaluation process recommended for government is also recommended for government contractors when they evaluate proposals from prospective subcontractors. The best practices research project that identified the best practices described in this book revealed both best practices and problematic practices. One troubling proposal evaluation practice revealed during the project involved the identification of weighted criteria that did not include price or life cycle costs. However, it was clear that price was a consideration. Although government contractors were not invited to participate in the best practices research project, the predominance of deficient proposal evaluation techniques discovered during the best practices research is an indicator that deficient proposal evaluation techniques are possibly practiced by government contractors as well as government entities. Implementation of the proposal evaluation method recommended for government entities by government contractors results in one combined score for each proposal that identifies the highest scoring proposal.

7.5 Perils of Selecting a Marginal Contractor

A flawed proposal evaluation plan, or the failure to conform to a well-constructed proposal evaluation plan, can result in serious consequences, such as selecting a less than optimal contractor, undue influence exerted on contractor selection by one proposal evaluation team member, failure to evaluate proposals according to the proposal evaluation process or criteria in the RFP, or a protest from an aggrieved contractor.

When all of the contractors competing for a particular contract are well qualified to provide the services or products required by the government, selecting the less than optimal contractor may not result in serious consequences for the government's program. However, when there is a wide variance in the qualifications of the competing contractors, selecting a less than optimal contractor is likely to have disastrous results. The minimal impact from substandard contractor performance is likely a strain on the agency's contract administration resources. If the substandard contractor's performance cannot be improved, the original contract may need to be terminated and a replacement contract awarded to a better qualified contractor. Contract termination and award of a replacement contract requires considerable human resources and is likely to also result in termination costs. Truly disastrous results from selecting a less than optimal contractor include the possibility of the government's failure to provide essential services, complete failure or cancellation of a program, or the involvement of contractor and government representatives in procurement fraud.

Selection of a deficient proposal scoring technique may permit one or a few members of the proposal evaluation team to exert undue influence on contractor selection. When this is unintentional, a less than optimal contractor may be selected, leading to problematic, yet not disastrous, results as discussed above. However, when the undue influence is made intentionally, government and contractor personnel may be involved in procurement fraud.

Failure to evaluate proposals according to the proposal evaluation process or criteria in the RFP is likely to result in selection of the less than optimal proposal. One might believe intuitively that the failure to evaluate proposals according to the proposal evaluation process or criteria is attributed to human error; however, dishonest government representatives may intentionally diverge from the proposal evaluation process or criteria to select their favored contractor. The motive for steering the contract award to the favored contractor may be merely to work with a known contractor that is believed to be able to meet the contractual requirements. However, there is also the possibility that the dishonest government representative colluded with a contractor representative to steer the contract award in return for some monetary or other personal reward. As discussed in Chapter 3, procurement fraud can have truly disastrous implications for the government, the contractor, and particularly for the individuals participating in the fraudulent activities.

Table 7.13 Sustained Protests Results Summary

Reason for Sustaining Protests	Frequency
Cost reimbursement for filing and pursuing protest was recommended due to agency delay in responding to protest allegations.	2
Source selection documentation discussed strengths, but not weaknesses, of higher priced proposal that had just a slightly higher rating.	1
GAO recommends that agency reimburse full cost of filing and pursuing its protest despite the fact that there were both successful and unsuccessful issues included in the protest.	1
Although the GAO denied four of five issues in the protest, the protest was sustained. Evaluators did not know or could not remember if they considered the successful contractor's adverse past performance. The agency did not properly assess relevance of past contracts.	1
Protest was sustained because the agency's evaluation of proposals was flawed in that the proposals were not evaluated according to the terms of the solicitation.	1
Protest was sustained because the agency's adjustment to offeror's price and cost proposals had numerous errors that materially affected the evaluation. Recommendation for termination of contract for convenience, reevaluation of proposals and reimbursement of the protester for the costs of filing and pursuing the protest.	1

Protests are filed by aggrieved contractors either when they contest the provisions of the solicitation or when they contest the proposal evaluation results. Protests are frequently based on the contention that the proposal evaluation was not based on the criteria contained in the solicitation or that other processes described in the solicitation were not followed. The GAO evaluates the merits of protests filed against federal government agencies. Table 7.13 illustrates the GAO decisions that were posted on their website on June 18, 2008. In addition to sustaining protests for the government's failure to conform to its practices, in several cases the GAO recommended that the government reimburse the contractor for its costs to file and pursue the protest. Such costs can be significant, especially when the procurement is for a large systems contract, when the evaluation of the merits of the protests continued over an extended time period, or when the contractor employs the services of a legal team to file or pursue its protest.

The National Institutes of Health (NIH) issued an RFP to acquire comprehensive chemical and low-level radioactive waste management services for NIH's main campus that identified the evaluation criteria, in descending order of importance, as technical, cost/price, and past performance. Clean Harbors Environmental Services, Inc., protested the award of the resultant contract to Clean Venture, Inc., based on NIH's failure during the evaluation to attempt to assess the relevance of the offerors' prior contracts although the solicitation required such an assessment.[6] In sustaining the protest by Clean Harbors, the GAO found that the NIH's failure to consider the comparative relevance of the offerors' past performance might have affected its source selection decision. Both companies, in this case, did receive ratings for past performance. However, Clean Venture's rating was based on smaller, less complex contracts when compared to Clean Harbors' contracts. Additionally, the GAO found that other contracts referred to in the offers could have been evaluated but apparently were not considered in the source selection decision. The GAO, therefore, found that Clean Harbors was prejudiced by NIH's failure to evaluate the comparative relevance of the offerors' past performance.

In addition to the costs associated with protests, especially protests that are sustained, risks resulting from protests filed by aggrieved contractors include damage to the agency's reputation, decreased confidence in government officials and employees, added workload to address the protest, delay in project commencement, and in unusual cases cancellation of the project.

Damage to agency's reputation: Sustained protests are an indicator that the agency is improperly evaluating proposals and improperly selecting contractors for awarding contracts. Continuing damage to an agency's reputation from repeated protests that are sustained is likely to cause a loss in confidence in an agency's credibility and competence. The Air Force suffered a damaged reputation through a series of discredited source selection actions. Following years of repeated missteps by the Air Force in the air refueling tanker replacement, Reuters reported[7] the unusual decision to remove SSA from the Air Force for the air refueling tanker replacement program and assign it to the Department of Defense. Defense Undersecretary John Young was slated to become the SSA with responsibility for determining the winner in the competition between the Boeing Company and Northrop Grumman Corporation/European Aeronautics Defence and Space Company (Northrop/EADS). However, the Air Force was scheduled to reconstitute the source selection advisory committee that evaluates proposals.

Decreased confidence in government: The transfer of SSA from the Air Force for the air refueling tanker replacement program also serves as an example of decreased confidence in government officials. Although career damage, short of termination, is not readily apparent in such cases at the federal level, it becomes more pronounced at the state and local government levels, especially when elected officials are impacted. The recall of Governor Gray Davis, discussed in Chapter 3, likely resulted from decreased voter confidence, beginning with energy contracts negotiated in secret during the California energy crisis of 2002 and culminating in the disastrous Oracle contract.

The GAO evaluates federal government agency procurements that are protested by aggrieved unsuccessful contractors. A review of the flawed proposal evaluation methodologies that led to protests sustained by the GAO provides an opportunity to learn from others' mistakes. The results of GAO determinations, minus information redacted for national security considerations, are regularly updated on their website: www.gao.gov.

One of the more notable GAO sustained protests was the protest filed by Boeing regarding the $35 billion contract for the KC-X air refueling tankers for the Air Force. The GAO report[8] revealed that Boeing challenged the technical and cost evaluations, conduct of discussions, and source selection decision. The GAO concluded that significant errors possibly affected the outcome of the competition between Boeing and Northrop Grumman/EADS. The specific reasons for sustaining the protest are summarized from the GAO report:

1. The proposals were not evaluated in accordance with the evaluation criteria stated in the solicitation. Although the solicitation stated that consideration would be given to non-mandatory technical requirements, Boeing did not receive such consideration despite the fact that they exceeded more of these requirements than Northrop Grumman/EADS.
2. Although the solicitation stated that no consideration would be afforded proposals that exceeded objectives, Northrop Grumman/EADS did receive credit for exceeding a key air refueling objective.
3. The contracting agency informed Boeing that it fully satisfied an operational utility key performance parameter objective. It was determined later by the contracting agency that Boeing only partially met that objective, but Boeing was not advised of this later determination. Meanwhile, the contracting agency continued to discuss the satisfaction of this key performance parameter objective with Northrop Grumman/EADS.
4. Northrop Grumman/EADS was selected for the contract award despite their clear exception to the material requirement to plan and support the agency to achieve initial organic depot-level maintenance within two years after delivery of the first production aircraft.
5. During the investigation of the protest, the contracting agency conceded that it erred in evaluating the most probable life cycle costs and that once the errors were corrected, Boeing displaced Northrop Grumman/EADS as the contractor with the lowest life cycle cost.
6. The contracting agency improperly increased Boeing's estimated nonrecurring engineering costs when it found that their proposed cost was unreasonably low. The contracting agency also used a flawed simulation model to evaluate the percentage of cost growth.

The GAO report continues with the following recommendations for the contracting agency:

1. Reopen discussions with the offerors.
2. Obtain revised proposals.
3. Reevaluate the revised proposals.
4. Make a new source selection decision consistent with the GAO's decision.
5. Amend the solicitation prior to conducting further discussions with the contractors if the agency believes that the solicitation does not adequately state its needs.
6. Terminate the contract awarded to Northrop Grumman/EADS if the agency selects Boeing's proposal.
7. Reimburse Boeing the costs, including reasonable attorneys' fees, of filing and pursuing the protest.

The determinations by the GAO reflected in the aerial refueling tanker case and the cases noted in Table 7.13 may cause some constituents to doubt the government's impartiality and ability to effectively evaluate proposals and select the contractor offering the best value to the government. However, posting the GAO's apparently impartial evaluation of source selection proceedings by federal government agencies provides the public with considerable insight into procurement actions and instills trust in government and respect for the GAO. The GAO's website on June 18, 2008, when the air tanker decision was posted, reflected their determinations on additional cases. Table 7.13 provides a summary of other sustained protests on that date.

The findings reported in Table 7.13, as with the Boeing protest of the KC-X contract award to Northrop Grumman/EADS, prominently reflect the continuing problem of failure to evaluate proposals according to the criteria in the solicitation. Although evaluating proposals by criteria that do not exactly match the criteria in the solicitation is most likely due to inexperience or carelessness, prudent agencies are aware that such a failure may also be an indicator of possible unethical or criminal behavior. The findings in Table 7.13 also reinforce the problem of excess costs associated with a flawed proposal evaluation, resulting in the need for the government to reimburse contractors for filing and pursuing protests.

Government contractors with flawed proposal evaluation processes do not face the same risk of receiving protests as faced by government. However, failure to employ a well-designed proposal evaluation methodology can result in serious consequences, such as selecting a subcontractor that does not best meet the prime contractor's criteria for contract award. Selection of a lesser qualified contractor increases the risk of receiving unacceptable subcontracted products or services. Selection of a less than optimal contractor might be attributed to undue influence of one of the proposal evaluators or failure to evaluate proposals according to the criteria in the RFP. Because the objective of a source selection process is selection of the contractor proposing the optimal combination of price, performance, and time-liness, selection of a contractor that did not propose the optimal combination could easily result in payment of a higher than market price for poor-quality products or services that are delivered late.

7.6 Rewards of Selecting the Superior Contractor

The recommended proposal evaluation process described in Section 7.4 is not necessarily the singularly effective approach for designing an effective proposal evaluation process. However, implementing this recommended process max-imizes the probability of selecting the contractor or subcontractor that best meets the agency's or contractor's requirements. Realizing the benefits from implementing an effective proposal evaluation process is contingent on earlier actions in the contracting cycle with respect to ensuring that the proposals were solicited in a full and open competitive environment, the selected pro-posal evaluation criteria describe the attributes of a contractor that effectively meets the agency's needs, the weighting of the criteria represents the relative importance of the criteria for program success, the proposal evaluation team members have the requisite qualifications to evaluate the contractors' qualifica-tions with respect to the criteria, the proposal evaluation team members have committed themselves to honestly evaluate the proposals, and the evaluation team members have been trained to perform the proposal evaluation function according to the agency's policies and procedures. The benefits of implement-ing an effective proposal evaluation process include award of a contract to the contractor most likely to achieve program success, assurance to prospective contractors of an equitable proposal evaluation technique, fewer protests, and competitive pricing.

7.6.1 Contract Award to Best Qualified Contractor

Selection of the contractor that best meets the agency's requirements is essential to program success. Employing a proposal evaluation process providing for compari-son of proposals by knowledgeable personnel according to the evaluation criteria established by the agency maximizes the probability of selecting the contractor best qualified to provide the needed supplies or services. Weighted criteria provide greater emphasis on the contractor qualifications that are more significant for pro-gram success and less emphasis on qualifications that are less significant. A pro-posal scoring technique that ensures an equal voice for all proposal evaluation team members for each criterion further increases the probability for selecting the best qualified contractor. Selecting the best from a field of contractors competing in full and open competition maximizes the opportunity for program success.

7.6.2 Prospective Contractors Assured of Equitable Proposal Evaluation Technique

The ranking method for scoring proposals ensures that all proposal evaluation team members exert equal influence on the scoring of each criterion. This, in turn, contributes to selection of the best contractor while minimizing opportunities for collusion, thus providing greater assurance of selecting the contractor most likely to perform to the agency's expectations.

Weighted criteria emphasize the qualities of the contractors with the best qualifications for the functions that have the greatest importance to the agency. The ranking method for scoring proposals combined with criteria weighting introduces an element of objectivity into the evaluation of otherwise subjective criteria. The formula used to convert price or life cycle cost to a weighted score while maintaining the objective nature of dollar figures promotes equity in the proposal scoring and contractor selection process.

ProTech Corporation's protest of the award of a contract to Atherton Construction, Inc., for the construction of military family housing is provided as an example of a protest that was partially sustained because the agency weighted the evaluation criteria differently from the weighting described in the RFP.[9] The digest of the GAO's decision is quoted here:

> Selection of higher-rated, higher-priced proposal over lower-rated, lower-priced one was unreasonable, where the weight applied to the evaluation factors in the source selection decision differed from that announced in the solicitation.

7.6.3 Contract Awarded at a Competitive Price

In addition to ensuring prospective contractors that the agency uses an equitable measure for evaluating contractor pricing, the formula used to convert price or life cycle cost to a weighted score incorporates an entirely objective measure for evaluating life cycle costs or pricing to take full advantage of competition in contracting. The amount of emphasis on life cycle cost or pricing depends on the weight assigned to this criterion by the contracting agency. As a general rule, weighting of price or life cycle cost is greater for the purchase of products than for services, and the weighting of life cycle cost or price for professional services is less than the weighting for standard services.

7.6.4 Superior Subcontractor Selection Benefits Prime Contractors

Government contractors benefit through implementation of the proposal evaluation process recommended for government entities by obtaining a solitary score for each proposal that clearly identifies the subcontract proposal that best meets the prime contractor's criteria. Although the agencies participating in the best practices research project that failed to identify price or life cycle cost as a proposal evaluation criterion did not provide details on their proposal evaluation process, it appeared that they developed two separate numbers for each proposal. The two separate numbers are a weighted score based on their stated evaluation criteria and the price or life cycle cost as the second number. In the absence of a weight assigned to price or life cycle cost, there is no apparent methodology for obtaining a combined weighted score for price and other factors. The recommended proposal evaluation process results in a solitary score for each proposal that distinctly identifies the proposal receiving the best score based on the prime contractor's proposal evaluation criteria. Selection of the subcontractor that submitted the proposal that best met the prime contractor's criteria presents the greatest probability for a successful subcontracting effort.

7.7 Conclusion

Implementation of the recommendations for evaluating proposals provides the government with considerable assurance that contractors will be treated equally, certain proposal evaluators will not have greater influence on the selection process than other evaluators, and criteria will be afforded consideration proportional to its relevance to the government. The recommendations in the previous chapter for the RFP to include weighted proposal evaluation criteria, the method for scoring proposals, and procedures for requesting a debriefing and filing a protest provide assurance to prospective contractors that they will be treated equally and that their proposals will be evaluated equally. Implementation of the recommendation in this chapter to evaluate the proposals strictly according to the process and the criteria in the RFP is essential. The most frequent reason cited for sustaining protests is the government's failure to evaluate proposals as described in the RFP. For example, the GAO considered a protest filed by Helicopter Transport Services LLC (HTS) regarding the award of contracts to Erickson Air-Crane, Inc., and Columbia Helicopters, Inc., by the U.S. Forest Service, National Interagency Fire Center in Boise, Idaho, for fire support helicopter services. HTS alleged that the government improperly evaluated technical factors on a pass/fail basis, resulting in identical scores for each criterion even though the RFP indicated the criteria were listed in the order of their importance. The GAO concurred with that allegation[10] and sustained the protest. The GAO also concurred with HTS's allegation that their past performance was also evaluated improperly. The evaluation of criteria without giving greater weight to the criteria identified in the RFP as the more important conflicts with the recommendations in this book to ensure that proposals are evaluated according to the proposal evaluation procedures described in the RFP. Proposals that are sustained typically delay implementation of the program, increase costs, and damage the government's reputation. In sustaining HTS's protest, the GAO recommended that the helicopters subject to the improper proposal evaluation be awarded to the contractor whose proposal represents the best value to the government and that the HTS be reimbursed its costs, including reasonable attorneys' fees, for filing and pursuing its protest.

Notes

1. *Los Angeles Times*, "Misconduct Taints the Water in Some Privatized Systems" by Mike Hudson dated May 29, 2006.
2. The discussion of the Sikorsky Aircraft Company and Lockheed Martin Systems Integration-Owego protest is based on GAO File B-299145; B-299145.2; B-299145.3; February 26, 2007.
3. Department of Defense Office of Inspector General, "Source Selection for the National Polar-Orbiting Operational Environmental Satellite System — Conical Microwave Imager/Sounder," Audit report no. D-2006-097, July 10, 2006.
4. U.S. GAO, "L-3 Communications Titan Corporation," File number B-299319; B-299317.2; B-299317.3; March 29, 2007.
5. U.S. GAO, "Global Analytic Information Technology Services, Inc.," File number B-298840.2, February 6, 2007.
6. U.S. GAO, "Clean Harbors Environmental Services, Inc.," File number B-296176.2, December 9, 2005.
7. Reuters, Andrea Shalal-Esa, "U.S. Plans Expedited Rerun of Aerial Tanker Contest," July 8, 2008.
8. U.S. GAO, "Statement Regarding the Bid Protest Decision Resolving the Aerial Refueling Tanker Protest by The Boeing Company," Report number B-311344, June 18, 2008.
9. U.S. GAO, "ProTech Corporation," File number B-294818, December 30, 2004.
10. U.S. GAO, "Helicopter Transport Services LLC," File numbers B-400295 and B-400295.2, September 28, 2008.

Chapter 8

Contract Administration

We could find no evidence of any cost controls over the project from its inception. There is no indication of any report issued on a definitive, periodic basis, i.e., weekly or monthly, to the Executive Director, or to the House or Fiscal Committees of the Board of Commissioners. Because there was no breakdown of the budget into constituent elements, there was no way to compare costs as they occurred to the authorized elements for those costs. In other words, there was only a gross budget, and therefore, no possible way to affect adequate cost accounting during the course of the project.

Michigan Bar Journal
Report on Building Renovation Overruns
September 2001

8.1 Contract Administration Fundamentals

The preceding chapter on proposal evaluation represents that portion of the contracting cycle that ends with award of the contract or the recommendation for the governing board or chief elected official to sign the contract. The agency's responsibility with respect to contracts is abruptly altered upon award of the contract. At this stage of the contracting cycle, the contractor begins to perform according to their contractual responsibilities.

This portion of the contracting cycle is referred to as the contract administration phase. It represents the contract period of performance. If the advance contract planning team provided for the contract administration phase by specifying a contract budget breakout and contractor periodic reporting requirements throughout the period of performance, and if the agency followed through on these requirements by including these features in the solicitation and the contract, then the government is prepared to effectively perform the contract administration function.

The quotation from the *Michigan Bar Journal* at the beginning of this chapter represents a real life example of the failure to prepare for the contract administration function. Despite the government's successful efforts to select the contractor best qualified to provide the required materials or services, failure to effectively administer the contract and ensure the contractor's compliance with its provisions occasions vulnerability to program failure. Contract administration involves monitoring the contractor's performance during the period of performance to ensure that contractor obligations are met, the quality of the work product meets the contract requirements, schedules are adhered to, all conditions with respect to deliverables are met, and billings are accurate and timely.

Relatively low-value fixed-price contracts likely do not justify monitoring the contractor's spending rate in relation to the contractor's progress. A recommendation was made earlier in this book to avoid cost reimbursement contracts if at all possible; however, it is understood that in certain circumstances the agency may need to resort to cost reimbursement contracts. In the event that an agency awards a cost reimbursement contract, especially a relatively large-value contract, effective contract administration requires monitoring the contractor's progress and spending rate. Agencies may also consider closer monitoring of high-value fixed-price or level-of-effort contracts. Level of effort refers to a type of contract where the contractor is engaged to provide a number of hours of a specified service at contractual billing rates. Such contracts typically have a firm fixed price or not-to-exceed (NTE) price. Cost reimbursement, high-value, and level-of-effort contracts are candidates for cost/schedule performance monitoring, as described in Section 8.3. Government entities that award a contract subject to cost/schedule performance monitoring improve the agency's ability to manage the contract by structuring the scope of work to correspond to measurable work elements, breaking out the contract budget to correspond to the work elements in the scope of work, requiring the contractor to report on its progress at the same work element level, structuring invoices according to the work performed within the defined work elements, assigning an agency representative to monitor the contractor's progress, and verifying the contractor's report of work progress prior to invoice approval.

The fact that the contract has been awarded when the contract administration phase of the contracting cycle begins does not eliminate the potential for unethical or criminal behavior while the contractor is engaged in fulfilling its responsibilities. Reliance on just one government representative to monitor a contractor's performance provides an opportunity for collusion between the contractor and the representative. The potential for such collusion is lessened when the government assigns multiple representatives to the contract administration function.

Contract amendments are, necessarily, made after award of the contract and are also considered a contract administration function. Recommendations for amending contracts and a suggested format for contract amendments are provided in Section 8.4.

Contractors do not invariably encounter problems during the term of the contract; however, addressing these problems when they do occur is also a function of contract administration. Approaches for addressing underperforming contractors are provided in Section 8.6.

Computer software packages are available to assist government entities in performing the contract administration function. Contract administration or project management software is useful for monitoring the contractor's progress on work elements, milestones, deliverables, and costs incurred to accomplish the elements being measured. Computer software programs are readily available and are more efficient and less labor intensive than manually tracking contractor progress, schedules, deliverables, and costs. Relatively low-value fixed-price contracts are monitored with less formality. Standard spreadsheets provided with desktop or laptop computers likely suffice for managing future delivery dates for relatively low-value fixed-price contracts. If project management software is used by an agency to track high-value, complex, cost reimbursement contracts, it is appropriate to use that software for tracking all active contracts regardless of contract complexity or value. If computer software is used to track progress and spending on major contracts, the same computer software can be used to also track less complex contracts with the same efficiencies afforded large complex contracts. Managing both complex, high-value contracts as well as less complex contracts with the same computer software avoids the inconvenience of using separate tracking systems.

Contractor performance monitoring during the contract administration phase involves tracking the contractor's performance with respect to quality, cost, and schedule. Relying on computer software to monitor routine aspects of the contractor's schedule and costs frees the project manager, contract administrator, or other individual to concentrate on contractor quality. It is essential, however, to address detected schedule or cost variances before they can threaten project success. Although the importance of contractor quality justifies constant monitoring, unattended schedule or cost variances can be as damaging to program success as quality deficiencies. Delayed reaction to contractor performance deficiencies consistently results in considerable added workload to address problems that have worsened while being ignored.

There are also opportunities, during the contract administration phase, for government and contractor representatives to collude for illicit personal or company enrichment. One example of a government employee who was eventually discovered colluding with a contractor involves a former state school superintendent and her former deputy superintendent, who conspired with a computer consulting firm that fraudulently received more than $500,000 in federal funds.[1] The maximum amount the former superintendent was authorized to approve by her signature alone was $50,000. To avoid this limitation, she directed the issuance of eleven checks, in one day, in amounts just under her $50,000 limit. The products and services were not provided. Approximately half of the ill-gotten funds eventually reached the former superintendent's campaign fund and to third parties for campaign expenses.

8.2 Invoice Analysis for Avoiding Overpayments

Recommendations for dealing with the contract administration functions of contractor invoice approval and for monitoring deliverables and milestone completions are provided below.

Verification that there are no mathematical errors, including the extension of unit prices, is a basic task in the approval of contractor invoices. Verification of mathematical accuracy is important; however, considerably more verification is required prior to invoice approval. Variances between billing rates on invoices and billing rates in contracts are likely more common than one might assume. Such errors are predominately in the contractor's favor. When payments are based on the completion of milestones or percentage completion of milestones, complete reliance on the contractor's determination of completion is not recommended. Differences between the contractor's perception and the government's perception regarding milestone completion, or especially percentage completion, can be attributed to the subjective nature of milestone completion as well as the fact that contractors occasionally submit an invoice in advance of the milestone completion in anticipation of completing the milestone by the date that the invoice is approved. However, the contractor may be overly optimistic and not have completed all the work claimed by the date when the project manager reviews the invoice. Based on these observations, agency officials responsible for approving invoices based on milestone completions are urged to verify the completion or percentage completion prior to invoice approval.

Anomalies discovered during the invoice review process normally are resolved by requesting the contractor to cancel the invoice and submit a revised one. Although revised invoices are normally requested for significant errors, pen and ink correction of minor errors are permitted if acceptable to the contractor and if this practice is consistent with government policy.

When one government representative is responsible for approval of contractor payments, there is an opportunity for collusion between the government representative and the contractor. Therefore, agencies are advised to provide verification that payment approvals are legitimate.

8.3 A Process for Forecasting Contract Cost Overruns

Monitoring the contractor's performance with respect to its expenditure rate compared to its progress on contract tasks is appropriate for high-value or high-risk contracts. The decision to monitor the contractor's cost/schedule performance is best made early in the contracting cycle. The RFP and the contract should include provisions that require the contractor to supply periodic performance reports, financial information, and cost breakouts on invoices during the term of the contract to facilitate cost/schedule monitoring. Agencies that elect to perform cost/schedule performance monitoring normally require the contractor to report on the percentage completion of various tasks in the scope of work and invoice the agency based on actual expenditures for the same tasks. A template (Table 8.1) is provided for readers to estimate the contract costs at the time of project completion based on the cost/schedule data. Use of the template permits the agency to determine if the contractor is able to complete the project without experiencing an overrun that might threaten project success. Although considerable reliance is placed on the contractor's input with respect to its reporting of progress on milestones and expenditure rate, it is prudent to have agency personnel or consultants verify the contractor's reporting of task completion percentages.

If sufficient information is available on the invoice to compare the amount of contract funding available to the percentage of completed work, that comparison provides the agency valuable insight into the contractor's financial management. If the contractor is spending funds at a rate faster than the work is being completed, then the contracting agency is likely to be concerned that the contractor may be in danger of realizing a loss, in the event of a fixed-price or NTE contract, or an overrun, in the event of a cost reimbursement contract. In either event, the detection of a spend rate in excess of the contractor's work progress requires discussions with the contractor to ensure that financial considerations do not interfere with successful contract completion.

Cost overrun occurs when the contractor expends funds in excess of the original target cost in the absence of a change in the scope of work. Target cost is the cost associated with a cost reimbursement contract that the contracting agency and contractor agree to as the expected cost for completion of the work described in the scope of work. This cost is normally determined through cost analysis and subsequent negotiation of the cost proposal submitted by the contractor. Underrun of cost is the exact opposite of overrun of cost. Cost growth occurs when a change in scope results in an amendment to the contract that increases the target cost and fee. Such a change in scope agreed to by both parties to the contract is considered cost growth rather than cost overrun. By contrast, an overrun occurs when the contractor expends funds in excess of the target cost without an associated change in scope.

Change in scope occurs when the work to be performed by the contractor is modified from the original scope of work by agreement of the parties to the contract. The details of the change in scope, and possibly associated changes to the price or schedule, are normally negotiated by the contracting parties and formalized through a written contract amendment.

Recognition of the impact on cost and schedule from scope changes is likely to be determined first by project managers. In an article on large complex project estimating, published in Chile,[2] the authors recommended the development of a "scope change form" and a procedure to encourage project team members to document the impact on cost and schedule for scope changes and scope creep. The information in such a form is relevant to agency personnel responsible for negotiating and effecting the resultant contract amendment.

Agencies may wish to perform in-depth analyses of the expenditure rate and schedule performance for high-value contracts to determine if the contractor is expected to complete the contract work without exceeding the NTE price or experiencing an overrun. To ensure that the agency is able to perform a sophisticated analysis of the contractor's cost/schedule performance, consideration is given, when the contract is first drafted, to making information needed for such an analysis available by including payment provisions and contractor reporting requirements that provide sufficient information to compare the percent of contract completion to the contractor's expenditure rate. Although the agency might consider the evaluation of this information at the total contract price level, schedule performance at this level is difficult to verify and it does not isolate the specific tasks where a problematic expenditure rate is occurring. Ideally, when the agency has a vested interest in monitoring the contractor's expenditure rate, the contract cost and invoices are broken out for analysis at the individual task level. When the agency structures the contract such that it knows the estimated costs for each task and the contractor is required to invoice at the task level, it is possible to require the contractor to report on the percentage of completion for each of the priced tasks and compare that percentage to the percentage of funds expended. This comparison can then be used to forecast the funds required for completing the tasks and the funds required to complete the entire contract. The resultant forecast of funds required to complete the contract tasks can be compared with the funds budgeted for that task to determine whether the spend rate is favorable or unfavorable. A tool and a formula for making an estimate of expenditures at completion at both the task level and the contract level are presented in Table 8.1.

Government entities that elect to award cost reimbursement contracts are urged to monitor cost and schedule performance for their cost-type contracts. Agencies are able to determine in advance if the contractor is likely to experience a cost overrun. The accuracy of the prediction improves as contract completion nears. Agencies might consider tracking cost and schedule performance on level-of-effort contracts when they are for high-value contracts or for challenging projects, or if they were placed with contractors lacking excellent financial strength. Agencies may also consider monitoring cost and schedule performance for contractors with certain fixed price contracts. Just as with the approval of contractor invoices, monitoring cost and schedule performance by a solitary government representative provides an opportunity for collusion between that government representative and the contractor. Therefore, government entities may prefer to have more than one individual involved

Table 8.1   Estimate at Completion

	Contractor:		Contract Number:		Project:	
Task	Contract Price	Total Invoiced	Percent Invoiced	Percent Complete	Estimate to Complete	
A	$500,000	$250,000	50	50	$500,000	
B	$2,000,000	$1,500,000	75	80	$1,875,000	
C	$3,000,000	$2,000,000	67	65	$3,076,923	
D	$6,000,000	$5,000,000	83	70	$7,142,857	
E	$2,000,000	$1,000,000	50	50	$2,000,000	
F	$500,000	$300,000	60	60	$500,000	
Total project	$14,000,000	$10,050,000	72	67	$15,000,000	

Instructions for calculation of estimate at completion:

1. The "Task" column is completed by listing the separately priced tasks in the scope of work, with the "Total project" at the bottom of this column.
2. The "Contract Price" column is completed by listing the price for each task in the scope of work followed by the total contract price.
3. The "Total Invoiced" column is completed by listing the cumulative amount invoiced for each task in the scope of work followed by the total amount invoiced for the entire contract.
4. The "Percent Invoiced" column is completed by listing the percent of the cumulative amount invoiced for each task in the scope of work followed by the cumulative amount invoiced for the entire contract.
5. The "Percent Complete" column is completed by listing the contractor-supplied (and agency-verified) percentage of completion for each task in the scope of work followed by the percentage of completion for the entire contract.
6. The "Estimate to Complete" is calculated by dividing the "Total Invoiced" by "Percent Complete" and multiplying by 100.

in tracking the contractor's cost/schedule performance or to have the cost/schedule performance verified by another government representative.

It is not normally possible to track cost/schedule performance on fixed-price contracts unless the agency is making progress payments and requires the contractor to deliver progress reports. However, it is not usually necessary to track costs on fixed-price contracts. Exceptions to this rule are made if the contractor is suspected of lacking the financial resources to continue performance on the contract if it experiences a cost overrun. Contractors with fixed-price contracts risk financial loss in the event of an overrun. If a contractor lacks the financial strength to sustain the cost of a significant overrun, there is a risk that the contract work will not be completed either because the contractor goes out of business or the contractor abandons the contract work. All but financially strong contractors will face great difficulty when they incur $11 million in costs on an $8 million fixed-price contract. Contractors experiencing such a loss may need to consider the alternatives of going out of business or abandoning the project. Agencies wishing to avoid being surprised by a similar situation may elect to track cost and schedule performance despite having a fixed-price contract.

The ideal time for an agency to decide on cost/schedule performance monitoring is prior to release of the RFP. The model contract will include the requirement for the successful contractor to structure their invoices and periodic progress reports according to tasks defined by the government. The progress reports, when verified by the agency, enable cost/schedule monitoring. When the decision to track cost/schedule performance is made prior to release of the solicitation, the RFP can include instructions for the contractors to break out their pricing at the task level, prepare invoices at that same task level, and provide periodic reports on their schedule performance at the task level.

The estimate at completion in Table 8.1 is computed at the task level by dividing the invoiced price by the percent of completion and then multiplying the result by 100. Once the calculations are completed for each task, the estimates to complete each task are added to obtain the estimate to complete the entire contract. One benefit of making this calculation at the task level is that it identifies the task or tasks where the problem or problems exist. When the problem is narrowed to the specific problem tasks prior to contract completion, it is possible to address those tasks to determine possible corrective actions. The formula is based on the assumption that the contractor's spend rate continues in relationship to its progress from the date of the analysis through task completion. For example, the formula assumes that if $750,000 was invoiced to complete 75% of a particular task, the remaining 25% of the task will be invoiced at the same spending rate, or for an additional $250,000. The estimate at completion for this task, therefore, is $1,000,000. This estimate at completion is favorable for a task budgeted at $1,000,000 or more. However, the estimate is unfavorable for a task budgeted below $1,000,000.

A template for the "Estimate at Completion" form is provided on the CD that accompanies this book for agencies that wish to adopt this tool that estimates final contract costs. The accuracy of the estimate at completion, however, is dependent on the accuracy of the contractor's estimate of the percent of completion for each task. Agencies may wish to have one of their employees or consultants monitor the contractor's progress to verify the percentage of completion reports submitted by the contractor. There is a tendency for contractor personnel to be optimistic with respect to their on-time and under-budget performance. Therefore, a critical in-house evaluation of their cost/schedule performance is likely to reflect more accurate results. Agencies that have just one representative to verify contractor-provided information are subject to the possibility that the agency representative may collude with the contractor to provide false verification in return for one or more of the rewards included in Table 1.1. Contractors can be asked to explain significant differences between their percentages and the agency's percentages for task completion. The contractor's explanation can be used as the basis for discussions to resolve the differences in task completion percentages. When the variances are not critical, the discussions may be delayed until the next periodic project meeting. If there is an impasse during these discussions, the agency might consider placing the contractor on notice via certified letter regarding the accuracy of their progress reporting. Documenting disagreements regarding schedule performance as they occur will prove helpful if it becomes necessary to resolve future issues regarding contractor schedules.

The template of the estimate to complete on the CD is a good tool for forecasting the contractor's final cost performance; however, contractors may have legitimate challenges to the agency's estimate. Certain contractor tasks may have been based on higher billing rates at the beginning of the project and lower billing rates as the project nears completion. If this is accurate, the contractor may justify a lower estimate at completion. To avoid this problem associated with changes in the predominate billing rates at different stages of project tasks, the agency can require the contractor to estimate their expenditures on a monthly basis to compensate.

This added level of sophistication, however, may not be justified for relatively low-value contracts where there is no need for a precise estimate at completion. Agencies that wish to consider cost and schedule reporting that is more sophisticated than the estimate at completion may wish to consider the guidelines in ANSI/EIA Standard 748 or evaluate the alternatives available through an Internet search on "cost/schedule-control-system."

Government entities may require the contractor to provide an estimate at completion in a format similar to that in Table 8.1. Agencies electing to have contractors develop the estimate at completion are encouraged to also require the periodic performance reports, financial information, and cost breakouts on invoices required for the government to calculate the estimate at completion. The rationale for requesting this full range of reporting is to provide insight into the contractor's calculation in the event of a disagreement on the estimate at completion. The added reporting is not costly because the information on those reports is required by the contractor to calculate the estimate at completion. As with the government-prepared estimate at completion, agencies are urged to have an agency representative verify the data reported by the contractor. The reason for verifying the reported data is, again, due to the contractor's tendency to be optimistic with respect to cost/schedule performance. The interpretation of the data in Table 8.1 is provided in Table 8.2.

Table 8.2 Analysis of Estimate at Completion

Tasks A, E, & F have all been invoiced at the same percentage as the percentage of task completion. Therefore, the estimate at completion for these three tasks is equal to the contract price and no overrun or underrun is anticipated.
Task B has a completion percentage less than the invoiced percentage. Therefore, it is expected that there will be a cost underrun for this particular task.
Tasks C & D and the project completion percentages are all less than the invoiced percentage. Therefore, it is expected that there will be a cost overrun for these two tasks and the overall contract.
Because the total contract price is $14,000,000 and the estimate at completion is $15,000,000, it is expected that there will be a total contract overrun of $1,000,000. NOTE: The total project estimate at completion is calculated without considering the percent invoiced for individual tasks; therefore, it is unlikely that the addition of the individual estimates at completion for the tasks indicated in the right-hand column will exactly equal the project estimate to complete.

8.4 Maintaining Program Integrity by Effectively Managing Contract Modifications

Contracts are normally modified either by amendments or by change orders. Contract amendments are negotiated and staffed modifications to the contract that may be approved, up to a specified dollar threshold, at a lower organizational level than the original contract. Contracts are normally modified by a change order when the urgency of the change does not permit time for a staffed amendment. Certain government entities are authorized to issue change orders unilaterally. Unilateral changes to a contract are those that are made with the signature of just one party to the contract: the government. Despite a government's authority to issue unilateral changes, however, it is preferable to hold discussions, if possible, to gain a meeting of the minds regarding the nature of the contract modification and to establish an NTE value for the change. Most organizations prepare a fully staffed amendment to incorporate the change order, or a number of change orders, when there is sufficient time to process the more time-consuming contract amendment.

Agencies that manage contracts or track milestone completions with computer software require a process for updating the database to incorporate the contract changes. Agencies that populate their contract management software database concurrently with the preparation of contract documents may elect to make database updates necessitated by the contract modifications by populating changes to the database while the contract modification is prepared. This task can be accomplished by developing contract modification documents structured just as the original contract with a variable information table. As the contract modification is prepared, changes to the software are made to correspond to any changes in the variable information on the contract modification. A contract amendment template, as illustrated in Table 8.4, designed to facilitate automatic updates to computer software databases during preparation of the amendment is provided on the CD.

Modifications to the contract, change orders or amendments, are considered as part of the contract administration effort. Although some organizations have personnel who concentrate their efforts on contract administration, numerous government entities rely on the employees responsible for selecting the contractor to also administer the contract. When contracts are administered by the same personnel who award contracts, contract amendments are normally processed by the same individual or team responsible for award of the original contract. However, agencies that maintain separate organizations for procurement and for contract administration are likely to have the procuring organization geographically separated from the administering organization. In such cases, the administering organization is normally closer geographically to the contractor. The procuring agency is likely to make initial contract modifications prior to delegating contract administration responsibilities to the contract administration organization. In the case of large government contractors, the administering organization may maintain offices within the contractor's facilities.

Contract modifications are made without the benefits afforded by competition. Because of the lessened control over modifications, versus award of the original contract, some skeptics believe that contractors routinely offer pricing at a loss to win the contract with the intention of making their profit through contract modifications. A contract administrator who is in collusion with the contractor certainly facilitates such a contractor strategy. Therefore, it is essential that agencies do not rely solely on one government representative to verify the contractor's claims regarding the pricing of proposed contract modifications.

Amendments require the same essential features as contracts. Because these essential elements are assumed to have been met when the original contract was awarded, one might assume that there is no concern about continuing to meet these requirements when modifying the contract. Although it is unlikely that illegal purposes, parties ineligible for entering into a contract, or other essential elements of a contract are introduced through contract amendments, a contract amendment may fail to include consideration. For example, a contractor that cannot meet the scheduled completion date may request an extension. If that extension is granted without obtaining something of value to the agency in exchange for granting it, then that amendment lacks consideration. A reasonable price reduction would constitute adequate consideration. However, other valuable consideration may be substituted for a price reduction. For example, helpful additional information on future reports, expanded performance of a task in the scope of work, a new task added to the scope of work, or any other item of equal value to the contracting agency may be acceptable as consideration for the schedule extension.

Contract amendments normally include a description of the contract modifications, any change in pricing, and any impact on the schedule. Providing a summary of price changes and schedule impacts resulting from contract amendments is recommended because this practice guards against the possibility that the contractor might subsequently claim greater schedule relief or a greater price increase. If the modifications to the contract do not impact the schedule or price, mentioning that fact on the amendment avoids the possibility of subsequent price or schedule disputes relating to the amendment. When there are numerous amendments to a contract, it may be difficult to track the total price or the pricing of individually priced tasks in the scope of work. A good practice to avoid encountering this difficulty is to include a summary of the pricing changes on each contract amendment. This can be accomplished by including a summary as shown in Table 8.3.

When the price does not change, this fact is normally reflected in the amendment using the format in Table 8.3 and showing the same value in both the "Previous total contract price" and "Revised total contract price" and with 0 in the space for "Price change this amendment," or simply by including a statement in the contract amendment that states "There is no change in contract pricing as a result of this amendment" or equivalent language.

Government entities generally include a boilerplate in their contract templates that includes provisions requiring all contract changes to be made in advance, in writing, and be signed by all parties to the contract. Although this is representative of good contract management practice, it does not ensure that oral changes are not enforceable. Generally, whenever a government employee instructs a contractor to perform work beyond that included in the scope of work, that written or verbal change is honored if the agency employee had the apparent authority to make such a change. The determination of which government employees have such apparent authority has historically been interpreted liberally. Complete reliance, therefore, cannot be placed on contract provisions for "written only contract changes that

Table 8.3   Summary of Price Changes

Task	Previous Price	Revised Price
A	$100,000.00	$100,000.00
B	$100,000.00	$100,000.00
C	$202,753.00	$181,131.00
Previous total contract price		$402,753.00
Price change this amendment		($21,622.00)
Revised total contract price		$381,131.00

are signed by authorized representatives of parties to the contract" to protect the agency from constructive changes. The recommended approach to minimizing constructive change orders is to train employees who have contact with contractors to refrain from giving verbal or written instructions to contractor personnel.

8.5 Ensuring Timely Milestone Completions and Deliverables

Managing contract milestones differs from monitoring cost/schedule performance in that managing milestone completions and deliverables is concerned with the contractor providing acceptable products or services on the contract schedule dates. Just as with other contract administration functions, attesting to the acceptability of contractor products or services provides opportunities for collusion between an agency representative and the contractor. Therefore, agencies are encouraged to provide verification of the acceptability of products and services provided by contractors. Agencies with small contract workloads may elect to manage key contract dates manually; however, contract management software is more appropriate for agencies with moderate to large contract workloads. Contract management software that includes the tracking of deliverables generally improves the contract management function while reducing reliance on human resources for this effort. Contract templates and contract amendment templates with variable information tables and other tables for entering other key dates can facilitate population of the database for milestones and deliverables tracking software concurrently with the preparation of contracts and amendments. Populating the database with key reporting information during preparation of the contract and amendments eliminates the need to perform subsequent data entry and avoids the problems associated with information in the contract differing from the milestones and deliverables tracking database that can result when a second data entry operation is necessary to populate the database. Agencies are urged to address problems discovered while tracking the contractor's contract milestones and deliverables with the contractor immediately upon making such discoveries. The failure of an agency to react in a timely manner to contractor performance problems will likely lead to a worsening of the problem. Timely intervention to contractor delinquencies ensures that the contractor will devote more attention to correcting the problems.

As mentioned in Section 8.4, agencies can populate their contract management software database concurrently with the preparation of contracts and contract amendments. The format for a contract amendment that facilitates the automated modification of database information changed by the award of contract amendments is provided in Table 8.4 and on the CD that accompanies this book.

Table 8.4 Contract Amendment

Amendment No.:		Amendment Date:

VARIABLE INFORMATION TABLE

Term of This Contract (Complete Dates in Just One of the Following Three Rows)

	Term Begins		**Term Completion Date**
□ Below	On Following Date		On Following Date
	Receipt of Notice to Proceed		□ Calendar Days Following Notice to Proceed
	Upon Execution by Agency		□ Calendar Days Following Agency Contract Execution

Agency Department		FOB Point	

Terms — Basis of Price (Do Not √ More Than One of the Following Four Blocks)

Price	□ Fixed Price	□ Annual Price	□ Monthly Price	□ Hourly Rate
Not-to-Exceed Price		√ If Reasonable Expenses Authorized in Addition to Hourly Rate		

Contractor Contact Information	**Agency Contact Information**
Contractor	Project Manager
Address	Address
City, State & ZIP	City, State & ZIP
Telephone	Telephone
Facsimile	Facsimile

Milestone No.	Milestone Description	Due Date

Item No.	Deliverable Item Description	Due Date

NARRATIVE

AGENCY

By_____

Name_____

Title_____

CONTRACTOR

By_____

Name_____

Title_____

The suggested template to update the information in the variable information table also provides for updating the schedule dates for milestones and deliverables. There is also space on the contract amendment template for a narrative explanation of the changes to the contract.

Agencies that do not elect the automation of milestone or deliverables tracking or do not elect to populate their computer database concurrently with the preparation of contracts or contract amendments, need not include a variable information table on the amendment templates. However, in the absence of using similar tables to collect milestone and deliverables tracking information concurrently with the preparation of contract documents, the agency might consider providing a summary of price changes as shown in Table 8.3. Providing the summary of price changes in this format ensures that the agency is managing the total contract cost, but not needlessly expending effort to format information not used to populate a database.

Tracking contract deliverables and milestones has historically been limited to providing notification after a key date has passed and the contractor becomes delinquent. When key dates are included in a computer database, however, it is possible to send computer-prompted reminders to the government staff and the contractor in advance of the due dates to ensure that upcoming events are not overlooked. When government entities elect to provide alerts to upcoming milestone or deliverable dates, the software is programmed to send reminders one or two weeks, or another appropriate time period, in advance of the dates for tracked events.

Agencies with a relatively small number of contracts may find that tracking contract milestones and deliverables manually or through desktop applications such as the scheduling feature on desktop computers may not require specialized computer software. However, large to medium size agencies with a relatively large volume of contracts may require an automated system to ensure that contractors are meeting their contract milestones and deliverable responsibilities. Regardless of the manner chosen to monitor deliverables and milestone completions, this task is simplified when dates for delivery of materials or services and for milestone completions are clearly indicated in the contract. Alerting government representatives and the contractor in advance of deliverable and milestone dates facilitates on-time completions. However, delinquent performance cannot be entirely avoided. When the government discovers that a contractor is not meeting milestones and deliverable responsibilities, and this problem is not addressed, the contractor's performance is likely to further deteriorate.

8.6 Energizing Underperforming Contractors

Timely reaction to substandard contractor performance is essential. Failure to react to the first sign of contractor problems invites continued substandard performance or even a further deterioration in performance. Agencies that delay their reaction until contractor performance has deteriorated to the point that they seek immediate termination for default is problematic. Failure to document the contractor's substandard performance may result in the need to pursue a termination for convenience in lieu of the default termination. Although initial contractor rebukes may be verbal, it is important to establish a record of such verbal rebukes to permit reference to the earlier agency actions in the event that continued contractor deficiencies require escalation to written advisories. Written notifications sent via certified mail with a return receipt requested are recommended when it appears that a contract may require termination. Certified mail with a return receipt provides the agency with written proof of delivery. The agency may elect to send such written communications via e-mail. If so, the agency may document the file with a printout of the e-mail as well as any response from the contractor. To ensure that the admonishment sent via certified mail is not unduly delayed, the agency may elect to also send a copy of the letter to the contractor as an e-mail attachment.

Establishing a record of the contractor's substandard performance and the agency's reaction is important if the contractor's performance deteriorates to the point that the agency wishes to terminate the contract. If provisions for liquidated damages are in the contract, it is recommended that the agency pursue collection of such liquidated damages from the contractor if completion dates are missed. When it is apparent that liquidated damages are due, the agency's initial contact with the contractor might be to ask if the contractor prefers to deduct the amounts due the agency for liquidated damages from future invoices, or if they prefer that the agency deduct the amounts due from contractor payments.

The U.S. Maritime Administration (MARAD) issued a solicitation for a contractor to purchase and dismantle certain vessels in the National Defense Reserve Fleet. The solicitation contained a liquidated damages clause. A contractor filed a protest claiming that liquidated damages were not appropriate for a sales contract, arguing that the agency would suffer no loss from breach because the contract generates revenue for the agency. In denying the protest, the GAO report[3] indicated that the record shows the agency had determined that it would be harmed monetarily if the purchased vessel was not dismantled in accordance with the schedule under the contract. The report also stated that the fact that the government would receive revenue from the sale of the vessel had no bearing on the propriety of the liquidated damages provision.

When a contractor's performance is not acceptable, but the agency does not have a strong case for terminating the contract for default, it may elect to terminate for convenience. If the agency elects to pursue termination of the contract for default, the recommended initial notification to the contractor is a show cause letter. If the contractor's response to the show cause letter presents a strong case supporting the fact that a default termination is not justified or that agency personnel were complicit with respect to the substandard performance, the agency may chose to either permit the contractor to continue performance on the contract or terminate the contract for convenience. When a case for a default termination has been established, the decision to convert to a convenience termination is normally based on the recommendation of more than one individual to guard against the possibility that the agency representative for this decision is colluding with the contactor to avoid the adverse consequences of a default termination. Agencies do not normally pursue a termination for default unless they have a strong, well-documented case. Contractors are likely to challenge default terminations because having a contract terminated for default may adversely impact the award of future government contracts. Therefore, the termination of a contract for default may result in a lengthy and costly court case.

A sample "show cause" letter is provided on the CD. One recommended feature for show cause letters is citation of all earlier infractions and agency admonishments regarding previous substandard contractor performance. Another recommended feature is to fully describe the immediate infraction(s) giving rise to the show cause letter. The termination for default provisions of the contract are normally referenced in the show cause letter as well as notification to the contractor that the agency intends to terminate the contract for default unless the contractor can show cause (provide justification) by a date certain why the contract termination is not justified. Including the contract provision in the show cause letter reinforces the agency's rights with respect to default termination, and indicating the date certain for the response clearly establishes this critical date. The show cause letter also normally includes a contract termination date (either the date the response is due or some subsequent date) in the event that the contractor fails to satisfactorily show cause why the contract termination is not justified. This establishes the date when the contract is terminated for default if the contractor does not respond or does not provide a satisfactory response to the show cause letter. A contractor's failure to respond to the show cause letter is the equivalent of not providing adequate cause why termination for default is not justified. Therefore, failure of the contractor to respond to the show cause letter by the due date is normally adequate justification to terminate the contract for default.

The contractor's justification for continued performance under the contract normally consists of the contractor's differing version of the performance cited as unacceptable, a description of the contracting agency's contribution to the performance considered unacceptable, a promise to improve future performance, or a combination of two or all three of these reasons.

As discussed earlier, contractors are likely to vigorously challenge a termination for default because a default termination blemishes the contractor's record and damages opportunities for obtaining future contracts from the contracting agency that is terminating the contract and from other government entities. If the contractor does contest the default termination, the contracting agency generally has three alternative reactions. The decision regarding what alternative to select is normally discussed with the agency's legal counsel.

The first alternative to a contested default termination is to keep the contract in force and permit the contractor to perform under the contract. This alternative is likely to be selected if agency personnel do not dispute the contractor's version of the performance failure or agency officials are convinced that there was contracting agency complicity in the contractor's substandard performance. Another reason for continuing to keep the contract in force is a determination by the contracting agency that it is satisfied with the contractor's promise to improve its future performance.

A second alternative is to terminate the contract for default despite the fact that the contractor has contested it. This decision requires careful consideration because the contractor has the option to contest the termination default through litigation. Pursuing the termination for default, therefore, is normally selected only if the agency has documented justification that it is certain to survive a court challenge. The agency terminating a contract for default must also be prepared to expend the time and funds required to pursue the default termination in court.

Another alternative to a contested default termination is to terminate the contract, but to terminate for convenience rather than for default. This alternative is likely to be chosen if the agency can afford the added time needed for the convenience termination, does not wish to risk the time and funds required if the contractor elects to contest the default termination through litigation, or determines that there is some chance that their justification for default termination or documentation of the contractor's unsatisfactory performance is not sufficient to survive the potential court challenge.

Regardless of the selected alternative to a contested default termination, once the agency makes a choice, it normally advises the contractor in writing of its decision. The letter may serve as the agency's documentation of its decision. If the second or third alternative is selected, the contractor's notification is normally sent via certified mail with a return receipt requested. The signed return receipt provides credible evidence that the contractor received written notice of the default or convenience termination.

8.7 Threat to Program Success from Flawed Contract Administration

The risk of program failure is the ultimate peril associated with a deficient contract administration program. Numerous risks are discussed in this section; however, all the risks contribute ultimately to program failure. The first risk to be discussed is that of constructive change orders, the costs associated with making equitable adjustments to contracts, and the government resources that are consumed in efforts to resolve the requests for equitable adjustments. An account is given of one contract that had fifty-eight requests for equitable adjustments totaling $39 million from constructive change orders.[4] Additional risks discussed include increased risk of procurement corruption; potential for substandard contractor quality or timeliness; inability to forecast cost, cost overruns, or cost at completion; approval of erroneous invoices; inability to react to underperforming contractors; commitment to an underperforming contractor; and the possibility of the contractor abandoning the project.

8.7.1 Risk of Constructive Change Orders

One way to potentially avoid constructive change orders is to train agency representatives who deal with contractors to guard against directing them to perform work beyond that specified in the contract. Constructive change orders may be written or oral direction, or acts of omission. One might assume that constructive changes do not result in a significant financial impact. However, in one case the special inspector general for Iraq reconstruction reported[5] that fifty-eight items were included in a request for equitable adjustment from one contractor for constructive changes in the amount of $39 million. As of March 17, 2006, fifty of the fifty-eight items had been resolved for $22 million. With the potential for obligating the government for such significant amounts, it is clearly worthwhile to train government employees in the hazards of constructive changes.

An example of a constructive change order is provided in the matter arising out of a contract for repair and related work to roof cells on a building at the Naval Operating Base, Norfolk, Virginia. The specifications called for waterproofing of roof systems that had been replaced. The contractor interpreted that to mean painting of the roof systems as they had done before and that was not uncommon in the industry. However, the Navy instructed the contractor to install a waterproofing membrane. The Navy and the contractor agreed to a specific product to use as the membrane. The Navy representative assumed the cost did not change. However, approximately one month later the contractor submitted a claim for an equitable adjustment for the added cost of installing the waterproofing membrane. The difference was resolved by the Armed Services Board of Contract Appeals[6] in favor of the contractor. The parties to the contract were directed to compute the number of square feet of the membrane installed and multiply it by $2.73 to determine the amount of the equitable adjustment. The contractor was also entitled to receive interest on the increased price of the contract.

8.7.2 Increased Risk of Procurement Corruption

The laissez faire approach to administering contracts places the government representative in close proximity to the contractor with neither adequate controls over the evaluation of goods or services provided by the contractor nor adequate controls over the approval of contractor payments. In most cases this does not result in procurement corruption. However, the lack of controls and close proximity does provide opportunities for dishonest government and contractor representatives to conspire to enrich themselves. Although this may seem impossible for the reader's organization. All contracting agencies are vulnerable to procurement corruption. The extent of the problem is illustrated by the previously discussed FBI statistics and the persistent media stories about contract corruption.

8.7.3 Potential for Substandard Contractor Quality or Timeliness

The most elemental contract administration effort, if conducted by a responsible government representative, results in the discovery of contractor quality or timeliness issues. However, lacking an effective contract administration protocol, with a conscientious agency representative ensuring that the contractor performs according to the contract terms, places the agency's interests in jeopardy. Establishing a formal approach to administering contracts, as recommended earlier in this chapter, better protects the government's interests in receiving the bargained-for value of goods or services provided by the contractor.

8.7.4 Inability to Forecast Cost, Cost Overruns, or Cost at Completion

Failure to require the contractor to provide reports on progress toward various tasks required by the contract and to prepare invoices that are tied to those tasks makes it impossible to calculate a meaningful estimate of costs at contract completion. Such calculations are essential for cost reimbursement contracts and may assist in contract administration for large fixed-price or NTE contracts. Estimates at completion are essential for cost reimbursement contracts because the government bears the ultimate risk for cost overruns. The quotation at the beginning of this chapter illustrates the perils associated with the failure to obtain a breakdown of the budget into constituent elements. Large-value fixed-price or NTE contracts that experience an overrun, despite the contractor bearing the risk of overruns, may also place the agency at risk. Consider the earlier example of the $8 million contract that had incurred costs of $11 million. A contractor that was not financially sound might find it necessary to abandon such a contract or risk bankruptcy. However, as shown by the Tomahawk weapons system example in Section 8.8, detecting an overrun in advance permitted the Navy to predict the tasks within the program that might experience cost overruns and make cost-cutting changes to eliminate the risk to program success.

8.7.5 Approval of Erroneous Invoices

Accounts payable systems may be helpful in detecting certain invoice errors; however, an invoice review protocol exercised by individuals who are familiar with the contract and the contractor's progress better positions the agency to detect a larger range of invoice errors. Although systems to prevent cumulative payments over the term of the contract may limit overpayments, payments up to the total value of the contract prior to completion of the work are possible. Although this condition does not deter dedicated, financially strong contractors from completing all the required contract work, less reputable contractors may assign a low priority to work that does not result in additional revenue and may be reluctant to perform any contract work that is essentially prepaid.

The sponsorship scandal in Canada was characterized by requests made to the former head of Groupaction Marketing for political donations and hiring of election workers as ghost employees who did little or no work in exchange for lucrative government sponsorship contracts.[7] Forensic experts were engaged to examine Groupaction's bank accounts and accounting records, where they discovered fictitious invoices created in an attempt to mask the transactions. Had the sponsorship contracts been subject to routine contract administration to include scrutiny of the invoices, the scheme might have been discovered earlier, thus minimizing the damage done.

8.7.6 Inability to React to Underperforming Contractor

Dealing with an underperforming contractor is similar to dealing with an underperforming employee. An employee who has not performed to the expected standards yet has received satisfactory performance ratings and has no record of disciplinary actions, absent a gross violation of agency policy, cannot be dismissed for continuing his or her past history of unsatisfactory performance. It is likewise necessary to establish a record of a contractor's misdeeds and attempts to have the contractor improve their performance prior to terminating a contract for default. Agencies that have termination for convenience provisions in their standard contract templates have the option to terminate the contract for convenience. However, convenience terminations typically have longer notification requirements than default terminations. Additionally, the agency may be able to offset damages against the defaulted contractor, have an option regarding acceptance of inventory from the defaulted contractor, and have the right to debar the terminated contractor.

8.7.7 Commitment to Underperforming Contractor

An agency that is inhibited from terminating a contract for default for lack of documented performance deficiencies, as discussed above, may be committed to continuing with the underperforming contractor for an extended time period while working with the contractor to improve its performance and developing the necessary documentation in the event it becomes necessary to terminate the contract. In either case, tone must be prepared to award a replacement contract to a different contractor. The extended commitment to an underperforming contractor can seriously affect the agency's ability to provide required public services or obtain needed supplies.

8.7.8 Possibility of the Contractor Abandoning the Project

Monitoring a contractor's progress in comparison to its expenditure rate can provide insight into the contractor's profitability on the contract being monitored.

Early detection of a probable loss on the contract provides the agency with an opportunity to work with the contractor to better align the contractor's performance and costs. If the projected loss is sufficiently serious to damage the contractor's survivability, however, there is the chance that the contractor will abandon the contract. In the event that the agency becomes aware of such a significant loss and the possibility of the contractor abandoning the contract, contingency planning for replacing the contractor is appropriate.

The failure of states and local government agencies to enact legislation similar to the federal government's False Claims Act, as did the City of New York, makes the agencies subject to continued undetected fraudulent activities and unable to recover funds inappropriately paid to government contractors.

8.7.9 Risks to Government Contractors That Fail to Implement Effective Contract Administration Processes

Government contractors that fail to implement effective subcontract administration processes risk failures by subcontractors that prevent the prime contractor from meeting delivery commitments to the government. Failure to meet government contractual delivery dates can reflect unfavorably on the performance of the prime contractor and is, therefore, detrimental to past performance ratings for future government source selection actions. Late deliveries to the government contractor also subject the prime contractor to liquidated damages that can have the effect of a reduction in the net revenues generated through the contract. Significant delinquent deliveries can lead the government to take escalating actions to obtain deliveries from the prime contractor. If the government's efforts to expedite delivery from the prime contractor are unsuccessful, the government may begin the process for a default termination, beginning with a show cause letter to the prime contractor. If the government is not satisfied with the prime contractor's reasoning for not terminating the contract for default, the government may proceed with a default termination. A default termination is a serious indicator of poor performance and may prevent the contractor from being awarded future contracts by the agency that terminated their contract as well as preventing contract awards from other government entities. The contractor may endure the effects from a termination for default for several years.

8.8 Administering Contracts to Promote Program Success

Improved probability for program success is the ultimate benefit available through an effective contract administration program. Numerous benefits are discussed in this section; however, all the benefits contribute ultimately to program success.

The first of such benefits to be discussed is the monitoring of contractor cost/ schedule performance and detecting cost or schedule anomalies in sufficient time to intervene and take corrective action. This discussion, however, is preceded by the account of a program that benefitted from cost/schedule analysis and the action taken to avoid a negative impact on program success that was detected. Additional risks that are discussed include detecting cost or schedule problems in sufficient time to intervene and take corrective action, improved monitoring and on-time completion of milestones and receipt of deliverables, assuring that contractor invoices are accurate prior to approval, and exercising knowledgeable decisions regarding the use of default versus convenience terminations. Implementation of legislation similar to the federal false claims act may help state and local government agencies discover a larger percentage of cases involving procurement fraud.

The success of a program may hinge on the effectiveness of the cost/schedule analyses and reaction to unfavorable cost trends. The program for installing the U.S. Navy's Tactical Tomahawk Weapon Control System (TTWCS) on eighty-five surface ships presents an example of prudent action taken in response to the detection of unfavorable cost trends. The Naval Surface Warfare Center, Port Hueneme Division (PHD), was responsible for executing the installation of the Tomahawk weapons system on surface ships. PHD's earned value management system (EVMS) projected an expected $2.3 million cost overrun by the end of fiscal year (FY) 2006, based on a December EVMS report. PHD manages Tomahawk tasks utilizing EVMS and performs monthly reviews. The only alternative appeared to be a reduction in the number of ships that received the latest version of the Tomahawk weapons system. PHD, with support from Performance Support Engineering, Incorporated (PSE), of Austin, Texas, led a cost analysis/recovery effort to understand the cause and effect of the variances being reported. EVMS provided crucial performance data on the major cost elements within the overall program with unfavorable cost trends. The cost analysis/recovery effort determined that some cost elements were controllable whereas others were not. PHD management and PSE developed cost savings targets for the controllable cost elements, identified individuals as target owners, and conducted weekly reviews to ensure that the targets were met. The continued review of EVMS and other cost data yielded two interesting results. First, as predicted, increased management attention to cost accruals resulted in cost savings. Second, some "uncontrollable" installation cost elements did not materialize, significantly reducing the projected overrun. As a result of a combination of these efforts and buy-in by personnel actually doing this work, the team succeeded by reaching $2.6 million in cost savings by the end of FY 2006, ending the FY with a cost surplus while executing the planned TTWCS installation program for this year.

8.8.1 Detecting Cost or Schedule Problems in Sufficient Time to Intervene and Take Corrective Action

As demonstrated in the previous example of the successful application of cost/ schedule analyses, preparing an estimate at completion or similar products from cost/schedule performance software products can certainly contribute favorably to program success. The estimate at completion tool discussed in Section 8.3 and available on the CD is suitable for projecting costs for many contracts and may be all that is required for some government entities. However, agencies that manage large, complex systems contracts may require more sophisticated tools, such as the EVMS used by PSE in the previous example. As in the PHD case, forecasting a cost overrun is merely the first step in this process. Effective cost/schedule analyses incorporate budget breakouts for lower level cost elements within the project. Once the overruns can be isolated to specific cost elements, it is possible to perform further analyses to determine whether the cost elements facing an overrun are controllable. If overrunning cost elements are controllable, the government is able to spend additional time to determine the cause of the expected overrun and establish steps that can be taken to implement sufficient cost savings to overcome it.

8.8.2 Improved Monitoring of Milestones and Deliverables

The existence of scheduled delivery dates in the contract administration computer software database provides the capability for updating the database when milestones are completed or deliverables are received, and to alert agency personnel when any schedule date is not met. This is superior to spending the time required to perform this function manually, and it is likely to be performed more accurately than the alternative of a manual comparison of actual dates to the contract schedule. In addition to the automated matching of actual dates to the contract schedule dates, computer software can be designed to check for future delivery dates and to notify both the agency and the contractor of upcoming scheduled milestone completions and deliveries. Advance notices of upcoming due dates contributes to improved on-time contractor performance.

8.8.3 Assurance of Accurate Contractor Invoices

Following the recommended process for evaluating invoices ensures the accuracy of payments to contractors and prevents overpayments due to invoice errors. As discussed earlier, invoice verification performed solely by one agency representative provides an opportunity for collusion between the agency representative and the contractor. Therefore, agencies are encouraged to provide a second invoice verification. Although accounts payable systems may verify the accuracy of certain invoice errors, following the recommendations for invoice approval guards against overpayments due to mathematical errors, incorrect unit prices or billing rates, extensions of unit prices or billing rates, payment for milestones that have not been completed or materials that have not been delivered, or overly optimistic estimations of task or milestone percentage completions.

A statement from the inspector general for the U.S. Postal Service to the Senate Committee on Governmental Affairs is provided as an example of the magnitude of costs that can be saved through a meticulous review prior to approving contractor payments. The inspector general made the following statement with respect to erroneous billings from just one contractor:

> As a result of our efforts and with the cooperation of Postal Service management, the Postal Service recovered over $12 million from a major telecommunications contractor and can avoid an additional $58 million in erroneous billings. Because the Postal Service did not adequately monitor contractor performance, it was repeatedly billed for work that was not performed and for substandard work. Postal Service management is reviewing all future bills to ensure correct billings, which should result in future savings.

8.8.4 Knowledgeable Decision-Making Regarding Use of Default versus Convenience Terminations

There are occasions when it becomes necessary to deal with a contractor to address substandard performance. Following the actions recommended in Section 8.5 regarding contractor notifications, establishing a written record of attempts to improve the contractor's performance, issuance of a show cause letter, and finding that the contractor's response was unsatisfactory or that there was no contractor response, the agency is prepared to make a decision regarding termination of the contract. If the contractor's response to the show cause letter convinces the agency to continue with the contract, there is no need to make a decision regarding the termination option. The discussion in Section 8.6 revealed that when terminating a contract due to substandard performance, the agency has an alternative to termination for default. Government entities have the option to terminate the contract either for default or for convenience. Agencies that are not confident regarding their justification, or the documentation of their case, for a default termination may elect to terminate the contract for convenience. Default terminations may adversely affect the contractor's ability to receive further government contracts. Therefore, it is important to heed the advice in Section 8.6 regarding the decision between terminating for convenience and terminating for default.

8.8.5 *False Claims Act Legislation*

The enactment of legislation by states and local governments, similar to the U.S. government's False Claims Act, is likely to result in increased detection of procurement fraud and the recovery of government funds.

In FY 2007/2008, the U.S. government recovered $1.34 billion through the False Claims Act.[8] Since 1986, when the False Claims Act was strengthened, the United States has recovered more than $21 billion through this program. Private citizens (referred to as relators) are authorized to file suit on behalf of the United States against those who falsely or fraudulently receive payments from the federal government. The false claims are based on cases such as Medicare, Medicaid, federal contracts, disaster assistance loans, and agricultural subsidies. Well over half of the recoveries result from suits filed by relators who file *qui tam* suits. Relators receive 15–25% of the proceeds when the U.S. government joins in a successful False Claims Act *qui tam* suit. When the United States does not join the suit, and the relator succeeds in pursuing the action, the relator receives 30% of the proceeds.

The U.S. False Claims Act rewards whistleblowers with a percentage of the proceeds from funds recovered from federal government contracts. Whistleblowers often receive approximately 15% or more of the proceeds. The False Claims Act works well in cases where disreputable government contractors are able to disguise their lack of contract compliance by falsifying work records and intimidating employees. A whistleblower notified the City of New York of suspected contract fraud regarding foster care services provided by St. Christopher's, Inc. Because her information was apparently ignored, she filed suit under the federal False Claims Act. The foster care case was investigated by the City of New York Department of Investigation.[9] The case was settled by the state and the city, resulting in the payment of $49 million to the federal government and $4.9 million to the whistleblower. Problems discovered during the investigation included St. Christopher's supervisory staff instructing caseworkers to change case records by fabricating visits to foster and birth homes, progress notes, case plans, and other activities that did not occur. The Department of Investigation also found that the records falsification activities potentially masked unacceptable conditions in the foster homes. The City of New York did not have such a false claims act at the time; however, the city did enact a law patterned after the federal law soon after the settlement was reached in the St. Christopher's case.[10] Other state and local government agencies may find that the performance of government contractors is more thoroughly scrutinized and there is a reduction in wasted funds when they too enact similar legislation.

8.8.6 *Benefits to Government Contractors That Implement Effective Contract Administration Processes*

Government contractors can generally benefit from implementation of all the contract administration practices recommended for government. Government contractors that do not award high-value or cost reimbursement contracts, however, may not need to perform cost/schedule analyses. The efficiencies gained through project management software are likely appropriate for government contractors because use of such products permits fewer people to administer more contracts. Software can be designed to perform routine tracking of milestones and deliverables without human intervention, unless there is an exception such as a missed milestone or delivery. This capability is especially attractive to government contractors because they typically have a high number of low-value deliverables to track. Computer-generated advance notifications of upcoming scheduled delivery dates can benefit government prime contractors by alerting lower tier subcontractors in advance of future due dates, thus preventing late deliveries and improving their on-time delivery rate.

8.9 Improved Profit, Quality, and Timeliness for Government Contractors

The approach to contract administration recommended for government is also recommended for the subcontracting function of government contractors. Federal government contractors in the United States are required to conduct their subcontracting function similarly to government contracting offices, including conformance with the *Federal Acquisition Regulation* (FAR). The contract management function for government contractors, however, is sales oriented whereas government's contract management function is responsible for the activities that occur during the contracting cycle. The subcontract management effort for government contractors is nearly identical to the contract management effort for government entities. Although government contractors typically have numerous purchase orders and subcontracts valued at considerably less than their prime government contract, the government contract provisions require contractors to conduct their subcontracting operations according to the FAR. One exception to the requirement to conform to strict FAR requirements is when the government contract is for the acquisition of commercial items.

Government contractors were encouraged in previous chapters to implement the recommendations for advance contract planning, features of the best practices RFP and model contract, and the proposal evaluation process. Government contractors are, likewise, urged to implement the contract administration practices described in this chapter for their subcontract administration function. Government contractors tend to have lower value subcontracts and a higher ratio of fixed-price contracts than government contracting offices. The lower value of subcontracts and lower ratio of cost reimbursement subcontracts for government contractors results in less need to perform cost/schedule analyses than government entities. Large systems contractors for the federal government, however, often do have high-value cost reimbursement subcontracts for which cost/schedule analyses are appropriate. The existence of a large number of lower value purchase orders and subcontracts makes computer-generated notices to lower tier subcontractors, alerting them to upcoming milestones and delivery dates, especially appropriate for government contractors. Such alerts to subcontractors and government program offices tends to result in improved rates of on-time deliveries and milestone completions.

8.10 Conclusion

The uncontested award of a contract represents the beginning of the contract administration phase of the contracting cycle. During this phase of the contracting cycle, the contractor performs contractual responsibilities while the government monitors the contractor's performance, evaluates and pays contractor invoices, and negotiates and awards modifications to the contract. The importance of effectively performing contract administration functions can be illustrated by reviewing the results of an audit performed by the Office of the Special Inspector General for Iraq Reconstruction (SIGIR) of DynCorp International's spending under its contract for the Iraqi Police Training Program.[11] The contract required DynCorp to provide housing, food, security, facilities, training support systems, and a cadre of law enforcement personnel in support of the Iraqi civilian police training program. The DynCorp contract is administered by the U.S. Department of State (DoS) Bureau for International Narcotics and Law Enforcement Affairs (INL). Selected facts determined during the audit, representing the tenor of the findings, are provided here:

- INL's ability to administer the DynCorp contract was inhibited due to a substantial increase in its workload without a commensurate increase in personnel.
- INL did not know what it had received for most of the $1.2 billion contract payments to DynCorp.
- INL's previous lack of management and financial controls left the government vulnerable to waste and fraud.
- There were duplicate payments of $1.8 million for an x-ray scanner that was never used.
- Payment of $387,000 was made for hotel stays of DynCorp officials who could have stayed in available living facilities.
- INL advised SIGIR officials that INL did not have the information needed to identify what DynCorp provided under the contract or how the funds were spent.
- Based on the lack of information on payments by INL and work provided by DynCorp, SIGIR was not able to complete the audit and issued an interim report with the intention to follow up later on INL's progress.

SIGIR found that INL is progressing in its efforts to improve its contract administration functions. The report indicated that INL's improvements included recovery of about $1.1 million in inappropriate payments to DynCorp, negotiated reductions of $113.7 million from cost/price proposals, and progress toward organizing the contract administration files.

Notes

1. U.S. Department of Education, Office of Inspector General, "Former State School Superintendant Linda Schrenko Sentenced to Eight Years in Federal Prison," July 12, 2006.
2. "Estimating Large Complex Projects," Cliff Schexnayder, Keith Molenaar, and Jennifer Shane, online version of *Revista Ingeniería de Construcción*, vol. 22, no. 2, pp. 91–98, August 2007.
3. U.S. GAO, "Southern Scrap Material Company," File number B-401059, April 29, 2009.
4. "Outcome, Cost, and Oversight of Iraq Reconstruction Contract W914NS-04-D-0006," Report number SIGIR-08-010, January 28, 2008.
5. Ibid.
6. The appeal of States Roofing Corporation under contract number N62470-97-C-8319, ASBCA Case No. 54854.
7. *CBC News* online posting, "Jean Brault's Testimony," March 2, 2006.
8. Department of Justice media release, "More Than $1 Billion Recovered by Justice Department in Fraud and False Claims in Fiscal Year 2008," November 10, 2008.
9. An account of the findings of the investigation into the foster care services is included in the Summary of Findings for Mayor Michael R. Bloomberg and Administration for Children's Services Commissioner John B. Mattingly, "The Department of Investigation's Examination of Foster Care Services Provided by St. Christopher's, Inc.," submitted by DOI Commissioner Rose Gill Hearn, January 14, 2005.
10. On May 19, 2005, Mayor Bloomberg signed into law the New York City False Claims Act, which permits the city to fight fraud perpetrated against it. The statute creates a way for people to help the city recover money lost through fraud. New York City's False Claims Act is patterned after the federal "*qui tam*" statute, which provides for citizen plaintiffs, under certain circumstances, to keep up to 30% of recovered funds.
11. "Interim Review of DynCorp International, LLC, Spending under Its Contract for the Iraqi Police Training Program," Report number SIGIR-07-016, October 23, 2007.

Chapter 9

Contracting during Emergencies

Emergency does not create power. Emergency does not increase granted power or remove or diminish the restrictions imposed upon power granted or reserved. The Constitution was adopted in a period of grave emergency. Its grants of power to the federal government and its limitation of the power of the States were determined in the light of emergency, and they are not altered by emergency. What power was thus granted and what limitations were thus imposed are questions [290 U.S. 398, 426] which have always been, and always will be, the subject of close examination under our constitutional system.

Chief Justice Hughes
Home Building & Loan Association v. Blaisdell, 290 U.S. 398 (1934)

9.1 Fundamentals of Emergency Contracting

Disasters call forth humanity's sincere concern for and generosity toward humankind as well as humanity's scourge of corruption and greed. Human reaction to calamities such as the 2010 earthquake in Haiti, 2008 earthquake in the Sichuan region of China, the 2008 Myanmar (Burma) cyclone, the 2005 Hurricane Katrina, the 2004 Indian Ocean tsunami, and lesser disasters is characterized by the compassion and generosity of donor countries, nongovernment organizations (NGOs), and individual responders. Indeed, some individuals interrupt their lives absolutely to offer assistance through their extended presence at the disaster site. While these heroic acts receive merely passing note, however, great notoriety is broadcast regarding the minority of opportunistic individuals and organizations that pilfer unconscionable profit following catastrophic events at the expense of the victims and heroic individuals as well as governments and the NGOs providing relief. Numerous examples of nefarious and amateurish contracting decisions made in haste, some paralleling the ethical lapses included in Table 1.1, are presented in this chapter. However, examples of agencies that have performed thoughtfully and appropriately will also be cited.

Sole source contracts during emergencies may be based on a disaster or other emergency conditions. In either event, sole source emergency contracting is performed under similar circumstances. An example of an unjustifiable sole source purchase based on emergency conditions without a declared emergency is provided in the case of medical equipment purchased in response to patient infections caused by use of obsolete medical equipment. Eye infections due to the use of certain medical equipment used in cataract procedures spurred the chief of ophthalmology in a U.S. Department of Veterans Affairs' (VA) facility to write a memorandum stating that the equipment was outdated and required replacement. The doctor's memorandum also included the statement that her doctors were familiar and comfortable with Alcon's Infiniti machine. Approximately two weeks later the VA issued a sole source purchase order for the equipment based on compelling urgent circumstances affecting patient care. On that same day the VA publicized the intent to award a sole source contract to Alcon for the medical equipment. Following award of the contract, the contracting officer prepared a sole source justification based on the urgent need and the fact that the Alcon equipment had advanced features not available through any other manufacturer. Bausch & Lomb, Incorporated (B&L) protested the award and stated that the sole source orders to Alcon were improper, that the VA failed to seek competitive offers, that the sole source justification was inaccurate, and that B&L's Millennium equipment was the most advanced equipment available and best meets the VA's needs. The protest was sustained by the U.S. Government Accountability Office (GAO) based substantially on verification of the rationale provided in B&L's protest. The GAO did not recommend termination of the orders because they had been fully performed. However, the GAO did recommend that the VA reimburse B&L its cost of pursuing the protest, including reasonable attorney's fees.

A GAO report[1] cited numerous instances of waste and potential fraud associated with FEMA's oversight of housing maintenance contracts in Mississippi following Hurricane Katrina. One particular example of excessive costs in the GAO report involved the placement of trailers at group sites rather than at private sites. The report indicated that FEMA will spend about $30,000 for each of the 280 sq. ft. trailers through March 2009. However, one trailer at the Port of Bienville Park could escalate to approximately $229,000. One major reason for the difference is that FEMA pays the same fixed costs for group site maintenance (GSM) regardless of the number of trailers at group sites. The GAO report indicated that FEMA spends $576,000 per year at the Port of Bienville Park. Because there are just eight trailers at Bienville Park, FEMA spends $72,000 per year for grounds maintenance and road and fence repair for each trailer.

Although noteworthy attempts have been made to limit opportunities for procurement corruption during emergencies, greater success has been achieved in the questionable practice of providing ever-increasing procurement flexibilities during and in the aftermath of disasters. Sole source and limited source contracting provide inherent opportunities for procurement corruption. Permitting sole source contracting at contract values where competition is normally required results in increased numbers and values for sole source contracts and the associated increases in opportunities for procurement fraud. Decreasing the incidence of competitive contracting by increasing the threshold where sole source contracting is permitted in reaction to disasters is not rational. Competition not only results in lower prices, but also encourages contractors to become more competitive with respect to timely delivery and the quality of materials or services. When timely delivery of materials or services is critical due to a declared emergency, the contracting agency may weigh availability higher than price and select the contractor that did not propose the lowest price but instead the fastest delivery. When delivery of a portion of the requirement is critical, but there is considerably less urgency for the balance of the requirement, the agency may be able to purchase the urgently required materials from the higher priced contractor, but order the less urgent materials from the lower priced contractor. To take advantage of this alternative, provisions of the solicitation need to permit the contracting agency the right to split the order between two or more contractors.

Obtaining competitive proposals or bids does not necessarily slow the contracting process because a solicitation can be sent concurrently to multiple prospective contractors that can, in turn, be required to return their proposals or bids in the same timeframe as for a sole source contractor. Placing more weight on the availability of the materials or services than on pricing permits the agency to select the higher priced proposal with the most immediate availability. In this scenario, competition likely results in faster delivery of the needed materials or services than a sole source contract. Although the selected contractor may not have been the contractor offering the lowest price, the mere existence of competition is likely to result in pricing lower than sole source procurement.

Competitive proposals or bids provide the contracting agency with alternatives for differing attributes for the offered materials or services from the prospective contractors. The sole source contractor may offer only one choice of attributes that disappoint the contracting agency. If the available attributes for products or services available through the sole source contractor are unacceptable, a longer delay is encountered if it becomes necessary to then request a proposal or bid from an alternative contractor. In this event, the attempt at sole source procurement results in significantly delayed receipt of the needed materials or services.

9.2 Private-Sector Contributions to Emergency Response

Recommendations for contracting in emergencies are provided on the topics of planning for contracting during emergencies, awarding contracts during emergencies, domestic emergencies, and international emergencies.

Disasters may occur with or without warning. When there is warning, as with hurricanes, government and the populace can take actions to prevent deaths, injuries, and property damage prior to the actual event's impact on the populace. When a disaster occurs without warning, as with most earthquakes, deaths, injuries, and property damage occur before the government and populace can react. Government can plan for future emergencies that occur either with or without warning. Planning for hazards when there is a warning includes actions such as evacuations and positioning materials and personnel for response during evacuations, rescue, and recovery. Planning for future emergencies is intended to help government meet the objective of responding quickly with the correct human and material resources in sufficient quantities to minimize loss of life, injuries, and property damage while continuing to provide essential government services. Because governments do not have all the necessary human and material resources for this endeavor, planning for response to future disasters is not complete unless there is a contracting component to the emergency plan. The ultimate dividend from an effective contracting component of an emergency contracting program is being prepared during future disasters by having indefinite delivery indefinite quantity (IDIQ) contracts in place for materials and services that can be anticipated and having contracting tools available for procuring materials and services that were not anticipated.

Regardless of the existence of a warning, not all harmful effects of disasters can be prevented. An effective evacuation is likely to minimize loss of life and injuries; however, in significant disasters there is always the risk for loss of life, injuries, and property damage. Therefore, there is a certain element of rescue and recovery efforts despite the warning. In this scenario, the benefits from an effective emergency contracting program are minimization of further loss of life, injuries, and property damage plus preventing illnesses and continuing essential government services. The recommendations in this chapter are intended to meet these objectives without providing unnecessary opportunities for charlatans to profit from the misery of others. Planning for and implementing a contracting process to obtain supplies and services from the private sector in support of the government's emergency response efforts constitutes a significant element of the effort to provide support to relief efforts.

Failure to develop advance plans for private-sector participation during emergencies results in hasty decision making or unwanted delays in awarding contracts for needed materials and services. Hasty decision making tends to result in overpriced contracts, slow response, and less-than-optimal quality for services or materials. Delays in awarding contracts results in an extension of the time when lives and property are threatened, as well as delays in the provision for essential government services. Needless loss of lives and damage to property may result from these unnecessary delays. The planning measures outlined below are offered to permit advance decision making prior to the next disaster in the absence of time pressures that are present during actual emergencies. These recommended measures involve planning for both contracts made in advance of emergencies and contracts awarded during emergencies. The specific recommended actions are to identify needed materials and services; award IDIQ contracts or purchase materials for warehousing; provide a template for expedited contract placement during emergencies; develop a process for obtaining competitive pricing, required quality, and expedited delivery during emergencies; and tighten contracting rules for rebuilding after the immediacy of the disaster has elapsed.

9.2.1 Identify Needed Materials and Services

Although it is not always possible to anticipate all services and materials that are required during emergencies, public servants and consultants who have been involved previously in declared disasters are able to identify services and materials that are needed for future emergencies. A comprehensive list of materials and services identified in advance of an emergency for placement on IDIQ contracts, or purchased and warehoused, not only significantly reduces the number of decisions made in haste for contracting during actual emergencies, but also results in lower prices, better quality, and improved availability.

9.2.2 Award IDIQ Contracts or Purchase Materials for Warehousing

Award of competitive contracts for the required materials and services identified in the preceding step results in improved pricing, better quality, and better availability when the contracts are placed in the absence of a disaster. Absence of an ongoing emergency provides government entities with the luxury of time available to not only identify the services and materials that are needed during emergencies, but also prepare comprehensive specifications to avoid exacerbating the disaster by purchasing dangerous materials such as the formaldehyde-tainted shelters purchased for Hurricane Katrina survivors. When it is practical to purchase the materials and warehouse them for use during emergencies, that option is worth considering. An example of materials that can be purchased and warehoused in advance of an emergency is prefabricated shelters manufactured from nontoxic but durable material. The shelters can be designed for ease of assembly, with minimal required warehouse space achieved by stacking floors, walls, and roofs that can be assembled on site when required. Services and some materials, however, cannot be warehoused. For such materials and services, award of IDIQ contracts may be appropriate. IDIQ contracts may be activated in the future for delivering supplies and providing services that are needed during actual emergencies.

9.2.3 Provide Template for Expedited Contract Placement during Emergencies

As mentioned above, all services and materials needed during emergencies cannot be anticipated in advance. Therefore, it is necessary to simplify the contracting process during emergencies for services and materials that were not anticipated. There is a discussion later in this paragraph of letter contracts that are practical for obtaining services and materials from the private sector when time does not permit the award of a fully staffed definitive contract. Providing templates for letter contracts, as well as solicitations for letter contracts, facilitates the award of contracts during and in the immediate aftermath of a disaster. This template, however, is not recommended for construction projects during the recovery effort when more time is available to use traditional contracting processes.

9.2.4 Develop Process for Obtaining Competitive Pricing, Required Quality, and Expedited Delivery

The provision for a letter contract template, as discussed above, does facilitate the award of contracts when they must be awarded without delay; however, the availability of a letter contract template does not negate the benefits of awarding contracts on a competitive basis. Full and open competition, as emphasized throughout this chapter and in Chapter 4, does not result solely in low prices but also discourages contract corruption and causes contractors to compete with respect to quality and timeliness as well. Since quotes can be obtained from multiple contractors in the same timeframe as a sole source quote, competition does not slow the contracting process for services and materials required during emergencies. In fact, obtaining competition may result in selecting a contractor that can provide materials or services delivery sooner than materials obtained from a sole source contractor. The process for awarding contracts on an expedited basis might involve soliciting contractors for pricing and availability via telephone, e-mail or by messenger. Selection of the contractor from the competing quotes, bids, or proposals can be considerably more informal than the formal process for evaluating proposals when there is no existing emergency.

9.2.5 Tighten Contracting Rules Following the Immediacy of the Disaster

Once the immediate threat to life, injury, and property damage has elapsed, governments err when they continue to use "procurement flexibility" to bypass full and open competition that is authorized to save lives, prevent injuries, and avoid property damage. Noncompetitive contracting is not recommended during emergencies because competitive proposals, bids, or quotes can be obtained in the same timeframe as sole source pricing, and as an added benefit, competition may yield faster delivery and superior quality materials or services. Therefore, continuing to avoid competition for reconstruction projects after the immediacy of the disaster has elapsed is, in most cases, irresponsible. Sole source justifications for multimillion or multibillion dollar contracts in the absence of an immediate threat to life, injury, or property damage are questionable. Legislation permitting the suspension of full and open competition in the absence of such threats is likewise questionable. Rebuilding infrastructure following a disaster is normally assigned a high priority; however, the suspension of competitive contracting requirements for high-value reconstruction projects is definitely not recommended.

Prudent agencies conduct exercises involving activation of their emergency operation centers (EOCs) periodically to ensure that personnel assigned to the EOC are well trained and that plans for future emergencies remain current. Although private-sector contractors are not likely required to provide services or materials during an EOC exercise, it is likely necessary during actual emergencies for private-sector companies to support government entities through providing both services and materials. When the materials and services that are required during future emergencies can be determined in advance, award of contracts in advance for activation during emergencies will prove beneficial to responding government entities. Such advance contracts may contain provisions, such as a notice to proceed, to initiate contract performance during emergencies when the materials and services are needed. Awarding contracts in advance of actual emergencies decreases the time required to employ private-sector materials and services during actual emergencies. Advance contracts, therefore, accelerate delivery of supplies and services where they are needed during actual emergencies. Additionally, placing contracts in advance of the emergency, in the absence of pressure to place the contracts with minimal lead time, permits agencies to ensure that contractors are selected on the basis of fair and reasonable pricing from companies that can provide appropriate materials and services in a timely manner.

When IDIQ contracts are awarded in advance of an emergency, the lack of pressure for dealing with an ongoing emergency permits the contracting agency time for discretion when developing the list of firms to be solicited, specifications, scope of work, preparation of a written solicitation, selection of the best contractor(s) based on competitive proposals or bids, and development of terms and conditions. Contracts designed for activation during future emergencies may be awarded routinely just as contracts awarded in the absence of an emergency.

Contracts placed in advance of emergencies need to be periodically reviewed to ensure that the product descriptions, scope of work, or contract provisions have not become obsolete. When such contract reviews reveal such obsolescence, the contracts may be updated by amendment or it may be necessary to award replacement contracts. The periodic reviews may include an evaluation of the contract ending date and a determination to extend the contract term or release solicitations for the competitive award of a follow-on contract.

The above discussion is not suggesting that there is a complete lack of planning for contracting during disasters. FEMA learned from the lack of planning in advance of Hurricanes Katrina and Rita. The placement of IDIQ contracts in advance of the 2007 wildfires in Southern California made the response to that disaster so successful that the fire was soon forgotten by nearly all that were not directly affected. Ongoing planning is evidenced by an RFP released in 2009 by the U.S. Agency for International Development (USAID) for a time and materials indefinite quantity contract (IQC) for worldwide emergency disaster response. The RFP was released by the Bureau for Democracy, Conflict and Humanitarian Assistance (DCHA). Other than the names, there is no discernable difference between IDIQ contracts and IQC. The services identified in the RFP include those listed below that are intended for immediate, short-term disaster relief:

1. Water, sanitation and hygiene, health and nutrition
2. Food and nonfood in response to disasters
3. Rehabilitation efforts in the areas of water, sanitation, health, nutrition, and shelter after an emergency response
4. Critical windows of opportunity for transition, conflict prevention, or democracy interventions
5. Services for requirements to conduct assessments of response mechanisms and strategies or interventions

An excellent example of pre-planning was described in a media release from the Canadian International Development Agency (CIDA) in May of 2008.[2] The media release mentioned that CIDA maintains a stock level of 5,000 kits containing two tarpaulins plus a shovel, rope, hammer, nails, hand saw, and other miscellaneous tools. The shelter kits were designed by the International Federation of the Red Cross (IFRC) to establish international specifications. The IFRC also coordinated the overall shelter response to Tropical Cyclone Nargis. The shelter kits, along with other relief supplies, were flown to Rangoon on one of the Canadian military's four C-17 Globemasters.

Once contracts are in place for future emergencies, it is necessary to ensure that they remain current. The failure of the U.S. Forest Service to renew an aircraft maintenance contract for the airport in Santa Maria, California, prevented the use of that airport in fighting the 2009 Jesusita fire.[3] The Forest Service may have renewed the contract in time, but the fire started ten days prior to the expected start of the fire season. Because the flight from Porterville to Santa Barbara takes approximately one hour and the flight from Santa Maria to Santa Barbara takes about twenty minutes, the reloading and refueling flights required triple the normal time, thus reducing the number of retardant drops that were made during the initial stage of the fire.

9.3 Improved Delivery and Quality while Controlling Emergency Contract Costs

Once an emergency occurs or appears imminent, there is insufficient time to award fully staffed contracts to private-sector companies in support of the contracting agency's immediate response. However, agencies can establish procedures in advance for awarding contracts in a timely manner during emergencies. The use of letter contracts is recommended to meet urgent continuing needs during actual emergencies.

The term "letter contract" refers to a type of contract used by the U.S. government when it is essential to award a contract without delay and there is insufficient time to prepare a fully staffed contract. The term will be used throughout this text to describe a contract designed for award on an expedited basis during an emergency. Although letter contracts are frequently awarded without competition, agencies are urged to stress competition when planning to award letter contracts. As mentioned earlier, competition does not necessarily slow the contracting process and may lead to faster delivery of supplies and services needed in the emergency response. Competition may also provide an opportunity to acquire supplies or services that are better suited than those offered by the presumptive sole source contractor. Although the evaluation of quotes, bids, or proposals may be abbreviated and less formal during emergencies, the existence of competition also reduces opportunities for ethical lapses.

Just as advance contract placement is appropriate for contract activation during both emergency and nonemergency conditions, letter contracts too are appropriate during emergency and nonemergency conditions whenever time does not permit the award of a fully staffed contract. Following the initial emergency reaction to a disaster, there is likely sufficient time to obtain full and open competition and fully staffed contracts for intermediate to long-term recovery projects.

Contracting agencies can better prepare to award contracts during emergencies by developing in advance a letter contract template, such as the one provided on the CD that accompanies this book. Development of a letter contract, containing provisions to minimize the government's exposure to risk, yet which can be awarded in time to address most emergencies, is recommended to minimize the contracting agency's risk exposure.

In the absence of a template for awarding letter contracts during an actual emergency, the need for the agency to act in haste may result in awarding contracts without incorporating basic contracting practices. Basic contracting efforts, often overlooked when acting in haste, include the selection of contractors on a competitive basis, incorporation of a scope of work that permits the contracting agency to mitigate risks, provision for some element of cost control, and incorporation of terms and conditions to protect the rights of the agency and the public.

Defending sole source contracting justified by the existence of an emergency is difficult to support. Competition is not employed solely to obtain the lowest pricing, but also to help obtain earlier service commencement or expedited delivery of materials. Competition is also used to acquire more comprehensive services or better quality supplies. Ideally, competition is used to achieve the optimal combination of price, quality, and delivery. Although most agencies are authorized to use relaxed contracting procedures during emergencies, the relaxed procedures do not necessarily relax the need to obtain competition for certain high-value contracts. To award a contract, even in an emergency, it is necessary to advise prospective contractors of the agency's needs and it is necessary for the companies to respond by describing how they can meet the agency's needs. Although the agency's inquiries to prospective contractors are informal (and possibly oral), their inquiries are, in fact, solicitations, and the contractors' responses (although informal) are, in fact, proposals. Informal solicitations can be delivered to multiple prospective contractors in essentially the same timeframe that a single solicitation can be delivered to a presumptive sole source contractor. Likewise, solicitations can indicate a mandatory response date and time to ensure timely receipt of all proposals. If the solicitation is sent to just one contractor, the government may be disappointed by both the delay before the contractor can commence delivery of materials or services and the nature of the service or materials proposed. Had multiple contractors been solicited, one or more of the added contractors may have proposed an earlier service commencement or commodity delivery date or better quality services or materials. Multiple contracts for the same service or product are appropriate when one contractor cannot meet the agency's total demand. Therefore, it may be in the agency's best interests to award multiple contracts for the same services or materials.

An example of a sole source contract that appeared to be unreasonably justified under emergency conditions was included in an audit conducted by the Office of the Auditor General of Canada.[4] The Royal Canadian Mounted Police recommended that the Public Works and Government Services Canada (PWGSC) award a contract for police training services valued at $362,000 on a sole source basis. The sole source justification was based on the work being urgent and confidential and that the firm had unique knowledge or experience. The audit findings, however, included the following statement:

> Normally, if the "pressing emergency" exception is invoked, the contract is let immediately to reflect the urgency of the requirement. However, more than four months elapsed between the foreign government's request for the assistance and the RCMP's request that PWGSC initiate the contracting process.

The advance knowledge of the need to contract for police training services makes this justification appear to be clearly a case where the pressing emergency exception was abused.

Including a description of the selection criteria in the solicitation is a basic tenet of standard government contracting. The existence of an emergency does not justify abandonment of this need to advise prospective contractors of the government's criteria for selecting the successful contractor. When selecting contractors during an emergency, the criteria is normally weighted heavily on (1) the timeline for commencing service or product delivery, (2) the service level or product quality, and (3) to a lesser degree, price. Prudent agencies minimize the importance of the price criterion when selecting contractors during an emergency. Depending on the nature of the emergency and available communication modes, the solicitation may be communicated via e-mail, facsimile, telephone, in person, or any other available alternative. By soliciting proposals from competing contractors, agencies can choose between multiple proposals in essentially the same time needed to place a sole source contract. If the presumptive sole source contractor had submitted a proposal for delayed commencement of service or product delivery or disappointing service level or product quality, the agency operating in this noncompetitive environment may have no alternative but to accept the minimalist proposal from the sole source contractor. Although the contractor submitting the more attractive proposal in a competitive procurement may have included a higher price, the agency is permitted to award the contract based on the more heavily weighted availability and quality selection criteria mentioned in the solicitation. Although price or life cycle cost may have a lower priority during emergencies, contractors tend to offer lower pricing when they are aware that the procurement is competitive. Agencies that are not presently authorized to contract in this manner during actual emergencies might wish to seek modification of their contracting authority to permit more timely response during emergencies.

Once the immediacy of the emergency is lessened, thus reducing the urgency of protecting life and property, the need to use accelerated procurement methods ceases. More emphasis can then be placed on pricing during source selection. Continuing to deemphasize pricing after the immediate threat to life and property has subsided is contradictory to good contracting practices and unnecessarily exposes the government to greater opportunities for contract fraud.

Precautions can be taken to reduce the risks associated with the award of contracts, such as letter contracts, that have not been fully staffed. Risks can be mitigated by incorporating a scope of work, establishing a process for cost control, and including the agency's standard contract terms and conditions in letter contracts.

> *Scope of work*: Providing a letter contract template with a scope of work helps ensure that contractors are obligated to provide the needed materials and services through contracting terminology that includes the word, such as "shall," that best compels the contractor to perform. A template containing the framework for a complete scope of work, wherein agency personnel completing the scope of work need only fill in blanks for the work to be

performed by the contractor, helps ensure that contractors are obligated to deliver products or perform services when needed.

Cost control: Letter contracts are appropriate in emergency conditions or in other cases when the time available before award of the contract precludes the ability to award a fully staffed contract. This does not imply, however, that the agency awarding the letter contract cannot include a fixed price, hourly rate, or not-to-exceed (NTE) price. The agency's informal solicitation normally requires the prospective contractors to include proposed pricing based on a fixed price or a not-to-exceed basis. As mentioned earlier, emergency conditions may dictate selection of a contractor that did not propose the lowest price. However, the NTE pricing, combined with the competitive environment, provides an element of cost control despite selection of a contractor that did not propose the lowest price.

Terms and conditions: The agency's standard terms and conditions are familiar to all contractors that provide goods or services during those times when there is no emergency. Those same contractors are likely to be represented on the list of firms solicited to provide materials and services during an emergency. Because those firms are familiar with the agency's terms and conditions, including insurance and indemnification provisions, letter contracts with standard terms and conditions can be awarded without delays incurred for contractors to review unfamiliar terms and conditions.

Contracting agencies normally permit award of high-value emergency contracts by an official who does not have authority to award a nonemergency contract at such a high price. However, those same rules also routinely require ratification of the contract, within some timeframe certain, by the official, board, or commission with authority to award high-value contracts during nonemergency periods. The timeframe established for ratification is normally the next meeting of the governing body when time permits placement of contract ratification on the agenda.

A letter contract typically has a limited effective life and requires replacement by a definitive contract. A definitive contract is a fully staffed contract executed by a government official authorized to approve contracts at or above the stated value during nonemergency time periods. The expiration date is normally stated clearly in the text of the letter contract as well as a statement to the effect that the agency will replace the letter contract with a definitive contract on or before the expiration of the letter contract. Inclusion of the expiration date and need to replace the letter contract with a definitive contract clearly informs the contractor of these agency requirements and reinforces the need to seek contract ratification. Government regulations typically specify the length of time, such as thirty, sixty, or ninety days following contract award, when the letter contract expires and requires definitization. If a definitive contract cannot be approved prior to expiration of the letter contract, the official, commission, or board responsible for ratifying the definitized contract may extend the expiration date for the letter contract.

9.3.1 *Domestic Emergencies*

In purely domestic disasters where the affected country has the resources necessary to save lives, conduct the cleanup, provide temporary housing, and finance the reconstruction efforts, there is no need for the complex relationships inherent to international emergency responses. This does not lessen the need to establish processes and procedures for preventing mismanagement and corruption even in prosperous countries. The measures in the Hurricane Katrina Accountability and Contract Reform Act were suitable, had the act been adopted, as the framework for preventing fraud, waste, and abuse during domestic emergency responses.

Catastrophic events occurring in prosperous countries prepared to deal with emergencies within their borders do not require the complexities of an international emergency response. Although such purely domestic emergencies are susceptible to fraud, waste, and abuse, response to purely domestic emergencies is not enmeshed in the intricate relationships inherent with international responses. However, the recommendations for planning, preparation, and response to domestic disasters are also applicable to international emergency responses. Despite this commonality, and because of certain significant differences, the response to domestic emergencies is presented separately from the recommendations for response to international relief operations.

Government entities must continuously be prepared to deal with domestic emergencies that threaten lives, property, or the continued provision of essential government services. Private-sector contractors are likely to contribute to the government's efforts to deal with such emergencies. Just as agencies benefit by planning in advance for employing government resources during emergencies, they similarly benefit by planning in advance to engage private-sector contractors during emergencies.

Despite exposure to notoriety, opportunists continue to seek unconscionable profit during disasters. The predictability of such despicable behavior has resulted in commendable efforts to establish processes for curbing corruption stemming from the recovery and reconstruction efforts for actual emergencies.

Although the Hurricane Katrina Accountability and Contract Reform Act (HR 3838), introduced in the U.S. Congress, was defeated by the administration, its provisions were suited for preventing corruption during domestic emergencies in prosperous countries. The Hurricane Katrina Act (or "the Act") included the establishment of an anti-fraud commission, increased transparency and accountability, and established contracting reform procedures to prevent and address corruption in the aftermath of Hurricane Katrina. Enactment of the Act would also have repealed the $250,000 threshold for debit and credit card purchases. Repealing the $250,000 purchase limit would have removed certain opportunities for fraud without overly restricting government officials responding to Hurricane Katrina.

An anti-fraud commission proposed by the Act was charged with reviewing contract awards to ensure compliance with competitive procurement requirements and the award of contracts based on merit, reviewing real-time spending through contracts and procurement cards, and evaluating the qualifications and number of contracting personnel monitoring federal contractors.

The provisions of the Hurricane Katrina Act for increasing transparency and accountability were proposed for facilitation through the establishment of a public database containing federal contracting information. The proposed Act also contained a provision that required the administration to disclose acts of corruption to appropriate congressional committees. Although this provision requiring one branch of government to disclose acts of corruption to another branch of government might be considered merely political, some requirement for public disclosure of acts of corruption is appropriate.

Another provision of the Hurricane Katrina Act was designed to prevent and address corruption in federal contracting by restricting sole source contracting. That provision limits sole source contracting to cases where competition is not possible due to emergencies or other justifiable circumstances, guards against contractor conflicts of interest by prohibiting a contractor having oversight over other contractors with which they have contractual or other business relationships, restricts the hiring of federal employees by government contract, and repeals the $250,000 micro-purchase authority. The micro-purchase authority establishes the threshold for procurement card purchases, which was increased in the aftermath of Hurricane Katrina to permit extraordinary noncompetitive procurements.[5]

The exception for sole source contracting due to emergencies is questionable. Discussion earlier in this chapter covered the fallacy of justifying sole source contracting on the basis of an existing emergency. Agencies and legislative bodies are urged to reconsider existing exceptions to competitive procurement based on an emergency. Timeliness of delivery is paramount during emergencies. However, sole source contracting does not guarantee the earliest delivery. Multiple contractors can be solicited and respond to the solicitation (written or verbal) in virtually the same timeframe as a sole source procurement. In a competitive procurement, all the prospective contractors are motivated to submit a proposal that best meets the agency's needs. Although product or service availability may be the highest weighted criterion and the agency may select the contractor with the earliest delivery, the pricing is likely to be lower than pricing in sole source procurement merely due to the existence of competition. Another disadvantage of sole source contracting is that the absence of competition provides expanded opportunities for procurement corruption.

Although the Hurricane Katrina Act incorporated a well-constructed approach to combating procurement corruption in the aftermath of Hurricane Katrina, it was defeated. In opposing the Act, President George W. Bush's administration stated that it felt sufficient controls were included in existing federal procurement rules to prevent abuse and fraud.[6] It is true that there were existing federal procurement rules, with the notable exception regarding the $250,000 threshold for the debit and credit cards, enacted to prevent procurement fraud. However, the extensive contract corruption, incompetence, or malfeasance experienced in the aftermath of Hurricane Katrina established the defeat of this Act as one of numerous monumental mistakes contributing to the government's failure to adequately respond to Hurricane Katrina.

The provisions of the Hurricane Katrina Accountability and Contract Reform Act, less the blanket exemption from competition during emergencies and disclosure of corruption acts to congressional committees, represented a good framework for preventing corruption in domestic disasters.

9.3.2 International Emergencies

The provisions of the Hurricane Katrina Accountability and Contract Reform Act, with the exceptions already noted, are also appropriate for international emergency responses; however, the complexities introduced when the response is international require extraordinary processes.

In the absence of an international agreement on the response to tragedies, it is necessary to develop processes for reacting to each emergency while, hopefully, preventing mismanagement and abuse after the disaster has occurred. Delaying the adoption of corruption prevention measures until the affected regions and populace have experienced the effects of the disaster unnecessarily exposes the international community to procurement fraud excesses for an extended period of time. The fact that approximately $10 billion is expended annually in emergency responses is justification for the expenditure of funds to establish a standing international organization with established processes and procedures in place for dealing with future disasters while preventing mismanagement and corruption. Therefore, an "Outline for a Predetermined Emergency Accord on Response and Readiness (PEARR) Program", contained on the CD, includes conditions and features for such an international organization and agreement based on the proceedings of the Jakarta Expert Meeting.

The recommended responses to domestic emergencies are also appropriate for international emergency responses and are therefore recommended for implementation in international relief efforts. However, it is naïve to ignore the obvious added complexities when the response is international in scope. The initial refusal of international assistance from the Myanmar government in the aftermath of the 2008 cyclone is a prime example of a seemingly unexplainable international relief effort complexity that compounded the suffering of the affected populace. Complexities in international disaster responses, however, are not unusual despite the fact that most governments welcome international assistance.

In contrast to the defeat of the Hurricane Katrina Accountability and Contract Reform Act, the Asian Development Bank (ADB), the Organization for Economic Co-operation and Development (OECD), and Transparency International (TI) organized the Jakarta Expert Meeting that was held April 7–8, 2005, in Jakarta, Indonesia,[7] resulted in agreement to measures for curbing corruption, waste, and mismanagement in the aftermath of the December 2004 Indian Ocean tsunami. The report of the proceedings from this meeting, "Curbing Corruption in Tsunami Relief Operations," makes it apparent that considerable success was achieved through this effort with 101 participants from ADB, OECD, TI, sixteen countries, and nine international organizations.

The report published upon the conclusion of the Jakarta Expert Meeting contained a framework for action that included country ownership, community participation, access to information, transparency of aid flows, monitoring and evaluation, complaints and reporting mechanisms, mutual accountability and coordination, and capacity development for improved governance and corruption deterrence. Although there appeared to be some reservation regarding the country ownership feature of the framework for action in the text of the report,[8] implementation of the other features, listed above and contained in the framework for action, do facilitate the prevention of procurement corruption during relief operations. Transparency is an especially helpful feature for preventing corruption because it permits the citizenry and the media to determine the value of contracts for specific products or services awarded to named private-sector companies.

The most evident detriment to this approach for development of such a framework is that the features were formulated, agreed upon, and implemented about four months after the tsunami occurred. This delay in the implementation of the framework for action meant that the initial response and short-term recovery efforts had already been made. The reservations concerning country of ownership justify reconsideration of the decision to establish country of ownership as one of the features of the framework. The reservations about the country of ownership were based on the concern that use of the procurement rules of the country that experienced the disaster might expose the contracting process to opportunities for corruption, incompetence, or malfeasance.

Government entities faced with an emergency involving an imminent threat to life, property, or its capability to provide essential government services do not have the advantage of time for preparing formal solicitations, conducting sophisticated proposal evaluations, and providing full staffing that is normally afforded contracts for materials and services awarded during nonemergency periods. Yet, seeking competitive pricing, good quality, and timely delivery is essential despite the existence of emergencies. Failure to plan in advance for contracting during emergencies results in hasty contracting decisions during future emergencies. Excessive pricing, suboptimal quality, and belated commencement of service or product delivery is the likely result of contracting decisions made in haste. Two approaches to planning for contracted materials and services during an emergency are to place contracts in advance of emergencies for products and services that can be anticipated, and to provide for a contract instrument, such as a letter contract, that can be awarded expeditiously during an emergency when the need for certain products and services cannot be anticipated.

When materials and services required during an emergency can be anticipated, agencies can release competitive solicitations for the selection of contractors and award of IDIQ contracts prior to the next emergency in the usual manner without the time constraints present during an actual emergency. Such contracts can be drafted so that they become effective upon receipt of a notice to proceed from the contracting agency. During an emergency, the contracting agency can quickly provide written direction to proceed via e-mail or a facsimile transmission. When such contracts have been in place for an extended period of time, say one year, it is appropriate to review the contracts to determine whether the provisions are current and the contractors continue to be prepared to provide the materials and services according to the provisions of the contract.

Agencies can best serve disaster victims when they solicit bids or quotes for products or services that were not anticipated in advance of the emergency, evaluate bids and proposals to select contractors, and place contracts in an expeditious manner during the disaster and immediately thereafter. The contractual instrument recommended for award during actual emergencies, as discussed earlier, is the letter contract. Letter contracts are intended for award in an emergency situation when there is insufficient time to seek formal proposals, conduct sophisticated proposal evaluations, and obtain approval of the official who normally approves such contracts at the applicable value. The award of letter contracts need not be made on a sole source basis. Indeed, competitive contracting in emergencies is recommended to ensure timely delivery of the appropriate products or services at competitive pricing while discouraging contract corruption.

The recommendations presented here for responding to international disasters are compatible with the discussions that were held and the framework for action that was developed during the Jakarta Expert Meeting. However, the recommendations in this book, although addressing the issues during the deliberations in Jakarta, differ in several respects from the final recommendations accepted in Jakarta. The most significant difference relates to the measure adopted in Jakarta regarding the country of ownership feature that was not unanimously embraced. The concern regarding the country of ownership feature appeared to be based on the fear that emergency procurement systems in certain countries are inherently infected by corruptive practices that threaten debasement of the process for dispensing international emergency aid.

As previously mentioned, the most evident detriment to the approach taken at the Jakarta Expert Meeting was that their framework for action was formulated, agreed upon, and implemented, understandably, months following the tsunami that devastated the area. This delay in the implementation of the framework for action necessitated dealing with the initial response and short-term recovery efforts prior to implementation of the framework for action. To compensate for this delay, the establishment of a framework in advance of future catastrophes is proposed.

9.4 Need to Establish Response Mechanism in Advance of International Emergencies

The only feasible solution for providing timely responses to international emergencies while preventing corruption, incompetence, or malfeasance is to establish an international accord in advance of future international emergencies. Although potential sponsors or specific instruments for such an accord are not recommended by this author, one potential sponsor is the United Nations and a specific instrument is an addendum to the World Trade Organization's (WTO's) General Agreement on Trade and Tariffs (GATT) Agreement on Government Procurement that was signed in Marrakesh in 1994. The Agreement on Government Procurement established international standards for good procurement practices.

9.4.1 Justification for Expenses Required to Establish and Maintain a PEARR

There are costs associated with the establishment and ongoing administration of a PEARR. However, implementation and ongoing costs are insignificant when compared to the expected savings through avoidance of future costs associated with corruption, waste, and mismanagement. The cost of humanitarian relief has been estimated as $10 billion annually.[9] This tremendous expenditure by donor countries and NGOs certainly justifies the expense of establishing and maintaining a PEARR to plan for future emergency responses, establishing standards and processes for providing humanitarian relief, and guarding against the rampant corruption that has historically diverted a significant percentage of the $10 billion cost for humanitarian relief.

The organization responsible for drafting, implementing, and managing the PEARR would benefit by assigning representatives from prospective donor countries, prospective recipient countries, and NGOs.

9.4.2 Motivation for Prospective Participants to Consent to the PEARR

The prospect of curbing corruption waste and mismanagement may provide sufficient motivation for the suggested participants to agree to embrace an accord such as a PEARR. However, reluctant signatories may require additional measures:

> *Prospective donor countries* can be encouraged to consent to such an accord if eligibility for participation in reconstruction contracting or subcontracting by companies based in their country is contingent on the country's consent to the provisions of the accord.
>
> *Prospective recipient countries* can be encouraged to consent to the PEARR if such consent is a prerequisite to receipt of international assistance. Additionally, eligibility to participate in reconstruction contracting and subcontracting efforts might also be contingent on consent to PEARR provisions.
>
> *NGOs* may be required to consent to a PEARR as a prerequisite for participating in international relief efforts.

The content of a PEARR requires the development of a lengthy, complex document that is beyond the scope of this book. However, a suggested framework, including conditions and features, similar to the provisions of the "Outline for Predetermined Emergency Accord on Response and Readiness (PEARR) Program," is provided on the CD.

9.5 Obtaining Private-Sector Buy-In to International Emergency Response Mechanism

Government contractors that delay marketing efforts for participation in emergency operations until the emergency is declared have limited contracting opportunities unless their company name is well known and associated with the materials and services required during the declared emergency. One option available after an emergency has been declared is to contact the managing emergency operations and advise them of the services and materials that they can provide in support of emergency operations.

Government entities with the foresight to plan for future emergencies are likely to award IDIQ contracts for materials and services that are likely to be needed during future emergencies. Once the emergency is declared and it is determined that the materials or services are required, the government contacts the contractors with IDIQ contracts to make releases (request deliveries) against the IDIQ contracts. The standard process for initiating the award of IDIQ contracts is for the government to release a solicitation (RFP or IFB) to the private sector. Contractors wishing to provide materials or services in support of emergency operations that receive solicitations for IDIQ contracts, naturally, must respond with a proposal or bid as appropriate. In the absence of a solicitation for an IDIQ contract, interested contractors may contact the agency purchasing or contracting office and request that their company be placed on the agency's approved supplier list.

Responding to government solicitations and requesting placement on the approved supplier list are positive steps toward participation in future emergency operations. However, there is a more proactive measure recommended for contractors that wish to be awarded an IDIQ contract for materials or services required during future declared emergencies. Although the contracting process is normally initiated through release of a government solicitation, this does not prevent contractors from submitting an unsolicited proposal. Contractors that can provide materials or services that are likely to be needed during future emergencies can prepare a proposal for award of an IDIQ contract and submit it to the government as an unsolicited proposal. Although government entities do not always welcome unsolicited proposals, the proposal for an IDIQ contract sent to a government entity that has not planned for future emergencies may be welcomed. The proposal may exhort the agency to pursue IDIQ contracts for other needed materials and services and to recognize the contractor for performing a public service by invigorating the planning effort for future emergencies.

A summary of the recommendations for contracting in emergencies is provided in Table 9.1.

Table 9.1 Recommendations for Contracting in Emergencies

Recommendation Topics	Recommended Practices
Planning for emergencies	Identify anticipated needs for emergency supplies and services; award indefinite delivery indefinite quantity (IDIQ) contracts; provide a template for awarding contracts during emergencies; develop a process for obtaining expedited delivery, required quality, and competitive pricing for emergency contracting; and create rules for tightening contracting restrictions following the immediacy of threats from disasters.
Awarding contracts during emergencies	Establish policies and practices for contracting during emergencies that include required competition to obtain expedited delivery, required quality, and competitive pricing; use letter contracts when necessary; include fixed price, unit pricing, or not-to-exceed price on letter contracts; include scope of work as well as terms and conditions in letter contracts; definitize letter contracts when time permits; use less formal and expedited evaluation of proposals to select contractors; and resist tendency to provide universal exception to competition during emergencies.
Domestic emergencies	Implement policies and procedures for contracting during emergencies; include means for guarding against fraud, waste, and abuse by including requirements for competitive procurements whenever possible; and use fully staffed definitive contracts awarded through full and open competition for rebuilding efforts following immediacy of threats caused by the disaster.
International emergencies	All of the above recommended practices are recommended for international emergencies. However, in the absence of policies and practices established in the absence of a disaster, the rules are not considered and agreed upon until after the disaster has occurred. Therefore, responsible countries, organizations, and individuals affected by the disaster are vulnerable to unscrupulous acts from the onset of each disaster until the processes and procedures are established for each disaster. Establish processes and procedures as described above in the absence of a disaster. Obtain buy-in from all potential participants, responders, and countries that require international assistance during disasters.

9.6 Failed Emergency Response and Corruption Exposure from Deficient Planning

The previously unimaginable terrorist attack on the United States at the World Trade Center in New York on September 11, 2001, was the catalyst for the Homeland Security Act of 2002, which, in addition to previously existing emergency procurement authorities, provided extraordinary added flexibility in the procurement of goods and services when reacting to terrorist threats. A memorandum from the administrator of the Office of Management and Budget to the President's Management Council[10] described the "flexibilities for emergency procurements" that became available through the Homeland Security Act of 2002. Although the memorandum mentioned the benefits of competition and the need to document the "cogency of the rationale for actions taken," the overall objective of the memorandum was to explain the extraordinary procurement flexibilities (or expanded sole source procurement authority) previously available and the new flexibilities available through the Homeland Security Act. The previously available flexibilities included simplified open market competitions for commercial items up to US$5 million, sole source procurements from historically underutilized business zone (HUBZone) participants, oral solicitations, letter contracts,[11] limited source selections, and innovative contracting that permit agencies to "innovate and use sound business judgment that is otherwise consistent with law and within the limits of their authority." The new flexibilities and expiration dates for the expanded procurement authority varied depending on whether the procurement was made by or for the Department of Defense (DoD), requiring obligation by September 30, 2003, or any other executive agency requiring solicitation issuance before November 24, 2003.

The new flexibilities were expansive indeed and provided unnecessary opportunities for procurement corruption. The simplified acquisition procedures for any executive agency modified the previous restriction pertaining to any acquisition under $100,000 or commercial items up to $5 million to *any product or service in any amount*. The waiver of certain accounting, compliance, and other laws for any executive agency, previously restricted to the acquisition of commercial items in any amount, was changed to *any product or service in any amount*. Micro-purchase authority for procurement card transactions (debit or credit card purchases) was increased from $2,500 to $7,500 for any executive agency and to $15,000 for the DoD. However, subsequent legislation greatly increased the threshold for purchase card transactions to $250,000. The simplified acquisition threshold for contingency humanitarian and peacekeeping operations was increased from $200,000 for contracts awarded and performed overseas to $200,000 for domestic and $250,000 for foreign contracts for any executive agency and to $250,000 for domestic and $500,000 for foreign DoD contracts. The general application for HUBZone contracting permits sole source contracting up to $5 million for manufacturing and up to $3 million for everything other than manufacturing. The increased flexibility for any executive agency references several subsections of U.S. Code (U.S.C.) 2304, which require competition unless the generally accepted exceptions to competition apply. However, there is also a reference to FAR 19.1306, which states that competition is not required unless there is more than one HUBZone small business concern that can satisfy the requirement. If the FAR 19.1306 exception is applicable, then the additional procurement flexibility changed the $5 million manufacturing and $3 million nonmanufacturing thresholds to sole source purchases in any amount if there is only one HUBZone small business that can satisfy the requirement.

These changes provide truly generous flexibilities for emergency procurements. The concern, however, is that in combination with more flexibility in reacting to emergencies they also further increase opportunities for nefarious, amateurish, and criminal behavior. In addition to these generous increases in government procurement flexibilities, the procurement card threshold was increased to $250,000 in reaction to Hurricane Katrina in 2005. Permitting noncompetitive procurement card purchases up to $250,000 further invites nefarious, amateurish, and criminal behavior.

There were a multitude of procurement disasters during the response to Hurricane Katrina, beginning with the initial response and lasting well into the reconstruction phase. As media reports have indicated,[11] the government purchased trailers and mobile homes without obtaining competitive bids shortly before Hurricane Katrina struck the Gulf Coast. That procurement action appeared to go beyond the "procurement flexibilities" the Bush administration urged contracting officials to use. The noncompetitive purchase of these 145,000 trailers and mobile homes at an average price of $18,600 each, for a total cost exceeding $2.5 billion, was apparently made solely based on the existence of the declared disaster. The lack of advance planning, failure to purchase the temporary shelters competitively, and failure to pre-position the temporary shelters when there was no emergency and no immediate threat of an emergency contributed to the nefarious, amateurish expenditure of $2.5 billion for temporary shelters that proved later to endanger the health and lives of the Hurricane Katrina victims. For several reasons, numerous communities refused to accept the temporary shelters. The primary problem was the use of formaldehyde in the manufacturing process that endangered individuals living in the shelters. *The Washington Post* reported that, upon realizing the existence of formaldehyde in the shelters, the government decided to sell the trailers at 40% of the original price to anyone who wished to purchase them. However, upon realization of the liability of selling the trailers containing formaldehyde, and following the sale of thousands of trailers, the government decided to repurchase the trailers and mobile homes for the full purchase price on the condition that they be delivered to FEMA drop-off points.

As discussed earlier in this chapter, the failure to plan for contracting during declared disasters leads to the need to make contracting decisions in haste. Relaxed contracting rules exacerbate the hasty contracting decisions by relaxing the rules requiring competitive procurement. The unfortunate combination of an absence of planning, relaxed procurement rules, and the fact that there are unscrupulous contractors who take advantage of any opportunity to gouge unearned profits to the detriment of the victims, government entities, and the public. "Procurement flexibility" permits sole source purchasing, in certain circumstances, from historically underrepresented companies such as HUBZone contractors and Native American tribally owned businesses. These relaxed contracting rules render these businesses as targets of dishonest contractors that wish to have the historically underrepresented companies awarded large sole source contracts when, in fact, the large business obtains the vast majority of the contract benefit while the historically underrepresented company retains a token amount of the proceeds.

Another problem during the aftermath of Hurricane Katrina was associated with the award of contracts to large corporations that did little work themselves, but subcontracted the work often through multiple tiers of subcontracts. A report by the NBC News Investigative Unit[12] revealed that four prime contractors were each awarded $500 million contracts with an option for an additional $500 million. One of the four prime contractors, Environmental Services Inc., reported limited subcontracting to two tiers; however, the company acknowledged that it had instances of five subcontracting tiers. Another of the four prime contractors, The Ashbritt Company, was reimbursed $23 per cubic yard through the prime contract. The first-tier subcontractor, C&B Enterprises, was reimbursed $9 per cubic yard through their subcontract. The second-tier subcontractor, Amlee Transportation, was reimbursed $8 per cubic yard. The third-tier subcontractor, Chris Hessler Inc, was reimbursed $7 per cubic yard. Finally, the fourth-tier subcontractor, Les Nirdlinger, was reimbursed $3 per cubic yard for the debris that it actually hauled. The Ashbritt Company was reimbursed $20 per cubic yard more than Les Nirdlinger for the debris Nirdlinger actually hauled. At $23 per cubic yard, the government contracted for the Ashbritt Company to remove 2,173,913 cubic yards. A contract for the removal of 2,173,913 cubic yards of debris at $23 per cubic yard equates to a total price of $49,999,999 versus $6,521,739 at $3 per cubic yard. Had the government awarded the entire debris removal effort through full and open competition, thus permitting small companies like Nirdlinger to compete, the potential savings would have been $43,478,260.

A summary of the perils emanating from the failure to plan for emergencies and for allowing overly permissive contracting practices during emergencies is provided in Table 9.2.

Contractors that fail to adopt the recommendations to respond to solicitations for IDIQ contracts, fail to contact government entities during declared emergencies to describe the materials or services they can provide to support emergency operations, or prepare an unsolicited proposal for IDIQ contracts for emergency materials or services significantly lessen the possibility for participation in emergency operations. Contractors that do not attempt to participate in IDIQ contracts in support of declared emergencies may also forfeit an opportunity to become established as a regular supplier of materials and services in the absence of an emergency.

Table 9.2   Perils of Failed Planning and Overly Permissive Contracting Practices during Emergencies

Specific Perils	Vulnerabilities
Expanded opportunities for procurement corruption	Providing widespread waivers of the requirement to award contracts through the competitive process during and following disasters creates expanded opportunities for corruption. This is especially damaging when one considers that expedited processes for soliciting proposals, evaluating proposals, and awarding contracts can be accomplished during the same timeframe as the award of sole source contracts. Delivery of materials and services needed in response to a disaster are accelerated through the competitive process if a competitor of the presumptive sole source contractor can more readily provide the needed materials or services.
Excessive pricing	In the absence of competition, contractors are prone to offer higher prices than they would propose in a competitive procurement environment. Therefore, it is likely that government pays a premium when contracting on a sole source basis. Consider the removal of debris following Hurricane Katrina where the government paid the prime contractor $23 per cubic yard while the fifth tier subcontractor, that actually performed the work, was paid just $3 per cubic yard.
Inadequate quality of needed materials and services	Agencies that fail to adequately plan for contracting during emergencies are faced with the need to purchase materials or services without having developed specifications or pre-qualified contractors. When there is urgency to provide such needed materials and services under pressure to preserve lives and property, there is a tendency to contract for whatever is available at the time. An extreme example of the disastrous results of failed planning and overly permissive contracting practices during emergencies is the purchase of formaldehyde-laden trailers during Hurricane Katrina.
Delayed availability of materials and services needed during emergencies	As discussed earlier, an expedited contracting process can result in the award of a contract through the competitive process in the same timeframe as a sole source contract. Had the government awarded the debris removal contract through "full and open" competition that included solicitation of all the subcontractors (even if they were solicited by telephone or e-mail) that had actually performed the work, there would not have been the delay necessitated by awarding subcontracts through five tiers of subcontractors. The existence of that level of subcontracting likely quintupled the time lag until actual debris removal commenced.

9.7 Protecting Lives and Property during Emergency Response

An effective emergency contracting program contributes to the objectives of the all-encompassing emergency response plan that is intended to save lives, treat and prevent injuries, prevent or minimize property damage, resume or continue essential government services, and rebuild the infrastructure. Implementing the recommendations in this chapter permits governments to meet these objectives while remaining conscious of pricing and the quality of supplies and services provided in response to the emergency while discouraging the corruption that frequently accompanies declared emergencies.

The extent of benefits expected from implementing the recommendations in this chapter for emergency contracting are dependent on planning and preparations made in advance of disasters, thus freeing relief workers to concentrate on implementing existing emergency contracting plans, activating existing contracts, and delivering pre-positioned materials to the disaster site. Pre-planning avoids the need for disaster responders to search for contractors after the disaster occurs and to establish what products and services are available, when they can be delivered, and what prices are charged.

Another advantage of pre-planning is the benefit of available time to ensure that materials meet expected quality standards. When contracting for temporary shelters, for example, following a disastrous event when time is of the essence, contracting personnel are pressured to obtain whatever is immediately available. As mentioned in Chapter 1, FEMA learned from its unfortunate experiences during the Hurricane Katrina disaster and had pre-competed IDIQ contracts in place when FEMA responded to the October 2007 wildfires in Southern California. During the time prior to the Southern California wildfires, when there were no declared federal disasters, FEMA was able to take advantage of the pause between disasters to plan for the materials that are required during emergencies, solicit multiple contractors, select the contractors that prepared their proposals in a competitive environment, and award IDIQ contracts that were activated during the next disaster.

Planning for emergencies and implementation of an effective emergency contracting program permit agency personnel to concentrate on their highest priorities of protecting lives and property, preventing injuries and illness, and continuing to provide essential services during actual emergencies. In the absence of an effective emergency contracting program, agency personnel are required to spend considerable time during an actual emergency performing tasks that could better be performed prior to the declared emergency. Placing IDIQ contracts during non-emergency conditions permits agency personnel to exercise decision making more rationally in the absence of an emergency and employ routine contracting processes that provide for full and open competition, do not provide invitations for procurement fraud opportunities, and facilitate the award of contracts to contractors offering the optimal combination of price, quality, and timeliness.

Submitting an unsolicited proposal for an IDIQ contract for emergency supplies or services may result in award of a contract to provide such supplies or services during future declared emergencies. The benefit to contractors submitting unsolicited proposals to government entities, however, need not be limited to award of an IDIQ contract. The contractor submitting the unsolicited proposal may also be recognized as a valuable supplier that, as a result of its unsolicited proposal, becomes established as a regular supplier to the agency during nonemergency conditions.

9.8 Conclusion

Among government's foremost obligations are protecting lives and property threatened by disasters and rebuilding following the emergency. There are numerous examples of governments' failures to meet these obligations in a reasonable manner. Too often the government reaction to criticism of the timeliness of its response and the excess costs is to streamline the process by ever increasing the threshold where contracts can be awarded without competition. Awarding sole source contracts, however, does not ensure timely response to disasters and almost certainly results in higher costs for responding to emergencies. When placing a contract during an emergency it is necessary to ask the sole source contractor its price, the nature of the product or service that it will provide, and the date when the product can be delivered or the service can commence. These basic facts are needed to award a contract regardless of the existence of an emergency. Government can request and receive a proposal from multiple contractors in the same timeframe as required from a sole source contractor. When timely delivery is of paramount importance it is better to evaluate delivery or commencement dates from multiple contractors than from the presumptive sole source contractor. In a competitive procurement, all the prospective contractors are likely to propose lower prices. Based on these realities of the procurement process, a competitive procurement is likely to provide lower prices and more timely availability of the required products or services than a sole source contract. The prospect for receiving lower prices and faster delivery through competitive contracting combined with government's obligation for a timely response to disasters compels governments to plan for competitive contracting during emergencies. The relaxation of the need for competing reconstruction contracts following emergency subsidence is not sensible because these contracts are awarded following the threat to lives and property. Governments, however, regularly waive competitive requirements for reconstruction contracts.

In addition to planning for competing contracts during emergencies, governments react faster and more economically when they plan for future disasters by awarding IDIQ contracts for products and services with a foreseen need during future emergencies. As mentioned earlier in this chapter, much of the criticism of FEMA's response to Hurricane Katrina might have been avoided had FEMA placed IDIQ contracts in advance of that disaster. To FEMA's credit, they had awarded IDIQ contracts in advance of the Southern California fires that occurred two years following Hurricane Katrina. Governments that prepare for future disasters by planning to award contracts competitively during emergencies and to award IDIQ contracts in advance of declared emergencies are better prepared to respond to disasters than governments that do not complete this requisite planning.

Notes

1. Committee on Homeland Security and Governmental Affairs, U.S. Senate, "Ineffective FEMA Oversight of Housing Maintenance Contracts in Mississippi Resulted in Millions of Dollars of Waste and Potential Fraud," Report number GAO-08-106, November 2007.
2. "Canada to Airlift 2,000 Emergency Shelter Kits to Burma," May 13, 2008.
3. *Santa Barbara Independent*, "Contract Glitch Blocks Air Tanker Drops," Nick Welsh, May 6, 2009.
4. The referenced audit report conducted by the Office of the Auditor General of Canada is entitled "1999 November Report of the Auditor General of Canada" dated November 1999.
5. In his September 7, 2005, letter to the Speaker of the House of Representatives requesting the Congress to consider an additional $51.8 billion for emergency FY 2005 supplemental resources, President George W. Bush made reference to details of his request, including an increase in the threshold for micro-purchase authority to $250,000. The micro-purchase threshold is equal to the threshold for government procurement cards.
6. U.S. House of Representatives, Committee on Government Reform — Minority Staff, Special Investigations Division, "Waste, Fraud, and Abuse in Hurricane Katrina Contracts," August 2006.
7. Asian Development Bank, "Curbing Corruption in Tsunami Relief Operations," Proceedings of the Jakarta Expert Meeting organized by the Asian Development Bank, Organisation for Economic Co-operation and Development, and Transparency International, and hosted by the Government of Indonesia in Jakarta, 7–8 April 2005.
8. The reservations regarding the country ownership feature resulted from concerns that the affected country may have an emergency procurement system inherently infected by corruptive practices that could debase the process for dispensing international emergency aid.
9. Asian Development Bank, "Curbing Corruption in Tsunami Relief Operations," Proceedings of the Jakarta Expert Meeting organized by the Asian Development Bank, Organisation for Economic Co-operation and Development, and Transparency International, and hosted by the Government of Indonesia in Jakarta, 7–8 April 2005, p. 41.
10. Executive Office of the President, Office of Management and Budget, Memorandum for the President's Management Council, "Guidelines for Using Emergency Procurement Flexibilities," May 30, 2003.
11. *The Washington Post*, "FEMA Flip-Flops Again on Trailers," Marc Kaufman, January 18, 2008.
12. NBC News Investigative Unit report, "Is Katrina Cleanup a Fleecing of America?" Lisa Myers & the NBC News Investigative Unit, June 5, 2006.

Chapter 10

Contract Completion and Audit

10.1 Fundamentals of Contract Completion

Contract completion occurs when the contractor completes the work described in the contract. The contractor may have some residual tasks such as honoring warranties and maintaining contractor records relating to the contract. The agency, however, has a number of tasks to perform following contract completion. Tasks typically performed include records retention, relief of financial encumbrances, evaluation of the contractor's performance, and audit of the contract. Eventually the contract records can be destroyed.

Contract closeout commences after the contractor has performed virtually all of the contractual responsibilities. Responsibility for records retention remains following contract completion. The agency's actions during contract closeout are straightforward. Agency representatives normally prepare a contractor performance report, disencumber all remaining funds and maintain contract records until they are eligible for destruction. Hard copy contract files, as opposed to electronic files, can normally be sent to a central records storage area one year after contract completion and maintained there until the records destruction date arrives. Clearly marking the record destruction date on the records storage container prevents storage of the records for an excessive time period.

10.1.1 Records Retention

Contract records, paper or electronic, need to be maintained for a period of time following contract completion in the event that a question, dispute, litigation, or other matter arises following contract completion. When a contractor has been found to be involved in conflict-of-interest or corruption cases, the agency may wish to review records of past contracts with that company to determine if similar problems may have affected earlier contracts. Government entities establish the time period for retention of completed contract files; however, a retention period that is frequently established is seven years following contract completion. Contract records for construction projects are often retained for the life of the capital asset that was constructed.

Upon completion of a contract by agencies that maintain hard copy files, all relevant contract documents are accumulated and inserted into the contract file. Agencies frequently maintain the completed contract files where they can be easily accessed during the first year following completion, when it is most likely that contract questions arise. After the first year, completed contract files are often removed to a more distant records storage area. Although most agencies have procedures requiring a destruction date on records sent to a central records storage area, those contracting offices that do not have such a policy may wish to require a document destruction date clearly marked on the file box for all records sent to the central records storage area. Failure to indicate the destruction date on records in central records storage can lead to retention of the contract records for an excessive time period. Maintaining expensive storage space for obsolete records results in excess costs.

As an alternative to maintaining hard-copy records on completed contracts, some agencies have converted to storage and maintenance of electronic records. Electronic storage requires significantly less space and also simplifies access to historical contract files. Maintaining a duplicate set of electronic files off-site is relatively simple and inexpensive in comparison to hard-copy files that are rarely duplicated and stored off-site as backup in the event that the original files are destroyed.

10.1.2 Relief of Financial Encumbrances

Contracting agencies typically encumber or commit funds in preparation for contract award, and the process for encumbering or committing funds on newly awarded contracts generally works well. However, numerous agencies do not have such an efficient process for removing excess encumbrances or commitments from completed contracts. In addition to the fact that it is a good contract management practice to remove excess funding from a contract when there is no chance of further expenditures, access to excess funding is often essential to ensure the continued provisioning of agency products or services. To ensure that excess funds are removed from the contract, the contracting agency might consider either developing a contract closeout checklist or including a space on the contractor performance report to indicate that excess funding has been returned to the general fund or the applicable department.

10.2 Contractor Performance Evaluations

A contracting agency report documenting the contractor's performance on recently completed contracts is recommended. Completion of the performance evaluation immediately upon contract completion, while the memories of the agency representatives are fresh, results in the most useful and accurate reports. The information in such a report becomes useful if and when the contractor is competing for, or otherwise being considered for, another contract at a later date or if another department or agency is checking references for a subsequent contract award. The following three measures of a contractor's performance are relevant for inclusion in the report: (1) cost management, (2) quality of the service or products that were provided, and (3) adherence to the schedule. Instances of lapses in ethical conduct or procurement corruption by the contractor, such as those indicated in Table 1.1, are also appropriate for inclusion in the contractor performance evaluation. In addition, the recommendation, or lack thereof, for awarding future similar contracts to the contractor being evaluated is useful for project managers and other agency representatives involved in evaluating past performance for future contract awards.

Contract completion occurs when all the tasks required by the contractor, including final reports, have been completed and all tasks required by the contracting agency, including final payment, have been completed. This differs from a notice of substantial completion that is typically issued upon completion of the contractor's portion of the work for construction contracts, and final payment is normally withheld until a specified number of days following the notice of completion for construction contracts.

The availability of financial information applicable to the contractor's performance and the significance of that information to the contracting agency depends on the type of contract. For example, very little information is available to the contracting agency when a firm fixed-price contract was awarded based on competition and there was no feedback on the contractor's profit or losses. However, under a cost reimbursement contract, the contracting agency obtains far more insight into the contractor's management of costs. When designing the format for contractor performance reports, it is appropriate to provide a space to report the contract type. Under a firm fixed-price contract with no profit or loss feedback to the contracting agency, the report on cost management is normally restricted to a statement to the effect that the contractor's cost management cannot be evaluated because the contractor was awarded a firm fixed-price contract. The contracting agency's project manager is able to provide information on the quality of the contractor's performance regardless of contract type. Accurate reporting of the contractor's performance is beneficial in the event that the contractor is considered for future contracts. However, if there were any quality issues that required resolution during the term of the contract, a discussion of the facts surrounding those issues will increase the report's usefulness.

The establishment of past performance as a criterion in contractor source selection is a common-sense approach, and a practice that is employed globally. A representative example of government direction to employ an evaluation of past performance in the contractor selection process is quoted below from a publication by the Australian Procurement & Construction Ministerial Council (APCC):[1]

> Performance will be a primary driver in tender selection with service providers competing on quality of performance. Clients may reward excellent performance on the part of service providers by improving their chances of winning work.
>
> Opportunities to win work will be enhanced in both open competition and through invitations to prequalified service providers. In both cases, past performance will be one of the criteria for the selection of service providers.
>
> Actions:
>
> 3.1 Recognise past performance when assessing tenders
>
> APCC members in each jurisdiction will incorporate past performance as a selection criterion in assessments of open tenders. The weightings given to performance will be of a sufficient level to convince contractors that performance has a defining impact on the tender assessment outcome.
>
> 3.2 Recognise past performance when prequalifying service providers
>
> Where prequalification schemes are in place, APCC members will include an ongoing assessment of past performance as a factor in increasing or decreasing a service provider's opportunities to bid for work.

Documents related to the contractor's performance, such as analyses, media reports, or legal documents, might also be considered for attachment to the contractor performance report.

The contracting agency's project manager and any other employees involved in the contract administration effort are normally best qualified to provide feedback on the contractor's schedule adherence. Obtaining feedback from all those involved in the contract administration effort contributes to the completeness of the resultant contractor performance report. Useful information for inclusion on the overall contractor performance evaluation includes conformance to the schedule dates for intermediate milestones, report submittals, and all deliverables. Although completion of the end milestone date is the most significant event, completion of intermediate milestones also reflects on the acceptability of the contactor's performance.

The usefulness of contractor performance reports is enhanced if there is a question regarding the reporting official's recommendation to award a similar contract to the contractor in the future. This is relevant because willingness or lack of willingness to use the contractor for similar contracts is one of the best indicators of the acceptability of a contractor's performance. It is recommended that, rather than report a mere yes or no, the reporting official be asked to report the reason for the recommendation regardless of whether the recommendation is favorable or unfavorable.

Although a copy of the contractor performance report is normally filed in the completed contract file, placing an additional copy in a central depository (as well as a shared database) where all affected parties may gain access to the performance reports for the agency's contractors is an additional good practice. A central depository for contractor performance reports makes the reports available to all agency departments as well as other agencies that may subsequently consider the contractor for similar projects.

10.3 Fundamentals of Contract Auditing

Contract audits may be conducted by a granting agency to determine whether the contracting agency complied with the terms of the grant. Contract audits may also be conducted by a central contracting office or audit function to determine the effectiveness of and compliance with policies and practices by departments with decentralized contracting authority.

Audits by granting agencies are typically performed following contract completion. Such audits are normally limited solely to a determination regarding the contracting agency's conformance to grant provisions. An audit determination of noncompliance with the grant provisions may result in a demand that the contracting agency partially or fully return the funds received from the granting agency.

Although contracting agencies may decentralize contracting authority to individual departments, centralized contracting offices are not necessarily absolved of responsibility for decentralized contracting activities. The agency that decentralizes contracting authority to distribute costs to the departments must necessarily maintain a contracting function, although leaner, to conduct contracting activities for the central agency offices. The centralized contracting function, consistent with retained responsibility for the agency's contracting program, normally implements and maintains contracting policies and procedures applicable to both the centralized and decentralized contracting activities. The centralized contracting function also normally provides training and guidance for the decentralized contracting offices. To ensure that the decentralized contracting offices have qualified employees and are conforming to the policies and procedures, the centralized contracting office might establish an audit program. Although the audit program may be limited to auditing a high percentage of completed high-value contracts and a declining percentage of lower value contracts, long-term high-value contracts are normally audited periodically during the term of the contract to measure program success and compliance with policies and procedures.

An example of an audit of completed contracts by an auditing agency to determine the effectiveness of contracting agencies is provided in a U.S. Government Accountability Office (GAO) report.[2] The report findings on ninety-six major defense acquisitions for programs from 2008 included cumulative cost growth of $296 billion and an average delay of twenty-two months. The report indicated that successful programs (an absence of problems associated with cost, schedule, or performance) were dependent on the following knowledge points and metrics:

1. Achieving a high level of technology maturity at the start of program development
2. Reaching design stability at the system-level critical design review
3. Demonstrating that critical manufacturing processes are in control before starting production

The GAO found that the poor outcomes were attributed to beginning system development without mature technologies and moving into system demonstration with insufficient design stability. These shortcomings led to significant cost growth and schedule delays.

A performance audit conducted by the Australian National Audit Office (ANAO)[3] provides an example of periodic audits conducted during the performance on a contract or contracts to measure program success and compliance with policies and procedures. This performance audit was a follow-up audit to the previous ANAO audit (number 3 2005-06) of the management of the M113 Armoured Personnel Carrier Upgrade Project. The upgrade to the M113 is a major upgrade that includes extending the length of the vehicles as well as installing new engines, gearboxes, and machine gun turrets. The audit report indicated that improvements had been made in all three management areas noted in the earlier audit. In addition to reviewing the contract files, the audit team visited the contractor's production facilities and a military installation where the upgraded M113s were being deployed. The standard three indicators of program success — performance, cost, and schedule — were all addressed during the course of the audit. The audit team noted technical, production, and contract problems encountered during the M113 upgrade and the impact on military units that were addressing problems associated with operating a mixed fleet of original M113s and upgraded M113s. The audit team concluded that negotiations between the contracting office and the prime contractor to address these problems were reasonable under the existing circumstances.

The preceding examples of weapons system performance audits are dissimilar from most government contracts in that technology that is often not completely mature at the onset of the contractor's work is required to be perfected during the course of the contract for incorporation in the deliverable products. This problem is also faced by any government entity that contracts for products incorporating immature technology, such as information technology products involving the development of new software as opposed to standard software products that merely require implementation.

Government entities that are not faced with technological development challenges are also audited regarding the cost, performance, and timeliness of contracted services and products. Therefore, audits focused on cost, performance, and timeliness are appropriate for all government contracts. Audit of the contracting function as performed throughout the contracting cycle, beginning with advance contract planning through contract administration and closeout, is also appropriate for all government entities. Government representatives who audit contracts are urged to be alert to indicators that criminal behavior or inept actions impacted decisions made regarding the contract being audited. Auditors seeking guidance on the methodology for auditing source selection actions are advised to review the process described in Chapter 7 for reacting to the receipt of a protest. The process for auditing the source selection phase of the contracting cycle parallels the process for investigating the merits of a protest. The audit of contracting functions is conducted to determine compliance with existing agency rules, policies, and practices. The purpose of such audits is to ensure that the contracting activities are being conducted appropriately and to identify any weaknesses that can be addressed by revising procedures, conducting training, changing the contracting workforce structure, or taking any other actions needed to address observed problems in the contracting function.

The contract document review conducted prior to execution of the contract normally includes evaluation of the reasonableness of the actions taken by agency personnel who prepared the contract document. (Note: Contract execution is synonymous with approval and award of the contract.) Time constraints existing due to the need for timely contract execution, however, may not permit verification of the information supporting contractor selection, detailed verification of the price reasonableness, and other functions performed during completion of the contract documents. To compensate for the lack of time for thorough analyses of all contracts prior to execution, agencies typically elect to audit a sample of the contracts after they have been executed, and often after contract completion. The contracts sampled normally consist of contracts that were either executed or completed during some recent time period, such as the fiscal or calendar year. The sampling process normally results in the selection of all high-value contracts for audit, as well as a decreasing percentage of contracts, correlated with the contract value, for mid-value and low-value contracts.

The healthcare field is especially vulnerable to contract fraud and is, therefore, likely to benefit from an effective audit program. According to an FBI report,[4] healthcare fraud investigations were lower in priority only to public corruption and corporate fraud in the FBI's White Collar Crime Program Plan. The creativity of individuals perpetrating healthcare fraud is illustrated in Table 10.1. An effective audit program is likely to discover incidents characteristic of the healthcare fraud schemes included in Table 10.1, thus permitting the government to react to the

Table 10.1   Healthcare Fraud Schemes

Billing for equipment not ordered by physicians and not received by patients
Billing for services not rendered
Billing excessively for services rendered
Billing for unneeded medications and services
Generating incorrect medical records indicating patients possessed nonexistent equipment
Provision of diluted, counterfeit, unregistered, expired, and substandard drugs[5]
Fraudulent laboratory tests
Patients undergo unnecessary or unwarranted surgery in exchange for a kickback
Pharmaceutical companies pay kickbacks to have physicians write prescriptions
Numerous empty offices in a single building listing sham suppliers that bill government for healthcare supplies and services[6]
Paying kickbacks disguised as administrative fees and sales and service agreements for marketing drugs
False claims for outpatient physical therapy not properly supported by plans of care administered by licensed physical therapists
Billing for unallowable costs such as lavish entertainment and travel to vacation resorts for meetings
Accounting fraud in the form of overbilling for hospital costs or home office cost statements
Paying kickbacks to physicians for referring patients to certain clinics
Pharmaceutical manufacturer reporting inflated prices for drugs knowing that those prices would be used by federal programs to set reimbursement rates

detected fraud case and implement improved contract administration practices to prevent further similar incidents.

Contracting professionals are likely best qualified to audit completed contracts, including the review of all aspects of the contract and the contracting process as described later in this chapter. However, price analysts or financial auditors might also be considered for participation on the audit team. Contract reviews by financial or legal professionals prior to contract execution likely are performed on all mid- to high-value contracts. Audits by financial auditors, therefore, are not normally required unless the contracts are selected for periodic financial audits or there is some subsequent indicator of a problem with a contract or contract review process. However, certain agencies maintain financial auditors who perform all contract audits.

A thorough audit of the contracting process is expected to include advance contract planning. Advance contract planning is normally performed by highly qualified agency officials or employees. Auditing advance contract planning with the benefit of hindsight that provides knowledge of the outcome, including problems that were encountered during contractor selection and contractor performance, may help the agency modify its advance contract planning process to compensate for any problems attributed to decisions made during this early phase of the contracting cycle. Advance contract planning team activities culminate in a myriad of decisions that impact the effectiveness of the solicitation, management of pre-proposal communications, contractor selection, and award of the contract, as well as the contractor's performance and the agency's contract administration process. Problems encountered in any of these subsequent phases of the contracting cycle that can be attributed to decisions made during advance planning may prove valuable in efforts to improve the advance contract planning process or training of agency representatives assigned to this function.

A deficient solicitation document also may have contributed to subsequent contractor selection or performance difficulties. Although earlier recommendations in this book included development of a template for solicitation documents, the availability of such templates does not ensure the absence of problems associated with the solicitation document. Problems attributed to the solicitation document may result from deficiencies in the RFP template, including attachments, or from modifications made by the agency representatives who adapted the solicitation template to their individual project. Problems attributed to the RFP, or other type of solicitation document, may be addressed by modifying the template to avoid repeating the same errors. Problems attributed to adapting the template for individual projects can be addressed either through additional guidance for using the solicitation template or by modifying the training of agency representatives who are expected to prepare future solicitation documents.

Protests, such as the protest of the contractor selection for the Air Force's air refueling tanker program discussed in previous chapters, create delays in the award of contracts and completion of contracts as well as the added expense associated with responding to protests. Protests are often filed due to a perception that the government did not treat prospective contractors equally during the pre-proposal phase of the contracting cycle. Protests during this stage of the contracting cycle often result from the government's failure to properly manage pre-proposal communications. Although there may not have been protests filed by aggrieved contractors, the lack of a protest does not eliminate the need to audit the management of pre-proposal communications. Auditing the pre-proposal communications management process may reveal deficiencies that were not detected by contractors even though the contractors may have had grounds for protesting the selection process or contractor selection. It is also appropriate to audit pre-proposal communications for a contract selected for audit that did have a protest filed by an aggrieved contractor. The fact that there was an agency investigation into the merits of a protest does not necessarily dispel the need to audit pre-proposal communications management. In fact, the existence of a protest provides an opportunity for auditing not only pre-proposal communications, but also the agency's response to the receipt of the protest. In this event, audit recommendations may result in improvements to both pre-proposal communications management and the agency's process for responding to protests from aggrieved contractors.

Review of the contractor selection process can determine whether the proposal evaluation team members complied with the description of the source selection process described in the solicitation, ensure that the team evaluated the proposals according to the criteria in the solicitation, determine whether weighted criteria were properly applied (if applicable), determine whether the team members used objective scores for the life cycle cost or proposed price (as applicable), as well as check for consistency between the instructions given to team members and the record of the proposal evaluation process. In the event that the contractor was selected without the benefit of competition, the sole source justification is normally reviewed to ensure that only one contractor was qualified and available for award of the contract. Department personnel preparing sole source justifications are prone to overlooking the existence of companies in competition with the contractor being recommended for a sole source contract. An Internet search often results in discovery of alternative contractors for the required products or services. Sole source justifications based on "only known supplier" are prime candidates for an Internet search for alternative suppliers. Routine Internet searches often result in the identification of a number of companies qualified to provide virtually all products and services. In addition to conducting an Internet search for competitors, ensuring that the justification convincingly establishes the fact that the selected contractor is the "only" contractor qualified to provide the needed products or services is recommended. Personnel auditing the contractor selection process are encouraged to consider the possibility of ethical issues or procurement corruption when they discover a variance from agency policy in the evaluation of bids or proposals, or when a less than convincing sole source justification is discovered in the contract files being audited.

Selecting contractors through full and open competition greatly simplifies justification of the source selection process. In addition to justifying contractor selection and the added benefits of providing the optimal combination of price, performance, and timeliness, full and open competition also greatly simplifies the determination that pricing is fair and reasonable. Fair pricing refers to a price that compensates the contractor for its costs plus a reasonable profit. Reasonable pricing refers to the receipt of products or services that are worthy of the price paid. When contractors are selected through full and open competition, the selection process normally justifies the existence of fair and reasonable pricing. In the absence of full and open competition, however, determining the fairness and reasonableness of pricing is more problematic. Making these determinations during the audit function is also complicated in the absence of full and open competition. Departments often attempt to justify pricing on noncompetitive contracts by the fact that the pricing from the previous year has either not increased at all or that any increase was consistent with inflation. However, if the previous price was based on a sole source contract without adequate price or cost analysis, then more justification is required to determine that present pricing is fair and reasonable. When considerable time has elapsed since a contract for a particular product or service was awarded on the basis of competition, the contract pricing may have since escalated well beyond the point of reasonableness.

An example of pricing that escalated to an unreasonable level is provided from a then active contract for industrial gases that had been awarded through full and open competition twelve years earlier. The contract had an evergreen clause, meaning that in the absence of a termination notice from the contracting agency the contract renews annually for one additional year. The active contract also had a price escalation clause with a maximum annual price increase of 8%. The contractor had increased the price by the maximum amount concurrently with each annual renewal during the duration of the contract. Upon discovery of this contract, without current substantiation of reasonable pricing, a solicitation was released to all local industrial gas suppliers to obtain competitive prices. A termination notice was sent to the then present contractor concurrently with the solicitation. The offers received in response to the solicitation revealed that pricing from all the suppliers, including the present contractor, was significantly lower than the current pricing. The lowest price offer was from the then current supplier. However, in a separate response to the termination notice, the current supplier offered pricing nearly identical to the pricing in its response to the solicitation. The separate response also included an offer to make the revised pricing six months retroactive if the contracting agency renewed the contract for an additional three years. The contracting agency agreed to the proposed three-year renewal if the annual 8% escalation clause was replaced with an annual price increase or decrease based on price indices published by the Bureau of Labor Statistics. Immediately following the three-year contract renewal, including a check to the agency for the retroactive price reduction and the revised escalation clause, the contracting agency sent the contractor a termination notice to nullify the evergreen clause in the renewed contract.

If a truly independent price estimate for the required products or services is prepared by an agency department prior to the receipt of proposals, then that independent estimate may be used to justify contract pricing. However, if that "independent" price estimate was prepared merely by contacting the contractor and asking for their estimated price prior to releasing the RFP, then that estimate is not acceptable. Pricing may be based on catalogue or published pricing if the contractor does not grant discounts to other customers that were not matched for the agency's proposed contract. Pricing paid by other agencies for the same or similar products or services may be used to justify contract pricing if the other agency established its pricing on the basis of full and open competition or another method acceptable to the agency. Caution is advised, however, when basing price reasonableness on the pricing obtained from another agency. If that pricing was based on a sole source contract or on limited competition, rather than full and open competition, then it is prudent to treat the reasonableness of that pricing as suspect.

When the time available for auditing contracts permits an in-depth analysis, it is recommended that the actions normally included in the review by the contract management staff prior to contract award be repeated during the contract audit. This repeat of contract review actions prior to contract execution assists in the identification of problems with the existing contracting process as well as problems with the contract review process. When time does not permit such an in-depth audit for all contracts, it may be preferable to restrict the more in-depth audit to the high-value contracts.

Audit of the contract administration phase, beginning immediately following contract award, is a critical part of the periodic audit of the contracting function. The contract administration function is discussed in Chapter 8. Audit of the contract administration function can usually be conducted by reviewing the agency's policies and procedures with respect to the administration of contracts and then reviewing the contract administration records, including contract modifications and their associated documentation, to confirm that this function is being performed in conformance with applicable policies and procedures. Determining the fairness and reasonableness of pricing for contract modifications is more challenging because change orders and contract amendments are made following contract award without the benefit of competitive bids or proposals.

10.4 Deficient Performance Evaluations and Audits Perpetuate Failure

10.4.1 Records Retention

Agencies lacking an effective records retention program and maintaining hard-copy contract files are not likely to discard the records prematurely; however, they are likely to encounter difficulty or the near impossibility of locating documentation if contracting files have not been consolidated and organized in a central repository or stored electronically. Missing contract documents can result in the failure to protect the agency's interest when evaluating past performance for award of future contracts, when there is a need to perform repairs that are covered under a warranty, when a dispute regarding contractual issues surfaces following contract completion, or when contracting issues result in litigation between the agency and the contractor. Although it is likely that the appropriate records required to develop a response to any of these eventualities will be found at some later date, the records may not be located in time to protect the agency's interest or not until considerable resources have been expended to locate the needed records. In either of these events, the delayed receipt of the contractual documents may hinder completion of the warranty repairs or needlessly expose the agency to financial risks in the event of a dispute or the filing of litigation following contract completion.

An additional detrimental effect from a deficient records retention program or the reliance on hard-copy contract files is the probability of maintaining records longer than required. In an extreme case, the agency may feel that it is necessary to construct, purchase, or lease additional office or warehouse floor space when destruction of the obsolete records would have eliminated that need. Private-sector companies that store retained records for government entities normally charge for their services based on square footage or cubic space used for records storage. It is obvious that failure to destroy obsolete records from a contractor's warehouse results in excess records storage costs.

Maintaining contract files electronically avoids the expense of warehouse space required to maintain hard-copy files, makes it practical to maintain a backup copy of contract files, provides simplified and timely access, decreases the chance that contract files will be retained beyond the destruction date, and significantly reduces the cost of inadvertent retention beyond the destruction date.

10.4.2 *Performance Evaluation*

The failure to prepare contractor performance reports during the period of performance or following contract completion impairs the agency's ability to consider past performance when considering previous contractors for future contract work. Relevant past performance information includes the contractors' financial management, quality, adherence to schedules, conflicts of interest, and possibly material on matters as serious as fraud and corruption. Lack of completed contractor performance reports also impairs the agency's response to requests from others that are considering one of the agency's previous suppliers for contract award. Lack of information on contractor performance that can be shared with others in the agency or in other contracting agencies impairs the evaluation of proposals and adds to document search costs.

Just as the existence of contractor performance appraisals encourage contractors to perform well, failure to rate contractor performance and share agency performance with other government entities may cause certain contractors to assign less importance to superior performance. Although it is not reasonable to expect the majority of government contractors to place less emphasis on performance excellence in the absence of a performance appraisal program, there is the possibility of such a reaction by individual contractor employees. Government contractors with limited resources, striving to satisfy the requirements of various government entities, may feel the need to minimize their performance for one customer. Determining the customer to receive the lesser service level may be based on selecting the agency that does not have a contractor performance rating program.

Contractor performance evaluations during performance of an ongoing contract and following contract completion are relevant to source selection considerations, determination of contractor responsibility regarding eligibility for contract award, and contractor debarment proceedings with respect to failure to satisfactorily perform under a government contract. The most typical use of contractor performance evaluations is in the evaluation and selection of contractors for new contract awards. There are numerous references in the *Federal Acquisition Regulation* (FAR) regarding the requirement to consider past performance in source selection actions. FAR Subpart 15-3, Source Selection, establishes a requirement for federal government contracting officers to document the reason past performance is not an appropriate evaluation factor during source selection [FAR 15.304(c)(3)(iii)].

10.4.3 Audit Program

Government entities that do not implement an audit program to evaluate the performance of their contracting program are likely to be unaware of weaknesses in their processes for planning future contracting actions, preparing solicitations, managing pre-proposal communications, selecting contractors, preparing contract documents, and administering contracts. The reasons for failing to reach the goals of achieving the optimal combination of performance, price, and timeliness for contracted services and products are likely to be revealed through a contract audit program. Failure to implement a contract audit program, however, prevents the agency from determining changes needed to improve their contracting function.

Advance contract planning failures are capable of contaminating all phases of the contracting process. The lack of an audit program, or lack of an effective audit program, may conceal the failure to plan for full and open competition, thus resulting in the failure to solicit the best-qualified contractors for providing the needed products or services. The ultimate consequence of failure to employ full and open competition and to solicit the best-qualified contractor or contractors is limiting competition to lesser qualified contractors that propose or bid noncompetitive pricing. Under this scenario, the agency is likely to receive substandard services or products for premium prices. Defective solicitation documents might result from a myriad of problems including inappropriate proposal evaluation criteria or inappropriate weighting of evaluation criteria. Selecting contractors on the basis of inappropriate criteria or improperly weighted criteria provides opportunities for procurement fraud or the selection of a corrupt contractor. A deficient audit program or complete lack of an audit program that fails to detect weaknesses in preproposal communications management is likely to contribute to unequal treatment of prospective contractors and a higher rate of protests filed by aggrieved contractors. Audit programs that fail to detect deficient contract documents may result in the award of contracts with provisions favoring contractors at the expense of the government or that place unnecessary risks on the government.

Audits that fail to detect deficiencies in planning for administering contracts can leave the government at an unquestionable disadvantage after the contract is awarded, and the government becomes responsible for monitoring the contractor's performance. The quotation at the beginning of Chapter 8, from the *Michigan Bar Journal,* regarding the agency's lack of any cost controls, periodic contractor reporting, or breakout of the budget below the total contract level, clearly identifies weaknesses stemming from advance contract planning. Such contract planning weaknesses could have been detected during a comprehensive audit program.

Failure to audit the proceedings of proposal evaluation teams on contracts selected for audit provides opportunities for an undetected pattern of source selection decisions intended to illegitimately steer contracts toward favored contractors. Proposal evaluation teams can steer contract award toward a favored contractor by evaluating proposals according to criteria that do not correspond to the criteria in the solicitation, by weighting the criteria differently than the weighting described in the solicitation, or by failing to score life cycle costs or pricing as objective data according to the method described in Chapter 7, and also in the "Example of the Evaluation of Proposals with Weighted Criteria" on the CD that accompanies this book. Although public servants generally perform their functions honestly and in the best interests of their agency and the constituency, prudent auditors are alert to the possibility of corrupt practices.

The lack of a contract audit program may also result in the failure to detect contracting practices that conform to the agency's policies and procedures but fail to meet the agency's goal for achieving the optimal combination of price, performance, and timeliness. In this scenario, a review of the agency's policies and procedures as well as contracting tools and templates is appropriate. The review might include a comparison of the agency's policies and procedures, contracting tools, and templates with the best practices described on the CD. Contract auditors who are familiar with government contracting practices are able to determine additional areas where changes to the agency's procedures, tools, and templates may contribute to the achievement of the agency's contracting goals.

Centralized contracting offices have limited insight into policy and procedure compliance by decentralized contracting offices with delegated authority to award contracts. Although centralized contracting offices gain insight into the practices of decentralized contracting offices when evaluating high-value contracts exceeding the decentralized offices' authority for awarding contracts, such insight is limited to a small sample of the total contracts awarded by the decentralized contracting offices. Implementing a program to audit a sample of all contracts awarded by decentralized contracting offices is necessary to ensure that decentralized contracting practices are in accordance with agency policy and procedures.

10.5 Utility of Effective Contractor Performance Evaluation

Contractor performance evaluations may be prepared both periodically during the term of a contract and following contract completion, or prepared solely following contract completion. In either event, contract audits are valuable tools for dealing with issues that may surface following contract completion, when contractor past performance is a criterion for contract award for future contracts, or when other agencies request information on a contractor's past performance for a source selection decision. An evaluation of a contractor's performance completed shortly after contract completion will prove helpful in the event that contractual issues emerge well after contract completion. Contractor performance evaluations are more reliable when prepared while memories of the contractor's performance effectiveness have yet to fade. Delaying completion of contractor performance evaluations may also be impacted negatively because knowledgeable personnel may no longer be available to provide input.

Past performance is often a criterion for evaluating proposals for future contract awards. A well-maintained file of contractor performance evaluations is valuable when assessing the past performance of contractors competing for future contracts. Depending on the agency's definition of contractor responsibility, the file of contractor performance evaluations may prove valuable in determining the responsibility of contractors. As discussed in Chapter 7, contractors that have been declared as being not responsible are excluded from participating in agency contracting opportunities. If the agency includes a certain level of poor performance, as indicated in contractor evaluation reports in their definition of responsibility, companies that receive ratings outside the range established for responsible contractors can be excluded from eligibility for award of future contracts. The definition likely includes scores for acceptable performance, a number of performance ratings or percentage of contractor performance ratings below a certain threshold, and a time period for reports that are considered in the determination of responsibility. A form that may be adopted for use in evaluating the performance of contractors is provided in Table 10.2, and a template is available on the CD. The sample form also contains a space for the evaluator to enter her or his recommendation for award of contracts to the contractor for future similar projects. Contractor performance evaluation forms developed by a number of states may be accessed by searching the Internet for "state contractor performance evaluation."

Agencies that wish to consider a contractor performance evaluation that is more comprehensive than the form in Table 10.2 are advised to search the Internet for "GSA forms library" and then search the GSA Forms Library site for "GSA 353." GSA Form 353, Performance Evaluation & Facilities Report, is a more comprehensive report that can be used as a model for designing a detailed agency form for contractor performance evaluations.

Table 10.2   Contractor Performance Report

Contractor Name			
Contractor Number			
Contractor Contact Name			
Street Address			
City, State ZIP+4			
Telephone			
Facsimile			
E-mail			
Project Name			
Project Completion Date			
Contract Number		Contract Type	
Agency Department		Project Manager	
Cost Management			
Quality			
Adherence to Schedule			
Recommendation for Future Similar Projects			
Report Completed By			
Signature			
Date			

Maintaining a file of contractor performance reports will prove useful if other agencies request feedback on the performance of contractors they are considering for award of a contract. Such requests from other government entities may result from a previous contractor's proposal to another government entity that required prospective contractors to list previous projects. Alternatively, government entities occasionally broadcast requests for feedback on contractor performance to a number of other government entities. When agencies plan to share information in the contractor performance report with other agencies, it is advisable to indicate on the form and in contract provisions that contractor performance evaluations are used internally and shared with other agencies to evaluate the contractor's past performance.

Agencies that implement the recommendation to rate contractor performance have information available on their previous contractors for evaluating past performance during future proposal evaluation efforts. Since numerous government entities use similar contractor performance reports, comparable reports may be obtained from other agencies. Placing a provision in the solicitation requiring prospective contractors to list references and to identify previous similar projects may help the agency obtain performance reports from others. Agency personnel evaluating past performance may request performance reports completed by other agencies identified in proposals either as references or as agencies that awarded contracts for similar projects.

10.6 Contributions of Effective Contract Auditing

As mentioned in the fundamentals of auditing in Section 10.3, contract audits are conducted by granting agencies to determine whether the contracting agency complied with the terms of the grant. Central contracting offices or audit functions perform audits of departments with decentralized contracting authority to determine contracting effectiveness and compliance with agency contracting regulations and policies. Granting agencies typically perform audits following completion of contracting activities associated with expenditure of the grant funding. Contracting audits performed by central contracting offices and audit functions may also be performed following completion of the contracted work. Long-term, high-value projects, however, are audited periodically during the term of the contracts.

Periodic audit of contracts by an agency, similar to the GAO audit report discussed in Section 10.3, is recommended for agencies with high-value systems contracts. The cited GAO report was based on an in-depth audit that investigated the government's success in meeting the basic contracting objective of achieving the optimal combination of cost, performance, and timeliness, which are the ultimate indicators for measuring the effectiveness of contracting activities. Noted deficiencies in these areas were further analyzed in the GAO audit to determine the causes for failure to meet individual goals for the three performance indicators. The audit revealed unacceptable levels of cost growth and delays in the availability of weapons systems. The poor outcomes for cost growth and delay problems were attributed to starting system development without mature technologies and moving into system demonstration with insufficient design stability. This is valuable information for government entities wishing to improve their systems contracting function. The audit results demonstrated that efforts to hasten the maturation of technology prior to beginning system development and to reach a higher level of design stability prior to starting system demonstration are likely to improve the price and timeliness performance indicators. Although agency personnel are likely motivated to enter system development and demonstration at an early date to hasten the availability of new weapons systems, premature initiation of system development and demonstration actually delay the availability of the weapons systems and lead to inflated pricing. While a minority of government entities contract for weapons systems, the complexities of weapons system acquisition parallels the challenges associated with contracting for all systems that require technology advancement. Regardless of the nature of the systems procurement undertaken, in-depth analyses of the performance indicators, identification of the primary causes for poor outcomes, and recommendations to avoid repetition of past mistakes are highly recommended for government entities that contract out for major systems development.

An example of such an audit for other than a weapons system was performed by the State of New York, Office of the State Comptroller.[7] The report issued on December 5, 2008, was a follow-up to an earlier audit report entitled "Capital Project Planning and Cost Estimation." The original 2003 audit report was conducted to determine whether final costs of individual capital projects were accurately estimated, if better planning practices could have reduced the number of change orders, and if there was compliance with the cost estimation procedures. The original audit contained eight recommendations. The follow-up audit was conducted to determine if the recommendations had been implemented. Conducting periodic audits of ongoing projects to ensure that departments are managing large-scale projects to achieve the goal of an optimal combination of price, performance, and timeliness is highly recommended. Follow-up audits to determine progress toward implementation of previous recommendations is also highly recommended.

Audits designed specifically to uncover procurement fraud and corruption may reveal agency practices that seriously impact agency effectiveness. As reported in the UN Convention against Corruption, implementing procurement-related aspects in Nusa Dua, Indonesia, in 2008,[8] the UN Office on Drugs and Crime (UNODC) issued guidance encouraging members to establish an independent agency or commission to address access to bidding procedures and to ensure access to contract documentation for auditing to identify fraud and corruption indicators, maintain lists of debarred contractors, and establish codes of conduct and asset declaration requirements for procurement staff and auditors.

Time does not always permit verification of all the actions taken during contractor selection and negotiation prior to contract award. Review of contracts following award, therefore, may be the original verification of actions taken during contractor selection and negotiation. Contract administration activities, following award of contracts, are also candidates to audit. Completed contracts, therefore, are normally selected for audit on a sampling basis. Effective audits performed on completed contracts include all activities throughout the contracting cycle from advance contract planning through contract administration and closeout. Contract audits are performed to verify that the contracting process was performed according to agency policies and procedures. Sampling for such audits is likely based on the selection for audit of a high percentage, possibly 100%, of the highest priced contracts, a lower percentage (say 40%) of the mid-priced contracts, and a considerably lower percentage (say 10%) of low-value contracts.

10.7 Benefits of Effective Records Retention, Performance Evaluation, and Contract Auditing

10.7.1 Records Retention

Maintaining well-organized, complete contract records for ready reference to support the agency's interests are greatly appreciated in the event that there is a need for warranty repairs, a dispute arises following contract completion, or if litigation is initiated by the agency or the contractor regarding contractual matters. Office space can be gained after one year by transferring files to a central storage facility. Central storage of contract records in a warehouse environment is likely more cost effective than maintaining sufficient office space to store seven years or more of completed contract records. Agencies that maintain hard copy contract records, either within the contracting office or in a central records storage area, benefit from an aggressive records destruction regimen that ensures destruction of records when the retention period expires. Conversion to an electronic records format makes access to records more convenient, reduces storage space expense, and simplifies records destruction.

10.7.2 Performance Evaluation

Contractors that are notified, through solicitation and contract provisions, that their performance is evaluated and shared with others within the contracting agency and with other government entities may be motivated to provide superior service and products. Contracting agencies also benefit from an effective contractor performance evaluation program through ready availability of excellent information on contractors' past performance for future contract awards. Performance evaluations may also prove beneficial in the event of a need for warranty repairs, post-contract completion disputes, or litigation that is initiated following contract completion.

10.7.3 Audit Program

An efficient contract audit program can greatly benefit government entities by identifying deficiencies to determine where improvements are needed. Evaluating the agency's success or lack thereof for obtaining the optimal combination of price, performance, and timeliness can lead to contracting process changes to improve the effectiveness of the agency when pursuing these goals. The audit program may reveal weaknesses at any phase of the contracting cycle, beginning with advance contract planning and proceeding through solicitation, pre-proposal activities, proposal or bid evaluation, and contract award through contract administration and closeout. Improvement to the agency's contracting process may be in the form of modifications to contracting policies and procedures; modification of existing contracting tools or the creation of new contracting tools; personnel training; or revisions to or development of templates for solicitations, contracts, or attachments to contracts. Deficiencies in an agency's contracting program may also be traced to weaknesses in the training program for contracting professionals as well as other officials and employees who are not contracting professionals, but who are involved in the contracting process.

Performing contract audits during the term of the contract or following contract completion may identify existing problems well beyond insufficiently trained or incompetent agency representatives who make ineffective decisions. Poorly justified sole source justifications; limited competitive contract actions lacking full and open competition; a pattern of sole source contracts awarded to a favored contractor or group of contractors; excessive price increases; a lack of actions taken to identify contractor deficiencies; and failure to take corrective actions against underperforming contractors are indicators that the agency may be experiencing contract corruption. Detecting indicators of contract corruption potentially benefits contracting agencies by eliminating the costs associated with it. Evaluation of agency officials and employees who apparently cooperated with contractors to inappropriately justify contract awards may reveal illegitimate compensation to agency employees or officials who conspired with corrupt contractors to limit or eliminate competition to favor one contractor over others.

The effects of procurement corruption are global and destructive, as evidenced in the following passage from the proceedings of the Conference of the States Parties to the UN Convention against Corruption [footnotes deleted]:[9]

> Measuring corruption is far from an exact science. Estimates of the amount of procurement-related corruption therefore vary widely, but all indicate that the sums involved are significant. For example, one estimate of the amount of bribery worldwide is US$ 1 trillion. Other estimates are that 20–30 per cent of the value of procurement may be lost through corruption where it is systematic, indicating very high amount as procurement itself is estimated to constitute 15 per

cent of gross domestic product in OECD [Organisation for Economic Co-operation and Development] countries, a higher percentage in developing economics and up to 45 per cent of government spending in some economies.

One consistent result of contract corruption is excessive contract costs paid to corrupt contractors. The risks borne by corrupt contractors are significant; therefore, the excess costs of the contracts must be significant to accept such risks. Audit results that reveal contract corruption indicators can eliminate the costs associated with ongoing contract corruption and discourage future excess contract costs associated with illegal contracting activities.

Agencies may delegate contracting authority to lower tier organizations because the volume of contracting activity for a fully centralized contracting office otherwise requires an excessively large contracting office. Another reason for decentralizing contracting authority is that the centralized contracting office is excessively remote from the needs of the subordinate organizations requiring the contracted products or services. The agency delegating contracting authority, however, normally retains authority for award of high-value contracts. The central contracting office also retains responsibility for the overall contracting program. As the organization responsible for the overall contracting program, the delegating agency normally issues contracting policies and procedures, provides contract training and tools, confers advice and counsel on contracting matters, and ensures compliance with the contracting policies and procedures. Assurance of compliance with contracting policies and procedures for high-value contracts is accomplished through review of contracts and related documentation for contracts that exceed the pricing threshold for the organization with delegated contracting authority. Assurance of compliance with contracting policies and procedures for lower value contracts can be achieved through a contract audit program. The audit program provides the agency that delegated contracting authority assurance that the organization with delegated authority is employing good contracting practices and is in compliance with applicable policies and procedures. If it is found that the organization with delegated contracting authority is not in compliance, the agency that delegated contracting authority can work with the decentralized contracting office to provide supplemental training or additional contracting tools to correct the deficiencies.

Grant-funded contracts are frequently audited by the granting agency following contract completion. Auditing such contracts prior to contract completion, however, may reveal noncompliance issues that can be brought into compliance prior to contract completion, thus avoiding adverse audit findings by the granting agency that might otherwise result in the demand to return grant funding.

The UN Development Agency agreed to return a portion of the grant funds provided by the U.S. Agency for International Development (USAID) for capital projects because of shoddy work.[10] A criminal investigation conducted by the

USAID Inspector General led to the demand for a partial return of the grant funds due to the construction of a central bank with no electricity, an unsafe bridge, and other shoddy projects. USAID reportedly asked for the return of $7.6 million; however, a UN representative estimated that the funding to be returned would not exceed $1.5 million.

10.8 Promises and Perils Following Completion of Contractor's Responsibilities

10.8.1 Disadvantages for Federal Government Contractors That Fail to Maintain an Approved Purchasing System

The disadvantages of failing to maintain an approved purchasing system include the need to expend considerable administrative effort and experiencing delays in the award of high-value purchase orders and subcontracts while seeking advance approval from the government.[11] Federal contractors without an approved purchasing system are at a competitive disadvantage when competing for contracts when management, cost efficiency, or subcontracting are included as criteria in the government's proposal evaluation process.[12] Finally, federal contractors are at a disadvantage when negotiating pricing on prime government contracts if they do not have an approved purchasing system.[13]

10.8.2 Government Contractor Records Retention

Contractors have records retention requirements similar to the government's need to retain contract records for a specified time period. Contract provisions may also require the contractor to maintain work records developed during contract performance for a certain specified time period following contract completion. Contract provisions may also require contractors to transfer certain work records to a successor contractor upon contract completion.

10.8.3 Audit of the Subcontracting Function for Federal Government Contractors

Contractors that provide significant levels of products or services to the U.S. federal government have contracting departments that interface in a sales role with the government contracting offices. These contracting departments for federal government contractors are involved in the response to solicitations from government contracting offices and, when successful, are awarded contracts that conform to federal government contracts as required by FAR. Because the function of these contracting offices is more characteristic of a contractor's sales function, their activities are not subject to audit for compliance with the FAR rules for releasing solicitations, evaluating proposals or bids, awarding contracts or subcontracts, and contract administration. The contracting offices for federal contractors are, however, subject to FAR requirements with respect to the sales function such as truth in negotiations. However, the function of contracting offices for federal government contractors is beyond the scope of this book. Federal government contractors, however, are often involved in large-scale subcontracting and purchasing functions that are subject to FAR in a manner similar to the requirements for federal government contracting and purchasing offices.

10.8.4 Audit Recommendations for Federal Government Contractors

As conveyed above, the subcontracting and purchasing functions of government contractors are expected to function similarly to government contracting offices. The contracting offices for government contractors are more closely aligned with the contractors' sales function. The U.S. federal government performs contractor purchasing system reviews (CPSRs),[14] which are not technically audits; however, CPSRs are performed similarly to audits and serve a similar purpose. The purpose of the CPSR, as stated in the FAR, is to evaluate the efficiency and effectiveness of the contractor's expenditure of government funds and compliance with government policy when subcontracting. The results of the CPSR are provided to the government's administrative contracting officer (ACO), who grants, withholds, or withdraws approval of the contractor's purchasing system based on the CPSR results.

Contractors with sufficient federal government contract volume to justify a CPSR[15] leading to the granting, withholding, or withdrawal of purchasing system review, yet do not have an approved purchasing system, are urged to perform an audit of their purchasing system in advance of the government's CPSR. Guidance for conducting a CPSR is available through an Internet search and is recommended for conducting the purchasing system audit in advance of the CPSR. The CPSR includes review of the backup documentation for purchase orders and subcontracts that were awarded during the review period. Documentation reviews reveal weaknesses in purchasing and subcontracting practices, procedures, tools, and training as well as the approval process for purchase orders and contracts. Once the weaknesses have been discovered, it is possible to update the practices, procedures, tools, and training. The next recommended step is the development of a checklist to ensure that the contractor employee reviewing or approving purchase orders and subcontracts considers all the relevant federal government requirements prior to recommending approval or approving purchase orders and subcontracts. A good checklist employed by an employee knowledgeable of federal government contracting practices helps ensure that the contractor remains in compliance with federal government requirements without conducting further contractor audits of the purchasing system.

Contractors that currently have an approved purchasing system, and that have personnel knowledgeable of federal government contracts reviewing purchase orders and subcontracts with the checklist discussed in the preceding paragraph, are likely able to withstand CPSRs without conducting periodic contractor audits. The one caveat for reliance on the internal review using a checklist rather than periodic audits is that the checklist reviews have been conducted during the entire period covered by the government's CPSR. If, for example, the government conducts the CPSR for purchases made during the past twelve months but the checklist review has been limited to the past three months, the contractor is likely to have its purchasing system approval withheld or withdrawn. In the event that the government notifies the contractor of a scheduled CPSR to consider purchases made prior to implementation of its enhanced review and approval process, discussions with the ACO may produce a delay in the CPSR date, a limitation of the review to purchases made since the enhanced review and approval process, or a combination of the two preceding alternatives.

10.8.5 Benefits to Federal Government Contractors That Maintain an Approved Purchasing System

Federal government contractors, by virtue of maintaining an approved purchasing system through a successful CPSR, benefit through attaining authority to award most purchase orders and subcontracts without the need for advance approval from the government, may improve their competitiveness for award of future government contracts, and may obtain higher contract pricing for negotiated contracts. These benefits are made possible because maintaining an approved purchasing system (1) allows the contractors significantly more flexibility in awarding subcontracts without obtaining ACO approval,[16] thus saving administrative costs and time required to award subcontracts; (2) contributes to contractors' competitiveness when competing for federal government contracts as reflected in source selection evaluation factors;[17] and (3) reflects favorably on the contractor during price negotiations.[18] To ensure that these benefits are realized when competing for future federal government contracts, contractors are encouraged to call attention to the fact that they have an approved purchasing system in their proposals with respect to materials procurement, subcontracting, general management, cost efficiency, and in the backup materials for their price or cost proposal.

10.9 Conclusion

Readers have been introduced to approaches for avoiding collusion and ineptness inherent to government contracting. The specific approaches and tools recommended are based in part on the results of a document review performed on solicitation and contract documents provided by government entities as a portion of their participation in a best practices research project. The government procurement principles cited throughout this book are based primarily on globally accepted government procurement principles, as evidenced by the similarities between the following extract from the *UN Procurement Practitioner's Handbook*[19] and the procurement principles expounded in this book:

> Fairness, integrity and transparency, through competition
>
> Competition conducted in a fair and transparent manner is the heart of procurement in the UN. In order for competition to work best, it must guard against collusion and be conducted on the basis of clear and appropriate regulations, rules and procedures that are applied consistently to all potential suppliers. The procurement process should be carried out in a manner that gives all interested parties, both inside and outside the organization the assurance that the process is fair.
>
> A transparent system has clear rules and mechanisms to ensure compliance with those rules (unbiased specifications, objective evaluation criteria, standard solicitation documents, equal information to all parties, confidentiality of offers, etc.). Records are open, as appropriate, to inspection by auditors; unsuccessful suppliers can be briefed on the strengths and weaknesses of their own offers. Transparency ensures that any deviations from fair and equal treatment are detected very early, and makes such deviations less likely to occur. It thus protects the integrity of the process and the interest of the organization.

The documents and tools described herein and provided on the CD that accompanies this book will likely require modifications to meet local policies and practices prior to implementation. Once the tools and documents are implemented, however, contracting efficiency is likely to improve and elevated ethical practices are likely to be realized.

Notes

1. Australian Procurement & Construction Ministerial Council, "Principles for Encouraging Best Practice Performance," South Australia, 2000.
2. "Defense Acquisitions — Measuring the Value of DOD's Weapon Programs Requires Starting with Realistic Baselines," Report number GAO-09-543T, April 1, 2009.
3. "Management of the M113 Armoured Personnel Carrier Upgrade Project," Report number 27 2008-09, Forwarded by letter to the President of the Senate and Speaker of the House of Representatives, Parliament House in Canberra, Australia, from the Auditor-General, March 27, 2009.
4. FBI, "Financial Crimes Report to the Public," May 2005.

5. In his statement of November 1, 2005, before the Subcommittee on Criminal Justice, Drug Policy, and Human Resources, Committee on Government Reform, Randall W. Lutter, Ph.D., Acting Associate Commissioner for Policy and Planning, U.S. FDA, stated that up to 25% of medicines consumed in poor countries are counterfeit or substandard, and that up to 50% of drugs for sale in some countries are counterfeit.

6. Report from the Office of the Inspector General of the U.S. Department of Health and Human Services, "Aberrant Claim Patterns for Inhalation Drugs in South Florida," Daniel R. Levinson, Inspector General, April 2009. While conducting 1,581 unannounced site visits, inspectors found that 491 suppliers did not maintain physical facilities or were not open and staffed during business hours. In 2006 those 491 suppliers billed Medicare for nearly $237 million.

7. Report number 2008-F-58, December 5, 2008. This is a follow-up to an earlier audit report entitled "Capital Project Planning and Cost Estimation (Report 2003-S-58)."

8. The report was submitted by the UN Commission on International Trade Law from the Conference of the States Parties to the UN Convention against Corruption, Second session, Nusa Dua, Indonesia, January 28–February 1, 2008.

9. The referenced UN proceedings on corruption resulted from the Conference of the States Parties to the UN Convention against Corruption, Second session, Nusa Dua, Indonesia, January 28–February 1, 2008.

10. *USA Today*, "U.N. Agency Agrees to Repay Part of Grant for Afghan Work," Ken Dilanian, April 15, 2009.

11. The differences in consent requirements for awarding contracts based on contractors that do or do not have an approved purchasing system are described in FAR 44-201-1, Consent Requirements.

12. Source selection evaluation factors are described in FAR 15.304, Evaluation Factors and Significant Subfactors. FAR 15.304(c)(2) lists "management capability" as one of the possible non-cost evaluation factors that shall be addressed in every source selection. Contractors with approved purchasing systems are encouraged to emphasize that fact in their proposals with respect to their management capability.

13. The following references to approved purchasing systems are from FAR subpart 15.4, Contract Pricing: 15.404.3(a), Subcontract Pricing Considerations and 15.405(a), Price Negotiation. FAR 15.406.3(a)(4), Documenting the Negotiation, requires the government contracting officer to document the extent that the approval status of the contractor's purchasing system affected the negotiations.

14. The CPSR program is described in Subpart 44.3 of the FAR.

15. In accordance with FAR 44.302, Requirement, the government administrative contracting officer (ACO) determines the need to perform a CPSR for government contractors. Contractors that are expected to have $25 million in government contracts during the following twelve months meet the criteria for a CPSR; however, the head of the agency responsible for contract administration may raise or lower the $25 million threshold if that is in the government's best interest.

16. The differences in consent requirements for awarding contracts based on contractors that do or do not have an approved purchasing system are described in FAR 44-201-1, Consent Requirements.

17. See note 12 above.

18. See note 13 above.

19. *UN Procurement Practitioner's Handbook*, United Nations, November 2006, pp. 1-5–1-6.

Appendix: Glossary of Terms

A clear understanding of terms used in the contracting field is essential to ensure that government officials and employees maintain exacting communications between themselves and their internal customers, contractors, and prospective contractors. To ensure that improper use of contracting terms does not result in confusion, leading to such avoidable problems, this appendix provides definitions for contracting terms used throughout this book. Relatively brief definitions are provided here; however, a thorough discussion of the more significant topics is provided in the book.

Acceptance: is the communication of the final, unqualified assent to an offer.

Addendum: is the term used to describe the instrument used to make changes to a request for proposals (RFP) or any other type of solicitation after the solicitation has been sent to prospective contractors and before contractor responses are due.

Advance contract planning: represents planning conducted in advance of efforts to draft the solicitation sent to prospective contractors to determine their interest in competing for a contract to provide the needed products, services, or capital project. This planning is not considered *advanced* contract planning because certain government entities have a long history of carefully planning their procurement efforts before they begin drafting the solicitation. Other terms that may be used in lieu of advance contract planning are "advance procurement planning" and "acquisition planning."

Affirmative action programs: can be differentiated from equal opportunity programs in that contractors that are targeted for a particular affirmative action program may be awarded a contract despite the fact that competing non-targeted companies may have proposed lower pricing, higher quality products or services, or earlier product delivery or project completion.

Agency official: is a term used to describe any government elected or appointed official or employee who is involved in the contracting process or has been designated to review or execute contracts.

Agency representative: is synonymous with agency official.

Agreement: is occasionally used in this book as a synonym for contract.

Allocable costs: are those costs that pertain to the contracting agency's contract or project. Costs that are expended to support one contract are not allocable to another contract.

Allowable costs: (See **Unallowable costs**)

Amendment: is the term used for the most formal type of modification to a contract. Amendments are normally staffed, reviewed, and executed in the same manner as contracts. However, some agencies permit limited staffing and execution at a lower organizational level for amendments below a certain value or percentage of the total contract price. Some government entities require the less formal change orders to be formalized at some subsequent time by an amendment. In this case, several change orders may normally be formalized by a single amendment.

BAFO: (See **Best and final offer**)

Best and final offer: is the term used to describe a basic approach to negotiations in which the agency asks one or more of the prospective contractors to submit a "final" revision to their proposal. In some cases the agency may provide a revised scope of work or other contract changes to be considered when the contractor(s) prepares their BAFO(s).

Bids: are responses received from prospective contractors or suppliers to invitations for bids (IFBs) released by government entities. Like quotations or quotes, bids are typically prepared by completing blanks on a bid form generated by the contracting agency. The information provided on the bid form by the prospective contractors is similar to that information provided for quotations or quotes; however, it may include added information that is required based on high-dollar-value projects solicited via IFBs as opposed to low-dollar projects solicited via requests for quotations (RFQs). Unlike proposals, statements of qualifications, and quotations or quotes, bids are opened publicly and the prices are read aloud for all to hear. Bids are normally recorded on a spreadsheet, and copies of the spreadsheets are also considered public information that can be provided to anyone who submits a request or provides a self-addressed stamped envelope.

Bilateral: refers to signing, or executing, a contract or modification thereto by both parties to the contract. In state and local government contracting, all contracts and modifications thereto are normally required to be bilateral documents.

Billing rates: in not-to-exceed price contracts or cost reimbursement contracts are typically hourly rates for each applicable employee classification, an amount certain for each mile driven such as $.50/mile or reimbursement at the then current rate allowed by the applicable taxing authority; meals and hotel expenses can be reimbursed at a per diem rate such as $50.00/day for meals and $150/day for hotels or at actual cost. When certain rates are based on actual costs, it is possible to include a ceiling cost to ensure that contractor employees do not select luxury accommodations and expensive restaurants.

Boilerplate: (See **Contract boilerplate**)

Boondoggle: is the term for a visit or trip by a government official or employee, funded by a contractor or the government, which is of no real value to the government or the constituency but is primarily for the personal enjoyment or pleasure of the traveler.

Cash discounts: are frequently offered by contractors to ensure that invoices are paid in a timely manner. An example of payment terms when a cash discount is offered is "2% 15, Net 45." This indicates that the contracting agency may deduct 2% from the invoiced price if payment is made within 15 days of receipt of the invoice and products and services, and that if the payment is not made within 15 days the full amount of the invoice is due within 45 days of receipt of the invoice and products or services.

Change in scope: occurs when the work to be performed by the contractor is modified from the original scope of work by the parties to the contract. The details of the change in scope, and possibly associated changes to the price or schedule, are normally negotiated by the contracting parties and formalized through a written contract amendment.

Change order: is a type of modification to a contract that is normally used to authorize a change in the scope of work. A change order is used when there is insufficient time to staff the more formal contract "amendment." Change orders can normally be approved, within certain price parameters, at a lower organizational level than the original contract.

Chief elected official: is the term to describe the ranking elected official for a particular jurisdiction, such as the governor of a state or mayor of a city.

Competent parties: means that all the parties to the contract are mentally competent and of legal age.

Conflict of interest, actual: occurs when some action certain by a government representative directly, or is reasonably certain to, results in a financial benefit or avoidance of a financial detriment to the government representative, a relative, or a company with which the government representative or her or his relative is associated.

Conflict of interest, apparent (or perceived conflict of interest): occurs when there exists a business or contractual relationship or activities that may be viewed by a prudent businessperson as a conflict of interest. An apparent conflict of interest normally refers to an organizational conflict of interest.

Conflict of interest, potential (or possible conflict of interest): occurs for a government representative when some action certain by a government representative results in a financial benefit or avoidance of financial detriment to the government representative, a relative, or a business with which the government representative or her or his relative is associated.

Consideration: is established when each party is bound by their promises that constitute a bargain for exchange. However, being bound to perform some preexisting promise does not constitute consideration.

Constructive change order: is the term for an unauthorized verbal or oral act or omission that adds to a contractor's work scope. Boilerplate contract provisions generally state that all contract amendments shall be in writing and signed by the contracting officer in advance. However, it is likely that constructive change orders are enforceable if a government employee with apparent authority directs a contractor in writing or orally or by omission to perform beyond the scope of work.

Contract: is the term used for an agreement that is legally enforceable and reflects the relationship between two or more parties for a specific time period. Contracts are normally crafted to identify potential risks and describe how these risks are to be mitigated. There must be a meeting of the minds wherein there is no ambiguity with respect to the understanding of the parties regarding the nature of the agreement. Contracts must include an offer, acceptance, consideration, competent parties, and a legal purpose.

Contract boilerplate (or boilerplate): refers to standard terminology that does not normally vary regardless of the nature of the products or services for which proposals are being solicited. Standard terms and conditions are an example of boilerplate.

Contract completion: occurs when all the tasks required of the contractor, including final reports, have been completed, and all tasks required of the contracting agency, including final payment, have been completed. This differs from a notice of completion, which is typically issued upon completion of the contractor's portion of the work for construction contracts, and final payment is normally withheld until a specified number of days following the notice of completion.

Contract execution: refers to the signing of a contract by an individual duly authorized to bind and commit her or his company or organization to the provisions of the contract being signed. Signature by staff personnel such as legal counsel to indicate concurrence that a contract is sufficient as to form does not constitute execution of a contract. A contract that is executed by all parties to the contract is considered to be fully executed.

Contract term (period of performance): is the phrase used to indicate the beginning and ending date of the work to be performed by the contractor.

Contracting agency: is used synonymously with government entity.

Contractors: are private-sector companies or individuals that provide products or services to government entities on a contract basis.

Convenience terminations: are made to discontinue work on a contract when one party to the contract has not defaulted. Absent a convenience termination clause in a contract, one party cannot normally terminate a contract for convenience without the consent of the other party. Provisions for convenience terminations may be constructed to provide this option to just one or to both of the contracting parties.

Cost elements: in not-to-exceed price contracts or cost reimbursement contracts typically include hourly rates that may differ for various employee classifications such as senior analyst or administrative support personnel, mileage rates for vehicles, per diem rates for meals, and hotel expenses. Cost elements in firm fixed-price contracts may be fixed payments paid for milestone completion or a fixed periodic payment that is invoiced monthly during the term of the contract.

Cost growth: occurs when a change in scope results in a bilateral amendment to the contract that increases the target cost and fee. Such a change in scope agreed to by both parties to the contract is considered as cost growth and not a cost overrun. By contrast, an overrun occurs when the contractor expends funds in excess of the target cost without an associated change in scope or contract amendment.

Cost plus a percentage of cost (CPPC): contracts are unlawful in federal contracting and in some states as well. The American Bar Association (ABA) also recommends the prohibition of CPPC contracts. CPPC contracts provide for reimbursement to the contractor for allowable and allocable costs plus a predetermined percentage of those costs. A cursory analysis of CPPC contracts might conclude that they are not significantly different than CPFF (cost plus fixed fee) contracts. However, there is a significant difference between CPPC and CPFF contracts. When CPFF contractors overrun their contracts, the fee remains fixed. Therefore, the CPFF contractor's fee as a percentage of the costs is reduced when they experience a cost overrun, and this reduction in the fee as a percentage of actual costs acts as an incentive to control costs. Contrast this to a CPPC contract wherein greater contractor expenditures result in higher fees, thus higher profits.

Cost plus award fee (CPAF): contracts are similar to CPIF (cost plus incentive fee) contracts except that they do not use an exact formula for determining the amount of the fee. CPAF contracts typically include goals or criteria on which the award fee is based. The award fee factors may be established at the inception of the contract for the first phase of the performance period, which might be, for instance, the first six months of the contract term. Long-term CPAF contracts typically provide for adjustments to the factors on which the award fee is based. At the end of each award period, the contractor submits a document that supports the award fee at the level at which the contractor feels is deserved. The contracting agency typically reviews the contractor's submittal, evaluates the contractor's performance with respect to the award fee factors, and then unilaterally determines the amount of the award fee.

Cost plus fixed fee (CPFF): contracts provide for reimbursement of the contractor for allowable and allocable costs plus a fixed fee that is determined at the inception of the contract. In the event that the contractor overruns the target cost, the fixed fee is not decreased. Likewise, a contractor underrun of the target cost does not result in an increase to the fixed fee. However, if the contract is amended due to a change in scope, the fixed fee is normally increased or decreased in proportion to the increase or decrease in the target cost. The fee normally established for U.S. federal contracts cannot exceed 10% of the estimated cost for CPFF contracts; however, the maximum is 15% for experimental, developmental, or research, and 6% of estimated construction costs for architect–engineering CPFF contracts.

Cost plus incentive fee (CPIF): contracts provide for reimbursement to the contractor for allowable and allocable costs plus an incentive fee that is based on a formula determined at the inception of the contract. The incentive normally includes cost containment and may include other factors such as technical characteristics.

Cost reimbursement contracts: unlike fixed-price contracts, reimburse the contractor based on predetermined rates for products or services that are priced on the basis of real or expected efforts to support completion of requirements specified in the contract. Just as with the fixed-price contracts, the definitions for cost reimbursement contracts are generally based on the definitions for contract types contained in the *Federal Acquisition Regulation* (FAR). Cost reimbursement contracts are not appropriate unless the contracting agency is prepared to employ considerably more resources during contract negotiations and contract administration than they normally employ for fixed-price contracts. Additionally, cost reimbursement contracts are not recommended for award to contractors that do not have sophisticated accounting systems that provide the capability to track contract or project costs at a task level. The FAR also includes an extensive list of unallowable costs. Some examples of costs that are unallowable according to the FAR include entertainment, advertising, taxes, interest, labor relations, and losses on other contracts. Including provisions for unallowable costs in contracts necessitates more than a mere listing of costs that are unallowable. For example, advertising costs that are considered unallowable are likely limited to product advertising whereas advertising to recruit employees or to announce upcoming procurement opportunities are normally allowable. Government entities that permit cost reimbursement contracts might consider establishing categories of costs that are or are not reimbursable. If unallowable costs are not defined in cost reimbursement

contracts, agencies may be embarrassed by some ca
they are required to reimburse.

Counteroffer: means that the party receiving the offer expre
accepting the offer with conditions. However, the existe
tions actually constitutes a rejection of the offer that was
expression of a new offer. If the party making the counte,   ,, or
her counteroffer rejected, he or she cannot then merely acce_ _ ne original
offer. The original offer that was rejected by the counteroffer can no longer
be considered. Of course, the party that had their counteroffer rejected
may then indicate that they now wish to accept the original offer. If the
party that had made the original offer again agrees to the terms of their
original offer without further condition, then acceptance has occurred.

Courtesy: (See **Gratuity**)

Debarred: refers to contractors that have been excluded from government contracting and government-approved subcontracting for a specified time period.

Default termination: is the term used to describe the termination of a contract
by one party to a contract due to the other contracting party's failure to
perform its contractual obligations. Ideally, the contract outlines the steps
needed to terminate a contract for default. Typically, the party that is considering taking action to terminate a contract for default notifies the other
party of this intent by providing a show cause notice that includes a period
of time for the contractor in default to show cause why it would be preferable for the contract to remain in place. If the party receiving the show
cause letter fails to respond within the time period stated in the letter, the
contract may be terminated for default. If the other party to the contract
responds by stating the actions they plan to cure their failure to perform,
the party issuing the show cause letter then evaluates the merits of the plan
to cure the failure. If the plan is accepted, contract performance continues. If the plan is determined to be inadequate, the contract is terminated
for default. If the party that initiated the default termination by issuing
a show cause notice does not feel confident that its default termination
will be upheld or is reluctant to incur the costs associated with pursuing
a default termination, that party may elect to terminate the contract for
convenience.

Definitive contract: is a term used to describe a fully executed, fully staffed contract
that incorporates all the elements of a contract, including a complete understanding of the risks and responsibilities assumed by the parties to the contract. A definitive contract is generally used as the successor for a letter contract
that was intended to remain effective for a limited time period. Fully staffed
contracts awarded routinely are also considered definitive contracts; however,
that term is normally not used unless the definitive contract is intended as a
replacement for a letter contract.

Equal opportunity programs: involve outreach efforts to discover prospective contractors that historically have had less than full access to government contracting opportunities. Contractors may be included in equal opportunity programs because they are small minority-owned, woman-owned, or veteran-owned or belonging to any other category for which an equal opportunity program has been established. Equal opportunity programs usually provide outreach efforts to identify such companies and offer them the opportunity to compete with traditional contractors, but they do not afford any competitive advantage with respect to price, quality, or schedule adherence. Equal opportunity programs are normally established on the assumption that the management of small, minority-owned, woman-owned, or other identified categories of contractors is not inherently less qualified to compete with more traditional contractors in a capitalistic environment. Therefore, to succeed as government contractors they need only be given the opportunity to compete. It is assumed that targeted companies do not require a competitive advantage that would be considered unfair by traditional contractors and the citizenry.

Evaluation criteria (or selection criteria): are the factors considered for evaluation of proposals to select the successful contractor from among the competing contractors. Evaluation criteria are normally described in the solicitation to permit the prospective contractors to understand the basis for selecting the successful contractor by the contracting agency. When proposals are evaluated, it is essential that the selection of the successful contractor be based solely on the evaluation criteria stated in the solicitation. Therefore, great care is required to ensure that the evaluation criteria included in the solicitation measures significant and relevant attributes of a contractor. In the event that an unsuccessful contractor protests the contract award or recommendation for award, proposal evaluation team records that indicate strict adherence to evaluation criteria in contractor selection help defend such a challenge to the contractor selection.

Execution: (See **Contract execution**)

Fair pricing: refers to pricing that enables a contractor to recover their allowable and allocable direct and indirect costs and earn a reasonable profit.

Firm fixed-price (FFP): contracts are contracts wherein payment is based on completion of milestones or all the tasks in the scope of work without providing performance or other types of incentives developed to encourage the contractor to provide a product or service that exceeds the minimum specifications developed by the contracting agency or for delivery in advance of the contractual delivery date.

Fixed-price contracts: are those contracts wherein payment to the contractor is based on a fixed price to be paid to the contractor for completion of specific elements of the scope of work or for completion of the entire contract requirements.

Fixed-price incentive (FPI): contracts are similar to firm fixed-price contracts with the exception that the contract terms may include monetary incentive payments in the event that the contractor exceeds the specifications or delivers the described product or service by some date certain.

Flow-down terms and conditions: may be required if the contracting agency is awarding a contract in support of a grant or contract awarded by a state to a county, city, or district, or awarded by a federal agency to a state, county, city, or district. Oftentimes grants, state contracts, and federal contracts include terms and conditions that are required to flow down to all government contracts awarded in support of that grant or contract.

Fully executed contract: is a term used to describe a contract that has been signed for all parties to the contract by representatives authorized to commit their respective organizations.

Governing body: is the phrase used to describe the county board of supervisors, city council, district board, or any other entity that governs a particular local governmental body.

Gratuity: describes any payment of anything of monetary value in the form of cash, travel, entertainment, gift, meal(s), lodging, loans, subscriptions, conference fees, advances, deposits of money, services, employment or promises of employment, contracts of any kind, or any other article or intellection having present or future pecuniary benefit, or other items of value to government representatives in the hopes that the government representative will treat the contractor favorably. Government entities normally limit the value and frequency that gratuities may be accepted by government representatives.

Incorporation: of documents in addition to the contract itself is essential to ensure that documents accompanying or attached to the contract are enforceable. Merely attaching additional documents to a contract does not make the provisions of those attachments enforceable upon the contractor. To ensure that the provisions of the attachments are enforceable, one must incorporate them in the contract by identifying them by number, title, date, and so forth, and then following that description with phraseology similar to "which is attached to and incorporated in this contract." A contractor's proposal is sometimes incorporated in a contract. This can be beneficial because it renders all the contractor's promises in their proposal as part of the contract. However, there can also be detrimental effects because undesirable provisions of the proposal also become a part of the contract. Hopefully, the detrimental effects are minimized by placing the proposal lowest in precedence in the event of conflicts between contract provisions. However, an undesirable provision that does not conflict with other contract provisions becomes a part of the contract regardless of the precedence assigned to the contractor's proposal if the proposal is incorporated in the contract.

Incorporation by reference: is similar to the incorporation defined above with the exception that the actual document is not attached to the contract. Documents cannot be incorporated by reference unless they are readily available to all parties to the contract. Acceptable phraseology for incorporating documents by reference includes "which is incorporated in this contract by reference."

Indemnification: provisions typically require one or both parties to a contract to accept responsibility for loss or damage to a person or entity and to compensate the other party for losses or expenses incurred that arise out of or in connection with the other party's negligence or willful misconduct.

Insurance: provisions typically describe the types of insurance coverage and limits of liability for insurance policies that must be maintained by the contractor during the entire term of the contract. Typical types of required insurance coverage are general liability, automobile coverage, and workers' compensation. Professional liability coverage is also required if the contractor is expected to provide professional services such as legal, engineering, architectural, or accounting, or the services of similarly trained professionals.

Internal customers: are other employees of the contracting agency who rely on the contracts professional to provide guidance in contracting matters.

Invitation for bids (IFB): is a formal solicitation normally used to solicit bids for high-dollar-value capital equipment or construction work. IFBs are normally not used to solicit bids for services. However, there are certain grants that require solicitation for services with IFBs. IFBs solicit bids that are opened publicly and result in award of a contract to the responsive, responsible contractor with the lowest price. When grants require solicitation through an IFB, an IFB template is normally provided by the granting agency for use by the government.

Legal purposes: means that the nature of the products or services being contracted can be performed legally in the jurisdiction where the contract shall be construed and interpreted.

Letter contract: is the term used for an agreement that must be executed prior to the time required for a formal contract to be staffed through normal channels. Letter contracts normally include all the features (such as terms, start and end dates, and a not-to-exceed price) that the parties can agree to at the time that the letter contract is executed. Letter contracts normally include provisions that cause them to expire after a certain specified time period, with the expectation that they are replaced by a definitive contract on or before the expiration date.

Level of effort: contract refers to a type of contract where the contractor is engaged to provide a number of hours of a specified service at contractual billing rates. Such contracts typically have a firm fixed price or a not-to-exceed price.

Life cycle cost: refers to the initial price as adjusted during the term of the contract, plus all other agency costs associated with the project, such as the incremental cost of personnel, training, materials, project phaseout, or any other applicable project costs not included in the contract.

Local government agency: is the phrase used to describe the county, city, or district that contracts with private-sector companies or individuals to provide products or perform services for the local government agency.

Model contract: is a contract that is included in the solicitation and is identified as the contract document, essentially in the form of the contract that the contracting agency intends to award to the successful contractor. Model contracts ideally include the contracting agency's standard terms and conditions, insurance requirements, and the scope of work. Including a model contract in the solicitation and advising the prospective contractors that the contracting agency intends to award a contract essentially in the form of the model contract helps to derail the contractors' attempts to enter into a contract in their format with their terms and conditions. Contractors' terms and conditions often favor the contractor and may require extensive negotiations to render them acceptable to the contracting agency. The model contract includes all the essential elements of the contract awarded to the successful contractor such as offer, acceptance, consideration, competent parties, and a legal purpose.

Modification: is the generic term for any alteration to a contract. Modifications are generally limited to amendments and change orders.

Negotiations: are considered to be undertaken when the contracting agency enters into discussions with a prospective contractor or successful contractor to attempt to modify the price, schedule, terms and conditions, or any other element of the contractors' proposal or resultant contract. Solicitations often include a statement by the contracting agency to advise prospective contractors that the contracting agency may enter into negotiations or award a contract based on the initial proposal without conducting negotiations. When such a statement is included in the solicitation, the prospective contractors are normally advised to include their best pricing and other terms and conditions in their initial proposal.

Nondiscrimination clauses: may flow down from federal or state contracts or grants, and may be included in the government's standard terms and conditions. The categories of characteristics that cannot be subject to discrimination in providing products or services or in employment practices typically include race, color, national origin, religion, age, sex, and physical or mental disability. Early, obsolete versions of nondiscrimination clauses referred to disabilities as handicaps. However, the terms "handicap," handicapped," and "handicaps" are obsolete. There is an admonishment against use of such terms in the *Code of Federal Regulations* (CFR) because they are considered to be "overlaid with stereotypes" or invoke "patronizing attitudes, and other emotional attitudes."

Not-to-exceed: refers to a ceiling price that cannot be exceeded, except when the contract has been amended to increase the not-to-exceed price.

NTE (see Not-to-exceed):

Offer: means the communication of one party's willingness to enter into a contract that shall be binding if accepted by the party to which the offer was made.

Offeror: is the term used to describe a person or organization making an offer.

Overrun: of cost occurs when the contractor expends funds in excess of the original target cost in the absence of a change in the scope of work. (See the definition of cost growth to differentiate between these two terms.)

Payment terms: in contracts typically describe the frequency with which the contractor may submit invoices; the cost elements and billing rates at which costs may be invoiced for level of effort, not-to-exceed price, and cost reimbursement contracts, the time in which the contracting agency must pay the invoices; and cash discounts that may be taken if payments are made expeditiously. However, the payment terms may be less complex and merely indicate that the full contract price is paid upon completion of the contract work. When no cash discount is offered by the contractor, payment terms are typically expressed as "Net 30," which indicates that the full amount of the invoice is due 30 days after the invoice and products or services are received by the contracting agency.

Preamble: refers to the first section of the contract that identifies the contracting parties and their intent to enter into a contract. The effective date of the contract is often included in the preamble.

Price: refers to the initial contract price paid to the contractor. This price may be increased or decreased through contract amendments based on changes in the scope of work. Price does not normally include agency personnel costs, training, or materials not provided by the contractor, contract phaseout, or other miscellaneous project costs not included in the contract.

Private sector: includes companies, corporations, partnerships, sole proprietorships, individuals, consultants, or other nongovernment entities.

Professional services contract: is the term for an agreement for the furnishing of professional services, such as those provided by an engineer, architect, attorney, accountant, professor, consultant, or a professional in another field that requires equivalent education and experience.

Proposal evaluation team: membership typically consists of employees from the contracting agency's department that requires the services or products from the contractor. In some cases consultants, who themselves are on contract, may also serve on the proposal evaluation team. Contracts or purchasing personnel are also frequently members of proposal evaluation teams. The departments participating on the proposal evaluation team are normally identified in the solicitation. A chairperson is typically designated for each proposal evaluation team. The team opens the proposals, evaluates the proposals based on the evaluation criteria, and either selects the successful contractor or recommends a contractor to the source selection authority, governing body or chief elected official for approval and award of the contract.

Proposal format: is the phrase used to describe the contracting agency's prescribed organization of proposals submitted in response to an RFP. Specification of topics presented in the proposal that have a direct relationship to the evaluation criteria simplify the work of the proposal evaluation team and help ensure that the prospective contractors are treated equally. Specifying the sequence of the presentation of topics also simplifies the efforts of the proposal evaluation team. Placing a limit on the number of pages for each topic presented is highly recommended to prevent voluminous proposals that require an inordinate amount of time to read and evaluate.

Proposals: are responses to RFPs from prospective contractors that describe the approach that the contractor intends to employ to provide products or meet the services needs of the government entity that released the RFP. Proposals also typically describe the prospective contractor's experience and qualifications to provide products or perform services as well as their proposed pricing and any other information requested in the RFP.

Proprietary or trade secret: are terms used to describe company confidential information that may be included in a proposal but cannot ever be released to the proposing contractor's competitors or to the public. Although virtually all other information in proposals may be released after the contract has been awarded or recommended for award, proprietary or trade secret information must remain protected as confidential by the agency until it is destroyed or until the contractor that provided the information advises the agency that the material is no longer proprietary or a trade secret.

Prospective contractors: are those contractors that are believed to be qualified to deliver the required products or services to the government and that, therefore, are included on the list of contractors solicited through the RFP or other form of solicitation.

Protest: is the term used to describe a challenge to the solicitation, procedure for selecting a contractor, recommendation to award a contract, or actual contract award. Protests are generally initiated by an unsuccessful contractor(s). Defining the method for handling protests in the contracting agency's published policies and procedures as well as in the solicitation may help to keep protests manageable; however, contracts that are approved by the contracting agency's governing body or chief elected official may be protested at a public meeting of the governing body.

Quotations (or quotes): are responses to RFQs received from prospective contractors or suppliers in response to RFQs released by government entities. Quotations, or quotes, are typically prepared by completing blanks on a quotation form provided by the contracting agency. The information provided by the prospective contractors on the quotation form may be limited to pricing, delivery time promised, payment terms, identifying company information, and a signature from a contractor representative.

Quotes: (See **Quotations**)

Ratification: of contracts refers to the approval of contracts that were originally awarded by an individual who did not have the authority to execute the contract. In some cases the contract may have been awarded during an emergency to help protect lives or property. In other instances the official, board or commission with authority to award the contract may have been asked to ratify a contract that had been improperly awarded by an individual who lacked the required authority to execute the contract.

Reasonable pricing: refers to pricing that provides the contracting agency with the receipt of products or services at a price that does not exceed the reasonable value of the products or services received.

Recitals: refers to the section of a contract that normally follows the preamble and describes the rationale for the parties entering into a contract. This section often includes the basis for consideration.

Request for contractor qualifications (RFCQ): is similar to the RFP except that its use is limited to obtaining information on the qualifications of various private-sector entities that may be qualified to provide products or perform services. Prospective contractors, in response to the RFCQ, submit a statement of qualifications to the contracting agency. The contracting agency, in turn, evaluates the contractors' qualifications to determine which firms or individuals are qualified. Once a list of qualified contractors is developed, an RFP is normally sent to all the firms that were determined to be qualified through the RFCQ process. The RFCQ is a type of solicitation that is normally not used when the contracting agency is familiar with the prospective contractors for the products or services to be contracted. RFCQs are also not normally used when time is of the essence for placing the products or services under contract, because the need to follow through with an RFP after the list of qualified contractors is developed significantly extends the time required to obtain proposals. Some agencies refer to RFCQs merely as requests for qualifications (RFQ) or requests for information (RFI). However, use of the RFQ term can lead to confusion between requests for quotations and requests for qualifications, and RFI is not sufficiently descriptive of the nature of the solicitation.

Request for proposals (RFP): is the type of solicitation normally used to solicit proposals for services provided by private-sector contractors. RFPs are also normally used in any procurement where contractors are selected on the basis of best value to the agency, and for design/build construction contracts. RFPs typically include a short introduction of the government entity soliciting proposals; background for the products or services to be contracted to include the present manner in which the products or services are being provided; a description of the products or services to be provided;

evaluation criteria to be used in selecting the successful contractor; rights reserved by the contracting activity; format for preparing proposals along with page limitations when appropriate; and a copy of a model contract that includes the terms and conditions, required insurance coverage, and scope of work.

Request for quotations (RFQ): is an informal solicitation normally used to solicit quotes for low-dollar-value merchandise that is easily described. RFQs are normally not used to solicit quotations for services.

Responsible: contractors are those that meet the contracting agency's standards with respect to a reasonable expectation that the contractor has the management, technical, financial, equipment, and human resources available to ensure adequate performance of the work described in the solicitation. Agencies may have established a policy that specifies certain criteria that contractors must meet to be considered responsible. Those criteria normally include companies that have not been debarred or suspended, have not been convicted of certain offenses, or have not had a contract terminated for default, all within certain specified time periods.

Responsive: proposals are those that satisfactorily address all requirements specified in the RFP. Because proposals, unlike bids, are subject to negotiation, certain omissions or variances may be resolved through negotiations to make the proposal responsive. An example of an omission or variance that can be resolved is a proposed period of performance that does not result in completion of the work within the required timeframe. If negotiation with the contractor results in an adjustment to the period of performance matching the required timeframe, the proposal then may be deemed to be responsive.

RFCQ: (See **Request for contractor qualifications**)

RFI: (See **Request for contractor qualifications**)

RFQ: (See **Request for quotations and Request for contractor qualifications**)

Rights reserved by contracting agency: are rights of the contracting agency that are enumerated in the solicitation. They typically include the right to cancel the solicitation, modify the provisions of the solicitation, refrain from awarding a contract, engage in negotiations with prospective contractors, or any other rights the contracting agency wants to include.

Scope of work: is the title of the document that describes the work to be performed by the contractor. The scope of work may also include additional information such as certain aspects of the work that is performed by the contracting agency. Some contracting agencies also include billing rates in the scope of work for level of effort, not-to-exceed price, or cost reimbursement contracts. To ensure that the contractor is accountable for performance of the tasks listed in the scope of work, the scope of work normally has a preamble that includes a statement to the effect that "the contractor shall provide all labor, materials, equipment, supplies, transportation, and pay all required taxes and fees to complete the following tasks." In jurisdictions where a word other than "shall" is used to compel a contractor to perform services or provide products, "must" or "will" are substituted for "shall" in the preamble to the scope of work.

Service contract: is the term for an agreement for the furnishing of all services including professional services. Services in addition to professional services include janitorial, pest control, landscaping, trash collection, security guards, or any other services not included in the definition for professional services. (See also **Model contract**.)

Set-asides: is the term used to describe procurements for which solicitations are sent only to a targeted class of contractors (such as small businesses or disabled-veteran-owned businesses), and responses to the solicitation are not considered unless the responding companies are members of the targeted class of contractors.

Socioeconomic programs: are equal opportunity or affirmative action programs that promote social or economic goals based on the award of contracts to targeted companies. Such programs encourage the award of contracts to contractors that fit certain criteria, such as a maximum number of employees or ownership of and management by women, minorities, veterans, or disabled persons.

Solicitation: is the generic term used to describe documents sent to prospective contractors to advise them that a government organization is seeking proposals, quotations, or bids for products or services provided by the private sector. Examples of solicitations traditionally used in government contracting are RFPs, RFCQs, RFQs, and IFBs.

Source selection authority (SSA): is used by some government organizations as the phrase to identify the official with authority to award the contract.

Standard terms and conditions: are "terms and conditions" prepared and staffed, normally in advance of releasing the solicitation or drafting the contract, by a government entity and incorporated in the model contract, letter contract, or definitive contract awarded by the government.

Statement of qualifications: refers to the responses to RFCQs from prospective contractors. They describe the contractor's qualifications to perform the services or provide the products to the government entity that released the RFCQ. A statement of qualifications does not normally include pricing.

Statement of work: is the terminology used by certain government entities for a scope of work.

Successful contractor: might intuitively be considered as a contractor that successfully completes the work described in a contract. However, for the purposes of this book, the successful contractor is the contractor selected for award of a particular contract.

Supplier: is another term that is often used to describe a contractor; however, this term is most often reserved for companies that provide materials rather than services.

Suspended: refers to contractors that have been proposed for debarment or have been debarred, excluded, or otherwise disqualified from government contracting and government-approved subcontracting.

Target cost: is the cost associated with a cost reimbursement contract that the contracting agency and contractor agree to as the expected cost for completion of the work described in the scope of work. This cost is normally determined through cost analysis and subsequent negotiation of the cost proposal submitted by the contractor.

Targeted company: is the generic term used for companies that an agency targets for increased contracting opportunities through the agency's socioeconomic contracting program. Examples of targeted companies include small business, minority-owned small business, woman-owned business, veteran-owned business, and disabled-veteran-owned business.

Terms and conditions: are provisions that describe the rights and responsibilities of all parties to the contract. Typical examples of terms and conditions include payment, term of the contract, indemnification, termination, insurance, contract modifications, independent contractor, and other terms and conditions such as those included in the model contract that accompanies a request for proposals (RFP). Ideally, terms and conditions are balanced to provide equivalent rights to all parties to the contract. An example of a termination clause that is imbalanced is one wherein one party has the right to terminate the contract either for convenience or for cause, whereas the other party merely has the right to terminate for cause. Contractors that propose their own version of terms and conditions often include provisions that favor their company over the rights and responsibilities afforded their customer.

Types of contracts: is a term that refers primarily to the basis for payment by the contracting agency to the contractor. The definitions for types of contracts are generally based on contract types defined in the FAR, because state and local agencies do not consistently define types of contracts.

Unallowable costs: need to be defined by the contracting agency prior to contract award, and the rules for disallowance of unallowable costs need to be included in the contract. If costs such as those listed in the definition for **cost reimbursement contracts** are not designated as unallowable, the contracting agency may be obligated to reimburse the contractor for inappropriate costs. To ensure that unallowable costs are not reimbursed by the contracting agency, a contract clause permitting audit of the contractor's financial records may be included in the contract terms and conditions.

Underrun: of cost is the exact opposite of overrun of cost.

Unilateral: changes to a contract are those changes that are made with the signature of just one party to the contract. State or local agencies normally require bilateral contracts and contract modifications.

Unsuccessful contractor: is any contractor that submitted a proposal but was not selected for contract award.

Vendor: is occasionally used to describe contractors; however, this term is recommended solely for the limited number of companies that sell products through vending machines or from vending carts.

Weighted evaluation criteria: are identical to evaluation criteria, defined above, with the exception that weights are assigned to each of the criteria to differentiate their importance. For example, if price has twice the importance of contractor reputation, price might be assigned a weight of 40 and contractor reputation a weight of 20. Although it is not essential, the sum of the weights assigned to the criteria typically equals 100. Weighted criteria are especially helpful when the contractor selection is contentious or controversial. Examples of weighted criteria are provided in the best practices RFP.

Wet signed contract: is the term used to describe a contract with original signatures. Due to the excellent quality of modern copying equipment, it is recommended that contracts printed in black be signed in blue and that copies of original contracts not be made on color copiers.

Zero tolerance: with respect to gratuity standards, refers to government gratuity standards that prohibit government representatives from accepting a gift of any value from a contractor. A personal zero tolerance gratuity policy refers to personal policy by a government representative who decides against accepting a gift of any value from a contractor despite her or his government entity's gratuity standard that permits the acceptance of gratuities up to a certain monetary value.

Index